Sisters in the Faith

Sisters in the Faith

Shaker Women and Equality of the Sexes

Glendyne R. Wergland

University of Massachusetts Press
Amherst and Boston

Copyright © 2011 by University of Massachusetts Press
ALL RIGHTS RESERVED
Printed in the United States of America

LC 2010050041
ISBN 978-1-55849-863-1 (paper); 862-4 (library cloth)

Designed by Steve Dyer
Set in Sabon by House of Equations, Inc.
Printed and bound by Thomson-Shore, Inc.

LIBRARY OF CONGRESS CATALOGING-IN-PUBLICATION DATA

Wergland, Glendyne R.
Sisters in the faith : Shaker women and equality of the sexes /
Glendyne R. Wergland.
    p. cm.
Includes bibliographical references and index.
ISBN 978-1-55849-863-1 (pbk. : alk. paper)—ISBN 978-1-55849-
862-4 (library cloth : alk. paper)   1. Shaker women—Religious
life.   2. Shakers—History.   3. Equality—Religious aspects—
Christianity.   I. Title.   II. Title: Shaker women and equality of
the sexes.
BX9789.W7W47   2011
289'.8082—dc22   2010050041

British Library Cataloguing in Publication data are available.

*Dedicated to those who helped me understand sisterhood—
my grandmother Gertrude (Cosper) Beemer Weber and her
sisters; the friends of my youth, Paula (Kessinger) Megorden
and Pat (West) Bigler; my daughters, Jennifer and Karyn;
my fictive sisters, Norma Ramos d'Oliveira, Fran Daly Kilts,
and Jane Freeman Crosthwaite—as well as the Shakers at
Sabbathday Lake, Maine, whose communal life is a beacon
of hope and peace in a troubled world.*

CONTENTS

Illustrations follow on page 84.

ACKNOWLEDGMENTS

My heartfelt thanks and appreciation go to the people who have helped me:

My husband, Gerry, whose support frees me to write.

Our daughters, Karyn and Jennifer, who humor me in most things, including road trips.

My mother, Dolores (Goin) Beemer Canfield, who offers encouragement.

Christian Goodwillie, who generously provides interesting tidbits and listens to research problems with patience and grace.

Magda Gabor-Hotchkiss, who gives invaluable help in the Hancock Shaker Village library.

June Sprigg, who introduced me to Isaac Newton Youngs, whose spirit draws me onward.

Jane Crosthwaite, who pushed me further in Shaker studies than I intended to go.

Elizabeth De Wolfe, Kathy Peiss, and Joyce Berkman, who helped me reason through equality.

Sharon Koomler and Jerry Grant, who are founts of information about New Lebanon Shakers, as was the late Tom Donnelly.

Ilyon Woo, Brother Arnold Hadd, Steve Paterwic, Mario De Pillis, and Larry Foster, who shared quotations and sources.

Randy Ericson, who invited me to give the Couper Phi Beta Kappa Library Lecture at Hamilton College in 2007, prompting me to rethink Shaker gender roles.

Clark Dougan, senior editor at University of Massachusetts Press, who believed in this project from the start.

Carol Betsch and Deborah Stuart Smith, who made a valiant effort to save me from myself.

Stephen J. Stein, Etta M. Madden, and Elizabeth De Wolfe, who made helpful suggestions.

And finally, the unnamed textile conference registrar who, checking names off her list, assumed that my husband was the "Dr. Wergland" who would be speaking. Her error reminded me that even in the twenty-first century, many women as well as men still make unwarranted assumptions about women, scholarship, and gender.

PREFACE

These essays explore the lives of Shaker women. I was curious to learn how individuals, and women in a group, got along in this communal society. I began my research informed by other scholars that Shaker sisters were not really equal to Shaker brothers. Nonetheless, I had questions about how Shaker society empowered women (or not), and in what ways. My research turned up evidence that Shaker sisters had both power and authority in their society from 1780 through the nineteenth century, which was the extent of my timeline.

I began with the New Lebanon Church Family because I had already done enough research on that community to see relationships between individuals, as well as tensions between men and women. Knowing that location is not necessarily characteristic of all Shaker villages, I widened my study when evidence drew me elsewhere and dipped into records for Canaan, Hancock, Harvard, Tyringham, Watervliet, and Sabbathday Lake. Eventually, though, all roads circled back to New Lebanon.

I might have named this book *Sisters and Brothers in the Faith*. After drafting ten chapters, I realized that brethren intruded in every one. Often they remained politely in the background, but there they were. Ironically, this study of Shaker sisters was born from more than a decade of research on a man, Isaac Newton Youngs. Brother Isaac, bless his heart, recorded tidbits on Lucy Wright and made a point of mentioning women's activities. To see how unusual his journals were, for a Shaker brother, one has only to compare his with those written by other brethren, such as Seth Youngs Wells or Elisha D. Blakeman, who rarely mentioned sisters. Some brothers lived up to the Shaker ideal of equality better than others. But because the Shakers' system of gendered cooperation, reciprocity, and union kept the sexes working so closely together, I made no effort to separate them. I did try, however, to keep the focus on the sisters as I examined how they lived together with brethren in their communal society.

This book is not meant to be the last word on Shaker sisters, just as my biography of Isaac Newton Youngs is not meant to be the last word on that esteemed brother. Hundreds of manuscripts remain to be mined by curious and persistent scholars. I hope this book will provoke others to do further research.

Despite the conflicts that surface here, it is evident that Believers worked hard to get along with each other and their neighbors. In our increasingly crowded and contentious world, we could take a lesson from them.

SHAKER TERMINOLOGY

A few notes about Shaker terminology may be useful for readers who are not already familiar with this communal group.

The society overall was administered by a central Ministry, a team of two men and two women called Elders and Eldresses who lived at New Lebanon. One individual (called the Lead) was recognized as the leader of the four. Several Shaker enclaves (known as *families* or *orders*) located close together were collectively recognized as a Shaker village. Each family or order also had two Elders and two Eldresses who served as spiritual leaders. Deacons and deaconesses, sometimes called trustees, were assigned to do the public work of business with outsiders.

Shakers referred to their individual peers as Sister or Brother. They called themselves *Believers,* meaning a group set apart from non-Shakers, who were referred to as *unbelievers, the world,* or the *world's people.* The adjective *worldly* was used to mean "of the world's people."

Union was an essential Shaker virtue, referring to the unity of the group as a whole. Divisiveness was discouraged as contrary to union. Party spirit, or factionalism, was prohibited for the same reason.

The terms *visionist* and *instrument* were used to refer to individual Believers who had visions or received messages from the spirits of the dead. A *gift* was an inspired message or idea that originated with the spirits.

Readers are referred to Stephen J. Paterwic's *Historical Dictionary of the Shakers* (Lanham, Md.: Scarecrow Press, 2008), for a more complete list of all the important Shaker terms.

Sisters in the Faith

Introduction

THROUGH MOST OF THE NINETEENTH CENTURY, SHAKER SISTERS
outnumbered Shaker brothers. To better understand why women chose
to join the society, consider the status of non-Shaker women in Anglo-
American society. Wives were disadvantaged under Anglo-American law.
For women of the world's people, or non-Shakers, marriage brought subordination and no guarantee of comfort, safety, or support. Nonetheless,
most women married. The principle of coverture meant that a wife's legal
identity merged with her husband's at marriage and essentially disappeared.
Legally, married women were classed with children and others incapable
of managing their own affairs. A married woman could divorce only with
difficulty and could not count on having custody of her children. A woman
who intended to marry could establish separate property rights with a
prenuptial agreement, but most did not. Some parents protected married
daughters by writing "sole and separate" clauses into their own wills to
stipulate that a daughter could control her inheritance without a husband's
interference. In the nineteenth century, those stipulations increased, as did
women's property ownership. Massachusetts wills from 1780 to 1860 show
that many testators recognized sons' intemperance, profligacy with money,
bad business decisions, and criminal behavior; those parents shielded their
female heirs with protective bequests. But most inheritance customs and
laws favored men. Daughters usually did not inherit as much from their
fathers as sons did. A widow's dower was the right to lifetime use of one-
third of her husband's land but did not include the right to sell it—a custom
that left many widows strapped for cash. The widows of propertyless men
might be left destitute with children to support.[1] A "grass widow" or "California widow"—essentially a deserted wife—was in an even more tenuous
position, unable to sell property or remarry.[2]

Some women avoided wedlock because by remaining single they avoided the unequal power relationship between women and men.³ For those who remained single, life was shaped by economic considerations. Through the nineteenth century, single women had most of the rights that single men had, with the significant exception of the right to vote. As long as a woman remained unmarried, she could own property, pay taxes, run her own business, and manage her own affairs without a man's interference. If a woman did not want to marry, she had several respectable ways to earn a living, including teaching, doing wage work, or opening a business. Although in the 1860s Virginia Penny documented more than five hundred honorable occupations pursued by women in New York City, many of those jobs were available only in urban centers. A small town would not support all of those trades, and most of the population lived in small towns through the nineteenth century.⁴ As employees, however, women were paid less than men were, so it was hard for women to secure assets sufficient to support themselves in hard times. If a single woman's health failed, she might end up as a dependent in a relative's home or in the poorhouse. For some women, a safer alternative was to join the Shakers, who offered comfortable houses, good medical care, lifetime support, protection from economic and physical abuse, and the hope of salvation. Many women found a good life in Shaker society.

Ann Lee and a small group of English Shakers established their first communal group in Watervliet, New York. Mother Ann preached thrift, celibacy, pacifism, humility, and a strong work ethic. After she died in 1784, Joseph Meacham established New Lebanon, New York, as the society's headquarters. In 1787, Meacham began the "gathering in" process, collecting scattered members into organized Shaker villages. "Great care was taken in the selection of members for the Church, or the central family of the new order," the early twentieth-century church historians Anna White and Leila Taylor wrote. "Unmarried persons were selected, free from all obligations, of good health, exemplary in character and sound in the faith; also some children, with the consent of their parents." Others were considered unsuitable: debtors, those who were not exemplary Believers, and those who were bound to their natural kin. About sixty men and fifty women formed the first New Lebanon Church Family. Calvin Green recalled the first few years as hungry times full of hard work and with poor accommodations, but the Shakers' situation improved as they built their village.⁵

In 1788, Meacham called Lucy Wright to join him in the Ministry. Together they created the gender-balanced government of Elders, Eldresses, deacons, and deaconesses that symbolized Shaker women's equality with men. They began building fine meetinghouses, shops, and dwellings with equal (but separate) exterior doors, stairways, and rooms for men and women. From the time of Meacham's death in 1796, Wright was the acknowledged head of the society until she died in 1821.[6]

The New Lebanon community grew rapidly at first. They made a good living from farming and community industries, and their beautiful village was visible evidence of their diligence and prosperity. The community membership was 351 in 1803, 587 in 1835, and 550 in 1860. It began dropping after the Civil War, however, and was down to 188 in 1895.[7] The society also declined in overall numbers, closing several villages before 1900, and more thereafter. Today, one Shaker group persists at Sabbathday Lake, Maine, carrying Shakerism into its third century.

Several aspects of the New Lebanon sisters' experience may be representative of other nineteenth-century Shakers. Women and girls came into the society for similar reasons, regardless of location. Wherever they lived they did the same kind of work, engaged in the same kind of peer surveillance institutionalized to reduce misbehavior, and encountered the same issues.

However, the New Lebanon Church Family was different from other Shaker groups, beginning with its being more selective than others in choosing members. Living in the Church Family was an honor because its members were considered to have shown the greatest spiritual travel. Church Family members were more likely to persist as Believers than those in lower orders.[8]

The Shaker concept of equality between the sexes was developed and maintained at New Lebanon. An undated note reveals the thought behind the concept and its relation to the unity of the society:

> It is necessary in the order of Families that both Brethren & Sisters should have Just & Equal Lots of Care & Government according to their sex & ought to Support union & Relation to Each other according to their order & Callings so far as is for their own good & the good of others both in things spiritual & temporal as their Lots & Callings may require. But all Privit union between Brethren & Sisters in Families is Contrary to Chh order either in Elder or younger.[9]

Equal partners had to support one another and consider the good of all. They had to avoid "private union" and "party spirit" or "party feeling," and therefore cliques, factions, and "particular affection" (as Wright would later refer to intimate friendships) were discouraged as contrary to order.

Equality, however, was not practiced evenly throughout Shaker society. Isaac Newton Youngs wrote in 1816 that the Elders told the New Lebanon Church Family "not to speak of our order, in relation to being placed in order, brother & sister in an equality—There is not any family or order among believers, except Watervliet & this Church, that support that order." Youngs noted that the Hancock, Massachusetts, society had tried practicing equality, but had "flung it up & laid it by."[10] The New Lebanon Ministry set the standard but could not enforce the policy at villages where members balked. Nevertheless, the society's pursuit of the ideal made a difference in sisters' lives. Because Believers fostered union through consensus decision-making, the opinions of women, who made up the majority of membership, carried considerable weight. To maintain union, Shaker men and women had to consider themselves equal partners in a joint enterprise.[11]

Scholarly views of Shakers and the status of women have changed in the past four decades. Edward Deming Andrews's book *The People Called Shakers,* published in 1963, was the first influential study of the Shakers. Andrews credits Joseph Meacham alone with institutionalizing the concept of equality of the sexes.[12] He makes no mention of his doing so in partnership with Lucy Wright. Andrews did his research at a time when, as James Gregory, in a 1984 study, points out, male ethnographers "rarely studied women because the discipline was androcentric; studies of women held little status."[13]

In the 1970s, however, scholars began making insightful observations about Shaker women, celibacy, and equality. D'Ann Campbell, for example, examined religious doctrines and government structure and in a study published in 1978, she concludes, "Shaker women were considered on equal terms with men." She points out that women did not have to do 50 percent of the blacksmithing, carpentry, or farm work to be equal to men, as some twentieth-century feminists thought was necessary for there to be equality.[14] Interestingly, those feminists did not suggest that 50 percent of "women's work" should be done by men, as well, revealing that they valued the work of men over that of women, thereby promoting the inequality they criticized. Furthermore, they assessed women's work only for its economic value and seemed not to recognize the difference between social value and economic value.

In 1975, anthropologist Susan Carol Rogers published an article that has come to be seen as a watershed in women's studies. She points out: "It is only when we stop looking at male forms of power as the norm and begin to look at female arrangements as equally valid and significant, though perhaps different in form, that we can see how male and female roles are intertwined and so begin to understand how human societies operate."[15] Shakers understood "equally valid and significant" more than two hundred years ago.

Gregory, Campbell, and Rogers were part of an ongoing debate about the status of women. In 1980, Michelle Rosaldo summed up the problem of "pervasive gender inequality" based on the division between women's domestic sphere and men's public sphere and criticized the model based on "opposed spheres."[16] Her analysis, however, did not go far enough. The public sphere exists only because it rests on the foundation of domestic life, which is often overlooked or devalued even though it is fundamental to human society. If the spheres are interpreted only by men (as they generally were until the last quarter of the twentieth century), it is likely that the interpretation will value the masculine/public over the feminine/domestic. The comparative value of gendered spheres is only perceived, however, not real.

In 1788, Joseph Meacham and Lucy Wright, to their credit, recognized the institutionalized inequality of the sexes among the world's people and tried to counter it within Shakerism. Their genius was in understanding that men's and women's spheres were not opposed; they were two halves of a whole. Union, one of the Shakers' core values, depended on partnership. Men and women had to work together for the whole group to succeed in their collective endeavor; each sex had to support and respect the other. Thus Shakers' nineteenth-century views of gender proved to be less rigid than those of many twentieth-century scholars.

In 1980, Mary Farrell Bednarowski assessed Shaker women's advantages in belonging to a religion that deemphasized the masculine, tempered the doctrine of Adam's Fall, and recognized that women were worthy of roles beyond those of wife and mother. She pointed out the Shakers' radical incorporation of both female and male qualities into their concept of divinity. She quoted Eldress Antoinette Doolittle, who wrote that the apostolic church lacked "the recognition of woman's rights, and her capability as a counselor and co-worker with man in all that pertains to physical and spiritual life." Bednarowski concluded that women may have been drawn to Shakerism by "the possibility of assuming positions of leadership which were denied them in the mainstream religions."[17] Doolittle believed that Shaker sisters were equal to Shaker brethren, and Bednarowski concurred—but other scholars seemed unconvinced.

And so the scholarly debate about Shaker sisters' equality continued. Louis Kern wrote in 1981 that Shaker women were socially inferior but religiously superior to their male counterparts; in their capacity as visionists, Shaker women spiritually outranked the Elders.[18] In his analysis, Kern overlooks the sisters' view of their equality. If sisters believed themselves equal, then they were; historians who contradict historical figures' own assessment of their status do so at their peril. During the Era of Manifestations, however, spiritual power proved so seductive that some could not resist the temptation to use it. My evidence suggests that some brethren were frightened by female visionists' power, so Kern may have been correct on that point.

In 1991, Jean Humez published a study in which she examines gender through brethren's resistance to "petticoat government" under Lucy Wright's leadership. The strain between Shakerism's linkage of conservative and radical gender ideology was apparent—but brethren who could not tolerate "female rule" either learned to live with it or left the society.[19] Those apostates, at least, believed that the society's female leader had far too much power—for a woman. Male converts came from a society where men had all the perks of patriarchy, and some resisted the change. If a man opposed a woman's leadership, he had to make the choice whether to stay and live with it, or depart—and some men opted out. Brethren who persisted as Shakers joined in the consensus on female leadership (or decided to live with it even though they privately disagreed). The departure of the disaffected helped to preserve the union that Shakers valued.

According to Priscilla Brewer, "the Shakers were never committed to the complete equality of the sexes"; they moved in that direction only when declining numbers of brethren required it.[20] It seems to me, however, that scholars should not so easily dismiss evidence of the Shakers' commitment to equality. Perhaps Believers did not construct equality exactly the same way we might today, but that difference does not make their vision of equality any less valid for their place and time. The Shakers' perceived reality was what mattered.

Analyzing Shaker celibacy's benefits to women, scholars have concluded that Shaker equality was based, in part, on that tenet and on the Shakers' rejection of marriage. In 1989, feminist theorist Sally Kitch pointed out that because marriage was a key to women's inferiority to men, celibate women moved outside of that hierarchy.[21] Her assessment is true, as far as it goes. Shaker women evaded the traditional subordination of marriage, which established a man as head of the household. Sisters certainly had more equality to brethren than worldly women had to worldly men. Some villages, however, may have been dominated by one sex or the other, even though an organization chart would have shown that their leadership was gender-balanced. The official lines of authority are not necessarily the actual lines of authority in any organization.

Continuing the discussion of sisters' equality, Lawrence Foster, in 1991, wrote that celibacy removed the burdens of marriage and childbearing to free women for full participation in their society.[22] True; by eliminating marriage, Shakerism freed women from the legal hierarchy of the sexes. However, equality had little to do with childbearing, which Shakers might have allowed without creating a hierarchy of the sexes. Shaker men and women shared the responsibilities of rearing the children who lived with them. Among non-Shakers, the gendered hierarchy of marriage was the reason for the lack of equality between the sexes, not reproduction.[23]

In a study published in 1992, Stephen J. Stein describes what he sees as "the gradual but real subordination of women" in Shakerism after Lucy Wright died in 1821.[24] Surely some brethren made the effort to subordinate women, but a systematic examination of evidence from 1788 through the 1890s reveals that the New Lebanon sisters mustered their resources to maintain both power and authority. In a group that governs by consensus, it may be difficult for men to dominate women who are organized to resist subordination, especially when the women outnumber the men.

In a 2002 study, Suzanne Thurman suggests that the "androgynous ideal" empowered Shaker women more than celibacy did. Echoing Bednarowski, Thurman maintains that the dual godhead, represented by Jesus Christ and Ann Lee, was the source of women's equality. At the villages Thurman studied, Shaker women crossed gender boundaries; they were "encouraged to develop" in ways "not merely associated with their biological sex." Thurman may overemphasize the "deconstruction" of female roles, but she makes an excellent point: "The communal nature of Shaker society erased the division of public and private spheres, forcing women's work and actions into the public realm to be evaluated on a par with male activity."[25] This is the essence of equality: that women's work is considered as valuable as men's work, regardless of what each sex does.

Some anthropologists might agree with Thurman. In the twentieth century, only a few assessed gender roles, but their findings are useful in studying the Shakers. In 1967, Ernestine Friedl pointed out that in women's roles, appearance differed from reality. She argued that though men held formal political power in the Greek village she studied, women's power lay in the households that constitute the village; thus men's power rested on a foundation of women.[26] Each sex depended on cooperation and reciprocity.

In her 1975 watershed article, which has been widely cited, Susan Carol Rogers assesses female power and "the myth of male dominance." According to Rogers, women hold domestic power in a French agrarian village while the men are away. Women run the village through their informal communication networks (also known as gossip).[27] They share what Beverly Chiñas calls "a social universe separate from men." Women "are privy to information which men either do not or may not circulate among themselves," and so women regulate social relations.[28] This is what another anthropologist calls "cryptomatriarchy." Women "see and know everything," using that information to maintain community standards of behavior.[29] Likewise, nineteenth-century Shaker women policed village social mores, as the apostate Hervey Elkins pointed out in his comments about their domestic espionage.[30]

In Rogers's study, women had the power to shape village life because they worked in the village while men were away, out in the fields or gone to the city. Rogers's women pretended that men were the final authorities in all things, even though the women often determined the best course of action and influenced men's decisions. Men and women alike acted as if men were dominant; their system of gender relations maintains that public fiction.[31] This is what I call the "Father Knows Best" syndrome, where the family seems to defer to a head of household while managing him to get what they want—and he is wise to go along with them. Power may have worked the same way among the Shakers, with sisters sometimes making decisions independent of the brethren and influencing consensus to get what they wanted.

It is worth noting, however, that Rogers amended her findings several years later, after studying another town where women did not assert the same influence. In the first study, she concludes that "the two gender groups wield different kinds but equivalent amounts of power, kept in balance by public posturing or a 'myth' of male dominance," due in part to the sexes' interdependence. In the second study, however, she concludes: "Where people perceive their universe in terms of social hierarchies, they may be more likely to define and order the gender groups, like other social categories, in a hierarchical mode, as well. Conversely, where hierarchies are masked, obviated, or eliminated, differences between the gender groups may be drawn so as to set them in a mode of equivalence or identity."[32] Shakers eliminated the hierarchy of gender to create equality of the sexes.

Rogers inspired other anthropologists to reconsider male dominance and the status of women, among them James Gregory, who observes that men "are not necessarily as dominant in public matters as they may superficially appear to be, and . . . women may often play a far stronger role in such matters than has generally been recognized."[33] Other anthropologists concurred, many of them recognizing the power of gossip.[34] In 1984, Rogers wrote: "Consensus on the universality of female subordination/male dominance has disintegrated and become a matter of definitional dispute; depending on how it is defined, it is or is not a universal fact of human social life."[35] The same could be said about scholars' views of Shaker equality of the sexes.

Christopher Boehm offers another view that pertains to the Shakers. In any society, he points out, the rank and file create a "reverse dominance hierarchy." If members do not like what their leaders do, the rank and file can expel them, or leave. In effect, Boehm adds, "societies may be considered to be intentional communities, groups of people that make up their minds about the amount of hierarchy they wish to live with and then see to it that the program is followed."[36] Among nineteenth-century Shakers, consensus decision-making meant that women's opinions mattered. Brethren disaffected with Lucy Wright's "petticoat government" did leave the society. The most significant thing about their departure, however, was that it revealed more than their objection to being ruled by women; it also showed that they were unable to succeed in challenging women's authority. Equality of the sexes was evidently entrenched in Shaker society as early as 1796.

In 1994, Susan Starr Sered assessed the advantages that some religions—especially those whose leaders and most members are female—confer on women. She notes that although all women's religions address issues of gender, "religions that serve women's ongoing and collective interests are especially likely to elaborate and institutionalize gender differences and/or sexual segregation." She continues:

> It seems to me that women's religions have selected the most efficacious strategy possible considering the limitations within which they operate: None of these religions are located in a truly nonsexist cultural context. In other words, if these religions were to claim that men and women are the same, *no one would believe them anyway!* Gender differences seem so obviously "true," that enhancing or reinterpreting those differences offers women an ideology that is both believable and empowering. Denying those differences might make intellectual sense, but lacks tactical sense. In a perfect world, gender might be a meaningless cultural category. In an imperfect world, it seems to serve women's interests to own a clearly bounded portion of the cultural map.

Sered cites the Shakers as a case in point. She concludes, "An ideology of gender difference . . . in the framework of an ongoing 'sisterhood' and coupled with women's control of sexuality, fertility, and significant economic resources does allow women to reap collective benefits."[37] In Shakerism, women are as important as men.

Among the Shakers, sisters' and brothers' working partnerships married their different roles in an equality that women and men did not necessarily have among the world's people. In the nineteenth-century United States, male authority was bolstered by Anglo-American common law and by male ministers selectively quoting scripture. Shaker men and women, in contrast, lived under a system that promoted egalitarianism. Maintaining good working relationships in a communal society meant showing respect for the other sex. And if all else failed, Shaker sisters had the example of Ann Lee's leadership to bolster their own position.

Celibacy was the key to Shaker equality. By eliminating marriage, Shakers eliminated the source of men's traditional authority over women. Living as virgins, male and female alike, Believers diverged from mainstream traditions that valued women's virginity but did not apply the same standard to men. The Shakers rejected the hypocritical double standard and established women's equality by applying the same norm of chastity to men and women—and upheld it in practice as well as in theory. This study shows how women working together consolidated their gains, then expanded their power. Here, then, are examples of women serving in equality with men, women in partnership with men, and women in ascendancy over men. By the end of the nineteenth century, even outsiders recognized that Shaker society had become a gynocracy.

Part 1

Joining the Shakers

1

Ann Lee

They will come like doves . . .

ANN LEE WAS A STRONG AND DETERMINED EVANGELIST. IN the late eighteenth century, when women rarely spoke before public groups, much less founded churches, she defied the Anglo-American mainstream's expectation of a religious leader.[1] She proselytized by publicly denouncing men and women whose sins caught her attention, and she gave her followers latitude in religious expression, far beyond what conventional churches tolerated. She addressed them as a mother would, and they recognized her concern for their welfare. Unlike the typical itinerant preacher who came to town, spread the word, exhorted, issued the altar call, and went on to the next venue, Mother Ann recruited proselytes who remained Shakers for the rest of their lives. Many American Protestants seeking religious ecstasy found a home among the "Shaking Quakers."

Ann Lee and a small band of followers emigrated from England to America in 1774. Their arrival was inauspicious. At first they had to split up and find jobs. But after several years of wage work in New York, they moved to Watervliet (also known as Niskayuna) to establish a communal family. In the obscurity of that wilderness, the newcomers lived their religion largely unnoticed. During those early years, they attracted only one proselyte, a neighbor named Eleanor Vedder, who joined them in 1778. They were poor, and the living was hard. Fifteen people slept on the floor in one room, some with only a blanket to cover them. But the Shakers were industrious and believed "a blessing attended their labors."[2]

When Ann Lee's followers asked her about opening the gospel of Shakerism to the world, she assured them that eventually converts would "come like doves." At planting time in 1779, Mother Ann insisted they sow more seed. She explained, "We shall have company enough, before another year comes about, to consume it all."[3]

The social and economic upheaval of the Revolutionary War had plowed and harrowed the ground for planting a new religion. By 1779, the conflict had worn down the population. So many of the young men were gone to war that it was hard to get crops planted, cultivated, and harvested. Provisions ran short, especially in late spring, before wild foods were available and gardens began to yield. In Albany, rioters demanded food, and along the New York–Massachusetts border, Yankees considered mob action to get wheat for bread. Moreover, the winter of 1779–1780 was unusually severe, so cold that cattle froze to death.[4] Politics turned neighbor against neighbor, sometimes sending civilian Tories or patriots fleeing for their lives. Conscription, battlefield casualties, deaths from smallpox epidemics that swept through military camps, and the economic hardship of rising taxes and inflation afflicted every American.[5]

Divine Providence sent three blessings that promoted Mother Ann's new religion. The first blessing was a bountiful harvest in late 1779 that allowed the Shakers to stockpile food—a commodity more precious than money in wartime. Deprivation was a potent factor in moving hungry people toward a religious group that could provide whatever potential proselytes lacked.[6] Feeding newcomers made them more receptive to Ann Lee's message.

Another blessing was a New Light Baptist revival in the Berkshire hills near New Lebanon, New York. Four women, gifted in prayer, held daily meetings that included extraordinary spiritual phenomena, speaking in tongues, and visions. The religious excitement moved into Massachusetts under the leadership of the New Light lay preacher Joseph Meacham.[7] An observer recalled:

> Vivid and intense were men's convictions for sin; cries for mercy rent the air; meetings were scenes of excitement, soul anguish, realistic portrayals of penalties about to come, as souls stood bare in their sins before the eye of God. Not alone were the vicious and reprobate thus overtaken by the realization of God and their own sins, but men and women of responsibility and position, church members of long standing, ministers, deacons and elders; their religion had failed; they were unconverted and lost; their cries mingled with the heart-broken pleadings for salvation of those who had been hardened revilers of goodness. Conversions were swift and powerful; joy was felt as intense as the

sorrow that had preceded. Visions of angels were seen; to some the heavens seemed opened.[8]

To another observer, "They were full in the belief that God was about to perform some unheard-of wonder for his church upon earth."[9] Elizabeth Johnson, the wife of New Lebanon's former Presbyterian minister, said, "The signs and operations, and the prophetic spirit which prevailed in these meetings, clearly intimated that Christ was about to 'appear the second time, without sin, unto salvation.'"[10] The New Lights, already out of the religious mainstream, were ready for change. A skeptical New Englander wrote of the revivalists:

> They considered themselves now, according to their own phraseology, in Babylon; but the time of their deliverance was at hand. Many of them were in frequent and sore travail for the deliverance of the church, and for individuals; others were fainting, crying out, falling down, and wallowing on the ground; whilst some were falling into trances, out of which they would emerge full of the spirit of prophesy. They predicted, either that God was about to deliver his people, or that the day of judgment was at hand, or that after so many days the door of mercy would be forever shut against the unbelieving world. Many of them dreamed extraordinary dreams, which were interpreted by others in as extraordinary a manner.[11]

The revival began in the spring and peaked over the summer. In autumn, the New Light stir died down, leaving the hopefuls feeling as if the spirit of God had been withdrawn.[12]

Near the end of the revival, however, a minister preached on Romans 8:8, "So they that are in the flesh cannot please God." A few New Lights had already reached the conclusion that a celibate life might be required for salvation.[13] Many Christians believed that Adam and Eve were expelled from the Garden of Eden for having sexual intercourse. Because sex was the cause of Adam's fall, only celibates could live without sin. Before Ann Lee spoke her first word, the New Lights were considering the possibility that they might have to live without sex in order to reach salvation.

Eighteenth-century evangelicals wanted the help of a higher power to live sinless lives. Deborah Sackett, for instance, said she "had often felt the sting of inward guilt, & a strong desire to be saved from sin, but knew not how" until she met Ann Lee. Martha Deming felt so guilty about her sins that she could not sleep.[14] The desire for sinlessness was the soil Ann Lee needed for planting her message of hope and redemption. What yet remained was a propitious moment for planting the seed.

The Shakers' third blessing was a meteorological phenomenon, the "dark day," May 19, 1780, that frightened many Yankees into giving their hearts to God. One New Englander recalled that the morning began with a thundershower, "followed by an uncommon darkness such as is not remembered . . . the night was Extraordinary dark until one o'clock that a person could not see their hand when held up nor even a white sheet of paper. . . . The cause was unknown." The phenomenon turned day into night; it was so dark at noon that candles had to be lighted. Issachar Bates saw neighbors "wringing their hands and howling, 'The day of judgment has come!!'" The phenomenon was so "very awful and surprising" that ministers preached on the coming Judgment Day.[15] For a population sensitive to portents of good and evil, the darkness must have been terrifying. Inexplicable natural phenomena, as the historian Ross Beales points out, "demonstrated God's displeasure with a sinful people." The darkness was the sign Ann Lee had awaited. An astute judge of human nature, she knew that a frightened population, already fearful of divine judgment, was now ready for her message about sin and salvation. On May 21, 1780, she began preaching to the public.[16]

Among her audience was the New Light, Talmadge Bishop, who "caught the spirit, and like a sheaf fully dry, immediately kindled into a flame." He rushed home to New Lebanon to spread the tidings. A revival participant, Bishop knew where to deliver the news of Ann Lee, and many other New Lights welcomed the message. The road to Watervliet was "instantly crouded" with prospective proselytes, including the Hancock, Massachusetts, Baptist preacher Valentine Rathbun and his congregation.[17] Likewise, the Presbyterian minister Samuel Johnson, who had despaired of "finding the real work of salvation upon the old ecclesiastical foundation," was convinced that the glory of God shone on Shakers.[18] When Johnson and other mainstream ministers joined Ann Lee's congregation, they inverted the traditional gendering of church: the woman spoke, and the ministers followed her lead.

Daniel Goodrich, one of Rathbun's Baptists, was immediately attracted to the Shakers. Years later, he recalled Ann Lee. "There was a woman with them that was called Mother—that all confessed Sins to her or to one another; . . . [she] was able to tell People of all theire Sins."[19] Goodrich was impressed by Ann Lee's ability to know of people's sins without being told—a sign to him of supernatural power. Hopefuls from New Lebanon and from

Hancock and Pittsfield, Massachusetts, came in groups, families and friends seeking to fill their religious needs. Some approached as skeptics. Among the hopefuls were Lucy Wight and some friends. On the way to Watervliet, a companion asked Wight whether she intended to join the Shakers. Wight replied that she had long searched after religion but had never found one with a solid foundation, and if the Shakers had nothing better to offer, she would not join. "They cannot catch old birds with chaff," she said. But after attending Shaker worship, she said, "The mighty power of God was evidently present in visible operations among the people." Wight was convinced that Shakerism was not chaff after all. Others were impressed, as well. Daniel Goodrich, his father, and several siblings, cousins, and neighbors "received faith and embraced their testimony."[20]

Visitors increased through the summer of 1780 until hundreds had heard the Shaker message that called on them to confess all sin and forsake it, right wrongs against fellow men, and take up the cross in the regeneration of souls. According to Daniel Goodrich, those who "gladley receved and From the heart Obayed these things—theire harts weare filled with joy and Gladness; while Songs of Everlasting Joy rested on theire heads[;] houses became Little temples and weare filled with the Songs of New Jerusalem—and others Speaking with New and unknown Tounges, Leaping and Praising God." Proselytes blessed Mother Ann and the Elders, "who had called them from Darkness to Light and from the power of Satan to God."[21]

Rachel Spencer said that Ann Lee's message was so powerful that a visit to the Shakers was enough to squelch youthful frivolity. "Many of our company had been very light and carnal while on our way there," she remembered. "But," she said, "they returned with very different feelings. On our way home, all were solemn, silent and thoughtful; scarcely a word was spoken by any of the company." Convinced that Shakerism was the work of God, most of Spencer's New Lebanon friends joined the Shakers and remained faithful to the end of their days.[22]

Ann Lee's personality was central to Shakerism's attraction, as her early followers testified. Their testimonies, however, might be construed as hagiography and thus suspect as the collected views of the faithful. For that reason, an outsider's view, with biases contrary to those of the Shakers, is useful in assessing her effectiveness as an evangelist. A thread of gendered incredulity, for instance, runs through one skeptical visitor's account: "It hath appeared to many persons a riddle altogether inscrutable how it was possible for an indigent stranger to effect what this woman effected, when labouring under all the disadvantages with which she was burdened." Because Ann Lee was a woman, an immigrant, illiterate and poor, she was "in the eyes of the world" disqualified for ecclesiastical office. Yet she was the leader of a church that demanded unusual sacrifices from its members—and the congregation was growing.[23]

Mother Ann's friendliness was perhaps the first draw. She smiled and laughed easily, and like a good public relations person, she made most visitors feel welcome. "Those who visited this Elect lady," one outsider wrote, "were treated with the greatest hospitality."

> They were admitted into the company of their new converts, who were rejoicing and singing most melodiously. Some words they could understand, and some were in an unknown language to them. The mother would walk around them, smile upon them, lay her hand upon their heart, then take their hand and press it upon her own bosom. She would stroke their arms, lay her hand on their heads, and many other things she would do of the like kind; all the while she would be singing and chanting forth a strange bewitching kind of incantation, until the person was wrought into a perfect maze.[24]

Ann Lee's touch added an important dimension to her welcome. Her physical presence was powerful, and she used her hands to establish rapport, even intimacy. Twentieth-century marketing studies show that touch can be an effective tool in selling. Touch is a form of communication as well as a marker of interpersonal involvement and can be associated with appreciation, support, attention, interest, friendship, and love. A salesperson's success, according to these studies, depends largely on her credibility, friendliness, and warmth, and touch can bolster the customer's perception of those qualities. Furthermore, those who are physically touched by a salesperson, as Ann Lee's proselytes were, are more likely to comply than those not touched.[25] Thus touch contributes to the interpersonal bonds essential to securing commitment to a new religion.[26] It worked for those who "bought" Ann Lee's gospel.[27] Convert Elizabeth Williams was touched emotionally as well. "I felt such streams of love from Mother flowing into my soul," she said.[28]

Some proselytes felt something extraordinary in Mother Ann's touch and were convinced that she had supernatural powers. From her hands, they felt what Thankful Barce called "the power of God." John Bishop said it was like an electrical shock. Peter Dodge said, "The moment she took hold of my fingers, I felt the power of God, from her hand, run through my whole body." Her followers received that physical sensation only from Ann Lee.[29]

It may have been an adrenaline rush generated by their thrill in meeting a woman they believed to be the second messiah, but, to the proselytes, the feeling was so unusual and so highly charged physically and metaphorically that they remembered it for the rest of their lives.

In addition, Ann Lee was reputed to have healing hands.[30] In true gospel tradition, her followers testified, she healed Daniel Goodrich's daughter of a dislocated hip and cast out an evil spirit from another child. Salome Spencer attributed her mother's "miraculous gift of healing" to Ann Lee. Sarah Kibbee was unable to walk without crutches when Ann Lee told her to lay them aside and lean on Christ, instead. "In obedience to Mother I did so," Kibbee recalled forty years later, "& immediately I felt the healing power of God, & my crippled leg was restored as sound as the other." Prudence Hammond said Mother Ann cured her deafness.[31]

Those individuals' improved condition convinced others that Ann Lee, like Jesus of Nazareth, possessed supernatural powers.[32] Her spiritual gifts gave her followers a sense of connection to a higher power. The sociologist Rosabeth Moss Kanter calls this essential commitment mechanism transcendence.[33]

Another attraction was that Shaker worship was exciting, offering the emotional catharsis of a camp meeting or revival. Services, which sometimes lasted from morning until night, included shaking, turning, dancing, and speaking in tongues. Shakers, according to Rev. Ezra Stiles, were accustomed "to work themselves up to high Enthusiasm, so as in Worship all the Congregation to get to speak^g, pray^g & singing all at the same time."[34] Valentine Rathbun, soon after his apostasy, wrote, "The manner and form of their worship is entirely new, and different from all others." He added:

> In the best part of their worship, every one acts for himself, and almost every one different from the other; one will stand with his arms extended, acting over odd postures, which they call signs; another will be dancing, and sometimes hopping on one leg about the floor; another will fall to turning round, so swift that if it be a woman, her clothes will be so filled with the wind, as through they were kept out by a hoop; another will be prostrate on the floor; another will be talking with somebody; and some sitting by, smoaking their pipe; groaning most dismally; some trembling extremely; others acting as though all their nerves were convuls'd; others swinging their arms, with all vigor, as though they were turning a wheel, &c.[35]

Shaker services at that time included no public prayer, no preaching, and little scripture reading. Believers worshiped as the spirit moved them. And their singing was wonderful, especially that of Ann Lee, which, according to Rathbun, "seemed to be a perfect charm." He described what he heard:

> One will begin to sing some odd tune, without words or rule; after a while another will strike in; and after a while they all fall in, and make a strange charm: —some singing without words, and some with an unknown tongue or mutter, and some with a mixture of English. [Ann Lee] minds to strike such notes as makes a concord, and so form the charm[.] When they leave off singing, they drop off, one by one, as oddly as they come on.[36]

Eliab Harlow said, "The beautiful singing of Mother Ann so attracted my feelings that I was really delighted with it, and indeed no one could listen to it without admiration." Eliphalet Comstock recalled, "Such singing I never heard before. My tongue cannot express the heavenly comfort I felt in their singing." Job Bishop called it "melodious and heavenly," and he said, "The manifestations of Divine power were too evident to be disputed."[37]

Shaker enthusiasm horrified mainstream Protestant clergy. A traveling evangelist who passed through town once a year was perhaps a good thing, if only to stir up a congregation. But a new religion that competed for members and drained existing churches was not, especially if led by a woman. They admitted, however, that Ann Lee's "extraordinaries" had the spirit and power that many New Lights sought.

Ann Lee's other unusual qualities impressed visitors. Some strangers she greeted by name, telling them she knew they were coming and knew where they had lodged along the way and to whom they had spoken.[38] Proselytes believed in her visions, prophecies, and revelations, which to them resembled spiritual gifts described in scripture.

Ann Lee worked within Protestants' religious frame of reference, marketing her gospel by adding it to their mainstream beliefs, using religious syncretism to merge her version of Christianity with theirs. One critic wrote:

> Many persons who have been the subject of these bewitching charms have related surprising effects of them on their minds. They affirm that all their former views of things were strangely obliterated; they could recollect nothing of their former notions of religion; every thing appeared dark and confused, and the new system now before them wholly

swallowed up all their attention, and their whole souls were irresistibly borne away by its bewitching energy.[39]

Rathbun, an early apostate, noted that converts experienced, "a total blindness, as to all their former views, of religion and the bible," making them susceptible to believe everything the Shakers taught.[40] That statement is not strictly true. Many of Ann Lee's sayings came directly from scripture, and she regularly invoked Jesus Christ. Nevertheless, modern researchers have been struck by how Ann Lee could draw proselytes away from other denominations. These churches had failed to prevent war, fill larders, or provide solace. In contrast, Ann Lee, who preached pacifism, offered a full pantry, and provided spiritual gifts, was an attractive alternative. She also called for renunciation of worldly views, which the sociologist Rosabeth Moss Kanter identifies as an essential commitment mechanism. When a newcomer reached that point, Mother Ann knew that she had "made the sale."[41]

Such dramatic changes in outlook caused many outsiders to view Shakerism as witchcraft or "the work of the devil." Angell Matthewson heard in 1780 that Ann Lee "bewitched everyone" who visited her. Prudence Hammond recalled that when she got to know Ann Lee, she found neither deception nor witchcraft—evidence that both possibilities had been suggested. Others had also heard those rumors. Elizabeth Wood confessed that she had called Ann Lee "a Witch & wished she was shot with a piece of silver."[42] By 1782, the "common knowledge" was that Lee was a witch.[43] Stories of her supernatural gifts could have brought charges of witchcraft in an earlier time. Moreover, Ann Lee fit the profile of a potential witch: female, middle-aged, of English ancestry, childless, poor, and outspoken, even abrasive.[44] One family asked an exorcist to save their daughter from Shakerism.[45] The followers of Ann Lee, however, viewed her paranormal abilities as gifts from God, just as the followers of Jesus viewed his healing powers as God-given. Her spiritual gifts convinced many that she was the second embodiment of the Christ spirit.[46]

Ann Lee's leadership was at odds with the norm. Outsiders questioned her theology as well as her gender role. But Mother Ann assured proselytes that she recognized the divinity of Jesus of Nazareth. To explain her position she used a husband-and-wife analogy that farmers and farmwives well understood. When the male head of household (in this case, Christ) was present, he headed the church. When he departed, however, the female head of household (Ann Lee), stepped into the leadership role. This is the "substitute husband" view of Mother Ann's divinity that convinced potential proselytes of her spiritual authority.[47]

After the initial meeting, potential proselytes' socialization to the Shakers continued through personal interviews, group discussions, and exhortations.[48] All the while, Mother Ann was sizing up prospects. She and the Elders must have paid close attention to each individual to determine the best way to secure a commitment. A visitor's history, interests, hopes, fears, biases, and earlier religious disappointments provided material that Shakers could use to "sell" their new religion.

The Shakers employed admonishment and peer pressure effectively. While Ann Lee and the Elders provided instruction, for instance, other converts confirmed the truth of the information imparted, drawing each visitor in by saying they had many more things to tell, which the visitor was "not yet able to bear." According to Rathbun, if prospects argued with any point of doctrine, converts told them not to dispute because their business was to listen and receive instruction. Continued opposition brought out operations of divine power, "quick, strong and violent," and the Shakers would "cry out on the opposer, that he will be damn'd for opposing the power of God"—a display that most visitors probably preferred to avoid. Such reprimands also tested their conformity and humility.[49] At this point, some prospective proselytes opted out. Others joined, but, like Rathbun, soon left.

Ann Lee's effectiveness as an evangelist was based in part on her ability to judge the worthiness of the hopefuls who flocked to her. Many were called to lead a more godly life, but some, Mother Ann determined, could not meet the challenge. Religion derives power from its authority to judge, and perhaps exclude, those deemed unworthy as it does from its ability to attract followers and influence human behavior.

Prospective proselytes had to shape their behavior to meet Ann Lee's standards. Angell Matthewson recalled that Ann Lee chastised her followers "with language that would have been destitute of delicacy in any other woman." Mother Ann reproved the Spencer family, saying "I don't like your idleness, nastiness, covetousness, & pride." Despite the criticism, the Spencers evidently changed their ways and several joined the Shakers.[50] Ann Lee rejected other potential proselytes, including Tryphena Perkins, whom she called "a filthy whore." Lee's denunciation was considered defamation at first because Perkins was "not formed like other women" and therefore could not be guilty as charged. But when Perkins, a single woman, was reported to be pregnant by a married man, Mother Ann's assessment was assumed to be correct.[51] Ann Lee had to use her keen insight to shun the sinful and unrepentant because their presence among her followers would make her appear hypocritical. Mother Ann's rejection of a prospective follower might also be construed, however, as a marketing ploy, adding to her legend as a charismatic leader with supernatural gifts, while also bolstering the Shakers' reputation for living without sin.

Ann Lee also allowed her followers to drive some prospects away. An early convert, Abijah Worster, recalled: "In the early days of our faith, there came a young woman here by the name of Polly Swan to see the [Shakers], and Elenor Pierce and Martha Prescot being full of zeal, and lacking both wisdom & charity, began to war at her for her lust and pride, and pushed her about . . . and Polly, when she got out of their hands, run." Disturbed by the assault, Worster questioned Ann Lee about it: "I thought the design of the gospel was to gather souls to the way of God, not to drive them off?" She replied, "They have received the power of God, and are full of zeal; but lack wisdom to know how to improve their gifts; and if you strike at their zeal, they will be likely to lose their gifts, and go back to the world and be lost; and better it is, that ten souls should go to hell that never heared the gospel, than one soul that has."[52] Ann Lee supported Pierce and Prescot's expulsion of Polly Swan because they had made a commitment to the Shakers, and Swan had not. By giving latitude to her followers, she validated their spiritual gifts, as well as her own.

For a prospective convert who passed the test of the first meeting, perhaps the most startling revelation was that the Shakers were celibate. One visitor, William Loughton Smith, explained, "They reprobate matrimony; if any married persons become members of this church, they must immediately live in a state of separation, and any connection between them is considered criminal and the parties expelled; they continue their sect by making proselytes." Another visitor wrote, "One of [the shaking Quakers], in speaking of marriage, called it contrary to the example of the Saviour who was never married,—to use his terms 'never had any carnal connection with a woman.'"[53] "The truth is," convert Daniel Moseley explained,

> Mother Ann had the revelation of the Lord Jesus Christ given her to search out all the crooked windings of the serpent, and all the deceit of the devil, which has been so craftily diffused into the nature of man; and she was thereby able to rend that glossy covering which, like a mantle, they have spread over their works of concupiscence. By this means she was enabled to unmask all the base and unclean desires and deceitful wantonness of both male and female, and detect all those

alluring charms of lust by which they entice and deceive each other. She
exposed the subtle craftiness of that filthy nature in the males, by which
they seek to seduce and debauch the females; and all the enticing arts
of the females to ensnare and bewitch the males, and draw them into
their wanton embraces.

Ann Lee, Moseley points out, declared that lust is the cause of all human
corruption, including deceit, hypocrisy, covetousness, dissipation, idleness,
envy, contention, and strife. "These things (said she) are the fruits of the
filthy gratifications of the flesh, which bring distress and poverty, shame and
disgrace upon families and individuals, and fill the earth with wretchedness
and misery." But those who could endure the "purifying fire of Zion" would
be saved.[54] By preaching publicly against sex, Ann Lee violated gender norms
yet again. The sacrifice of sex, however, was a test of Believers' willingness
to forgo the pleasures of the world. That shared sacrifice, and the effort to
maintain celibacy, Kanter suggests, kept Believers' commitment strong.[55]

Ann Lee practiced celibacy herself after the death of her children and gave
practical advice to married women trying to end their conjugal relations.
She told them that her husband had complained to her former church and
her family that she remained chaste. "The church opposed my testimony
& tried to persuade me to give it up; & I had to stand the test against my
husband, my relation, & the church. I soon received that power of God
that my bed would rock under me & my husband was glad to leave it."[56]

If the idea of celibacy did not squelch interest, a potential proselyte would
return for another visit and perhaps take the next step toward commitment: confession of sins from childhood to the present. Stephen Marini
asserts that a proper confession took an "elaborate series of individual,
subgroup, and collective transactions—interviews, discussions, meals, and
worship—that created a richly textured spiritual environment in which
confession became natural, meaningful, and effective."[57] Ann Lee or an
Elder told the individual that they would "travail for him, that he may be
born again."[58] Confession, advocated in James 5:16, was one of the keys
to their success. A humbling sort of mortification, it was another commitment mechanism. The process demonstrated a proselyte's acceptance of the
Elders' authority—an important hurdle that had to be crossed before a
convert could move wholeheartedly into a new religion.[59] Ann Lee astutely
warned her followers that confession was "the only way in which they could
expect forgiveness. This confession must be in public, and every sin of heart
and life, though ever so secret, must be disclosed." Their future salvation

depended on this "all-important duty." To mainstream Protestants, such a confession was excessive, even indiscreet, and had a popish taint.[60] Daniel Goodrich remembered Ann Lee's request for his confession.

> Mother informed me that if I desired to find the way of God, and obtain salvation, I must confess my sins to God, in the presence of his witnesses, and forsake them forever; and take up my cross against all those propensities which caused me to commit sin; and in so doing, I should find forgiveness, and obtain the favor of God, and have power over sin. She said, "It is a shame to commit sin; but no shame to confess it."[61]

Confession was humbling, by design. It went beyond the public rite of repentance that Congregationalists required of erring members suspended from church membership until they read a public confession for a particular misdeed, often premarital fornication or intemperance. "Here was an exhibition really humiliating to every feeling and sober mind," a skeptical witness observed of the Shakers, "to behold multitudes of deluded mortals at once disgorging every abomination they had ever practiced, or even thought of in their lives." But confession was essential. The process gave a Believer the opportunity to purge sin, prove humility, show repentance, and receive forgiveness, while demonstrating acceptance of church leaders' authority. Many Protestant churches required sinners to publicly confess, and scripture shows the precedents.[62] Among the Shakers, a proselyte traded confession for salvation, showing that he or she had "bought" Shakerism.

Few early converts volunteered to confess their sins. Ann Lee convinced some that their errors were already so evident that they might as well confess. She overcame John Farrington's reluctance with practical logic, as he testified:

> When I was about to take my leave of them to return home, Mother Ann told me I might open my mind and confess my sins, if I was so minded, before I returned home. I said I believed it to be right to confess my sins: but I had thought to return home and labor to get a deeper sense of sin, and try to mend my life a little. Mother replied, "That is very good; but you can gain a deeper sense of sin after you have confessed them, as well as before, and be better able to mend your life."

In marketing terms, Mother Ann wanted to close the deal. She knew that if she could get Farrington to confess before he went home, his commitment to Shakerism increased. If she did not ask for a commitment, she could not be sure that he had converted. By hearing his confession and dispensing forgiveness, she boosted the likelihood that he would return. Determined to secure his conversion, she persuaded him; he confessed as thoroughly as he could (or would). When he finished, however, Mother Ann told him that he had omitted his secret sins, "unknown to any living mortal" but himself. His certainty that she knew them by the revelation of God increased her spiritual authority in his eyes.[63]

Mother Ann sized up her prospective proselytes and secured commitments with exquisite timing. Hannah Chauncey recalled, "I knew that she saw me through & through. She told me she knew every sin I had ever committed." Chauncey felt that Ann Lee spoke the truth.[64] When Lucy Wight first went to the Shakers, she, too, believed her sins were as plain and open to their view as to her own, but she did not confess until James Whittaker and Ann Lee asked her. "They then told me that there was a way of God for me," she said, "if I would confess and forsake my sins." Wight did. "I found that releasement from the burden of sin which I had never felt before," she recalled, "and which I had never been able to find in any other way, tho I had long sought for it." Elizabeth Johnson had a similar experience. She confessed because she believed Ann Lee could tell the state of her mind as easily as she could see her own face in a mirror. Ann Lee read Samuel Johnson's intentions before she asked him to make his confession. "This was just what I desired," he said, "and by this I perceived that she knew the state of my mind. I opened my mind and confessed my sins."[65]

For a newcomer, confession speeded a sense of belonging. According to one apostate, however, confession also told the Elders the "thoughts and feelings, purposes and propensities, character and condition" of every member, so they knew "exactly what influences to exert to keep them in subjection." Confession was the "secret lever" for manipulating individual Believers.[66] Ann Lee and the Elders pushed many into confessing; few were eager to expose their faults. Passing that test, however, meant that they were ready to make a commitment to their new faith.

Confession attracted criticism from skeptics, one of whom revealed what he considered Ann Lee's ulterior motive in exacting confessions. Once the confessions had been "effected," he pointed out, "the mother [Ann Lee] then warned them of the danger of pride, the great sin of following the foolish and vain fashions of the world; and after having fleeced them of their jewels, ear-rings, necklaces, buckles, and every other thing that might feed their pride, or rather enrich herself, and having cut off their hair hard by their ears, would then admit them into her fraternity."[67] Indeed, Ann

Lee expected her followers to invest in their new religion, giving up their material possessions for communal use. Every Believer did so, whether they owned a lot or a little. That investment, Kanter points out, was yet another commitment mechanism that held individuals in place as Shakers.[68] Without an investment in the society, it would be easy to walk away.

Ann Lee knew how quickly her followers could be seduced back to the world and its comparatively easy Christianity. She and the first Elders told proselytes after confession that having received the faith, they could go to heaven, but if they slid back to the world, the flesh and the devil, they would be doomed to hell. The effect, according to one apostate, was to terrify a convert into the sect.[69]

Though today's Shakers seem benign, in the eighteenth century they were a threat to the social order. The Shakers' insistence on celibate communalism, for instance, Rathbun explained, meant that "men and their wives have parted, children ran away from their parents, and society entirely broke up in neighborhoods."[70] Elderly parents depended on their adult children for support and care in old age. When children joined the Shakers, however, parents lost that security. When husbands joined and their wives did not, those women were reduced to poverty and had to be boarded at town expense, auctioned off to the lowest bidder.[71] Thus Shakerism had a bandwagon effect; when several family members joined, others followed. In return for covenanting themselves (and their property) to the society of Shakers, each proselyte received a guarantee of lifetime support—a reciprocal contract that worked as long as the society attracted new members.

Having handed over their property, some Believers may have felt that they could not afford to leave and simply reconciled themselves to their situation. Others left the society. Some went quietly. A few, however, made their apostasy profitable, writing and publishing derogatory pamphlets about the Shakers with the authority of former members who had seen the inner workings of the church. Moreover, those who entered the society with kin often left with kin, as well—or tried to. In the nineteenth century, after Shakers became sticklers for holding legally indentured youth, parents who seceded often had to leave without their children.[72]

Mother Ann's effectiveness as an evangelist can be measured in the longevity of her religion, which persists today. Shaker society's success can also be measured through outsiders' views. Even critics had to admire the Shakers' work ethic. In the mid-1790s, Elkanah Watson extolled their temporal success in "accumulating the common stock." William Loughton

Smith, a visiting congressman, reported, "Their neighbors give them a good reputation for their scrupulous observance of farming industry and attention to agriculture."[73]

In 1794, Benjamin Waterhouse described the New Lebanon Shaker village.

> The cultivation of this large farm is beyond any thing in this quarter. Their houses have a very neat appearance, being all painted white Barns, Cribs, and other out-houses very commodious, and in perfect order. Their horn cattle, their sheep, & their swine are the finest & fattest in the whole country. Their fences, gates, yards, and walled enclosures are as neat as their houses; but their meeting house or place of worship is neatest of all. It seems as if they meant to express by it an holy place, pure and undefiled. . . .

Their gardens and workshops were "distinguished by the same neatness which reigns throughout every part of the settlement." Shakers appeared to work diligently, but deliberately. "They pursue their business with a grave & serious air," he added, "without the least trace of anxiety, or mark of discontent." Such was the appearance of the Shaker settlement at New Lebanon. "By their fruits shall ye know them," he concluded.[74]

Ann Lee's spiritual children lived communally, maintained the cross of celibacy, and kept the faith. By revering their female founder, eliminating marriage (along with the legal disabilities it imposed on women), and providing leadership opportunities for women, Believers offered a strong incentive for women to join. The next generation of leaders, handpicked by Mother Ann, would reshape Shaker society based on the radical notion that women and men are equal in the eyes of God and should be, in human terms, as well.

2

The Short Marriage
of Mother Lucy Wright

He could not bear to spoil her with the flesh.

THE SEPARATION OF THE NEWLYWEDS LUCY WRIGHT AND Elizur Goodrich is a case study in Shaker history. Their matrimonial union was among many that crumbled under Shaker celibacy.[1] Because Lucy Wright subsequently became the Shakers' leader, however, her marriage and its dissolution are documented better than others. Furthermore, Wright's choices highlight Shakerism's benefits to women. Lucy Wright gave up her marriage (a civil contract that kept women in legal dependency) in favor of a Shaker covenant, which allowed her to rise to leadership with the kind of power that, among the world's people, was usually held by men.

In the late eighteenth century, most women expected to marry and bear children who would support their elderly parents until they died. Shaker celibacy was at odds with the tradition of the nuclear family because celibacy ended reproduction as well as the traditional hierarchy of marriage that privileged men over women.[2] For women who took to heart Romans 8:8 ("Those who are in the flesh cannot please God"), Shakerism took the place of the natural family and met the need for lifelong support, as well as sanctifying them through spiritual practice.

When Lucy Wright awoke on the morning of December 15, 1779, she probably felt the anticipation typical of a bride on her wedding day. Perhaps the first thing she did was look out the window to check the sky. Aside from bad weather hindering guests traveling to her nuptials, she had another reason to be concerned. Wedding-day weather forecast a marriage. The old saying, "Lowering sky, lowering bride" meant that a woman married on a stormy day would have an unhappy marriage. And, as the Pittsfield parson Thomas Allen wrote, that winter was "as long and severe a winter as almost was ever known." If Lucy Wright believed in omens, she had a reason to worry.[3]

At age nineteen, Lucy Wright was ready to change her status from single woman to wife, the traditional calling of eighteenth-century New England women. In keeping with the lessons she would have been taught from Matthew 19:5–6 and Genesis 1:28, she would have expected to become one flesh with Elizur Goodrich, bear his children, and serve as his helpmeet for the rest of her life, modeling herself on the biblical wife of many talents who looked well to the ways of her household and never ate the bread of idleness. She may have hoped that her offspring would bless her name, as did the children of the virtuous wife in Proverbs 31. Lucy Wright's willingness to marry showed that she was conventional in that respect. On her wedding day, however, no one could have guessed just how unconventional her life would become.

Lucy was born February 5, 1760, the daughter of John and Mary (Robbins) Wright of Pontoosuck plantation (later Pittsfield, Massachusetts), in the Housatonic River valley of the Berkshire hills, just a few miles from the New York line. Her parents were respectable middle-class landowners.[4] They must have been ambitious to risk the hardship of a near-wilderness where lonely log cabins stood scattered in small clearings and the roads were only paths wide enough for pack horses. Sarah Deming, the first white woman settler, had ridden into the Berkshires with her husband in 1752. They were so isolated that when a pregnant woman went into labor at Pontoosuck, the midwife Granny Dewey had to be fetched from Sheffield, more than twenty miles away. At first, the closest minister was at Jonathan Edwards's Indian mission in Stockbridge. The Pontoosuck settlement had no church until Lucy Wright was almost thirteen. The woods were so thick that newcomers had to girdle trees to clear land for planting.[5] Most families kept a cow or two, and women made butter and cheese for home consumption and trade. About a third of the households owned sheep. Lucy probably learned in early childhood to process wool and flax into textiles. Settlers had to barter goods or trade work with neighbors for whatever they could not produce themselves because the nearest shopkeeper was probably in Stockbridge near the Indian mission where Timothy Edwards had merchandise for sale.[6]

Worst of all, the French and Indian wars were not over. In 1754, many residents evacuated the Berkshires after Indians attacked Pontoosuck plantation and destroyed Hoosack, New York. Settlements north of Stockbridge emptied out because their homes were too far apart for mutual defense. Those brave enough to stay fortified their houses as garrisons and established a fort with eight soldiers at Pontoosuck. Settlers believed that the woods were filled with Indians, few of them friendly, so the persisting yeomen tended their crops with firearms within reach. Because they had to be prepared to defend themselves at a moment's notice, they practiced to stay proficient. Josiah Wright, a militiaman at Fort Pontoosuck, described a shooting match in 1756. "Shoot at marks," he wrote, "Both men and women." On the frontier, gender roles bent. Women had to learn marksmanship as well as housewifery.[7] Lucy Wright grew up understanding that women had to rise to meet challenges.

Lucy was a lively, black-eyed child, brighter than average. She made good use of her schooling. Massachusetts's "Old Deluder Satan law" required towns to hold public school, to ensure that children could read well enough to study scripture. Though attendance was not compulsory, Lucy Wright went to school, perhaps in Mrs. Phineas Parker's class in the west district of Pittsfield. According to Calvin Green, who knew her later, Lucy was an excellent reader and writer with a precise command of grammar and high standards in verbal expression.[8] As a girl, she longed for a sky-blue silk gown, a luxury in color, fiber, and expense.[9] That she eventually got one suggests that her parents indulged her and probably were not New Lights who frowned on prideful luxuries in dress. In evangelical households, clothing was a point of discipline, and simplicity was essential.[10]

Lucy Wright grew into an attractive woman, tall and graceful, with strong shoulders and arms. Her upper-body strength suggests that she had performed enough heavy labor in her youth to build visible muscles. Her face, according to Calvin Green, was "neither round nor long, but fair and symmetrical," with a bold forehead. By all accounts, she had dark hair, a good figure, and a beautiful smile. Lucy was energetic, with "an elastic step," well-behaved, "modest and unassuming," with "gentle manners and amiable disposition." She had "quick, lively ways [that] made her a pleasant companion, easily winning respect and affection." The "very handsome" girl was popular, a leader among her peers.[11] Such a girl attracted suitors, and Lucy singled out one for her favor.

Lucy and Elizur Goodrich, whose families were among the town's earliest settlers, probably met through the web of social, religious, and commercial relationships that connected everyone in the area. When they married, Elizur was twenty-eight and a veteran of the Revolutionary War. Like his father, his ten brothers, and all other able-bodied men and boys over age sixteen, he was a member of the town militia. During times of peace, they mustered once a year for training day, to elect officers, and practice shooting. During the war, however, militiamen could remain in the home guard or enlist in a state unit or the Continental Army. Elizur served two limited enlistments, the first with Colonel James Easton's Third Berkshire regiment under Major John Brown and Captain James Noble in the Canada campaign from May through December 1776.[12]

On August 16, 1777, the Berkshire militia responded to the call to battle at Bennington, Vermont. They marched thirty miles through a rainy night to Bennington, rested a while, and went into battle fortified by a prayer from the fighting parson, Rev. Thomas Allen. Veterans of other campaigns said the fire at Bennington was the hottest of the war, like one continual clap of thunder. During the battle, the soldiers watched Tory troops, some of them former friends and neighbors, picked off one by one as they tried to scale the steep, slippery slope to take refuge behind the earthworks.[13]

After the Battle of Bennington, Elizur never went to war again. He had lost three of his brothers. Benjamin, wounded during the siege of Quebec, was invalided out of service, but died on May 30, 1776, before he reached home. Samuel was killed in battle in December 1776. Josiah died at age eighteen, a prisoner of war, in 1778. The surviving brothers were disinclined to re-enlist even for the substantial bounties the Continental Army offered to induce men to join for the duration of the war. Instead, the Goodrich family became pacifists. Between 1780 and 1788, seven Goodrich brothers and most of their children joined the Shakers.[14]

Elizur and Lucy wed in 1779 but soon realized they were mismatched; they did not share a commitment to the physical union of husband and wife, despite the Anglo-American tradition, supported by the teaching in 1 Corinthians 7 that a husband and wife should become one flesh. In theory, a married couple's rights and duties were reciprocal. Physical access was not to be withheld except by mutual consent, and then only for a short time of continence. Marriage was the one legitimate outlet for sexuality; the assumption was that newlyweds' sexual union would affirm their lawful bond.[15] No so for Lucy and Elizur.

Although the couple viewed their partnership as profoundly meaningful, they did not truly cleave unto one another. To Elizur Goodrich, "Lucy was so beautiful & amiable that he could not bear to spoil her with the flesh." The two lived "uncommonly continent," according to Lucy Wright's biographer Calvin Green.[16] This description of the newlyweds' physical relationship is, of course, one-sided, depending as it does on the words of only one partner, reported by a third party many years after the fact. Furthermore, because this recollection was recorded after Wright and Goodrich became Shakers, it is possible that Elizur Goodrich described his newlywed life in a way that served his status as a celibate Believer. Besides adhering to the conventional view that relating intimate details of marital sexuality was indiscreet, Shakers avoided conversation that might "excite lustful sensations."[17]

We might deduce from Elizur Goodrich's reported words that his sexual drive was not up to the norm for a man of his age. The most likely explanation for this anomaly is religion. The Goodrich family included several generations of New Lights. Their earliest ancestor in the Berkshires, Charles Goodrich, "obtained a hope under Whitefield in 1741," according to his epitaph, which suggests that the preaching of the English evangelist George Whitefield reassured Goodrich of his salvation.[18] Several Goodrich family members belonged to Valentine Rathbun's New Light Baptist congregation. Lucy Wright and Elizur Goodrich's subsequent history shows that they were evangelical Christians. Many evangelical children were taught from an early age to associate guilt and shame with their sexual impulses. What made them behave (even in the absence of an authority figure) was their active conscience, the "inner disciplinarian" that governed their actions. Elizur's beliefs and feelings were probably much like those of his cousin Daniel Goodrich, who described feeling accountable to God throughout his childhood for his falsehoods and wickedness. Even though Daniel wanted to do good, evil tempted him. Finally he was convinced that his best hope for salvation lay with the Shakers. His "inner disciplinarian" was not satisfied until he found a more rigorous route to redemption.[19]

"Self-suppressed" eighteenth-century evangelicals used prayer, hard work, and constant self-control as "remedies against uncleanness." Nicholas Gilman, a guilt-ridden young man who later became a New Light preacher, made a list of antidotes to lust: fleeing temptation, avoiding idleness, joining a company of others when tempted by unclean thoughts, and praying. Such habits, long practiced to repress lust, might have made legitimate marital sex difficult. Some evangelicals viewed sexual contact as filthy and sinful even after marriage.[20] Thus, Elizur Goodrich may not have been able to set aside his inhibitions once he was married. Furthermore, the fact that many of the Goodriches joined the Shakers suggests that the family shared the view that celibacy was the route to redemption.

One might conjecture that Elizur's unusual continence was reinforced by incompatibility with his assertive wife. She was already a proven leader by the time of her marriage, and she may not have relinquished authority under her husband's roof.[21] It is possible, too, that Elizur Goodrich had physical reasons for his lack of interest in sex—factors unlikely to be preserved for posterity. His documented attraction to his wife, however, makes it improbable that homosexuality was among those factors.[22] Equally conjectural are similar possibilities for Lucy Wright.

To their credit, the young couple made the best of their situation. According to Shaker sources, both felt that marriage was "a nobler state, with deeper and higher meanings than licensed sensuality can realize." It is unclear, however, whether Elizur, Lucy, or their Shaker biographers made that assessment, so it is hard to say whether it is an accurate representation of the facts or just an attempt to portray their marriage in the best possible light. The comment, however, suggests that the young couple believed that their partnership could transcend physical love.[23] Their sexual continence was the first pivotal circumstance in their marriage. The second was their new religion.

Lucy (Wright) and Elizur Goodrich, like many other New Englanders, were driven by the social and economic upheaval of the revolutionary era to look for a new source of religious inspiration. Wartime inflation left even thrifty Yankees in debt, among them the merchant Elizur Goodrich, whose father may have had set him up in business for his portion. Elizur, however, did not increase his assets enough to buy land, an indication that his prosperity must have been limited.[24] Moreover, he was in debt.[25] The established order was ruinous economically and socially, as well as a challenge to Christian virtues.

The couple seem to have been dissatisfied with their religious options, and sought something better. In their seeking, they were caught up in the revival of 1779. Elizur, especially, was "an ardent sharer in the hopes inspired by its exercises, visions and rhapsodies." The revivalists hoped for Christ to reappear and warfare to end. But they were disappointed. "Like many before them and many since, they saw suns rise and set, winter unfold into spring . . . [but] no change appeared. Their emotions subsided; the meetings, so intense and absorbing, ceased; farmers and mechanics went about their work; the war went on." New religions offer new hope, and so, when Ann Lee opened Shaker worship to the public in May 1780, "thousands flocked from the neighboring towns in New York and Massachusetts to listen to her novel and marvelous doctrines."[26] Lucy (Wright) and Elizur Goodrich were soon among them. In early summer, perhaps six months into their marriage, the couple left the Berkshire hills of western Massachusetts and crossed the Hudson River to Watervliet to see the shaking Quakers. Around the same time, at least twenty-five of the Goodrich family went there seeking religious perfection. Most of Ann Lee's proselytes were former New Light Baptists who appreciated the spiritual excitement of the 1779 revival but were disappointed by its failure to bring change. Thus, Elizur and Lucy were open to the Shakers' "spiritual dynamo," though they had to be persuaded that Shakerism was their best hope.[27]

Ann Lee's message moved many members of the Goodrich family. In June 1780, Elizur's brother and sister-in-law Nathan and Hannah (Fuller) Goodrich arrived at Watervliet to find a crowd with Mother Ann, some of them sharing "sharp testimony against sin." The first words they heard were Mary Partington's. "Strip off your pride and abominations!" she exhorted. "We know you; but you do not know us—We have men here that are not defiled with women, and women that are not defiled with men!" Nathan and Hannah stayed overnight with the Shakers, as did Elizur. The next day, Ann Lee berated Hannah with the words, "Let your husband alone—fastening your lust upon him!" Hannah may have been embarrassed, but she knew that celibacy would require changes in her behavior. Seeking guidance, she asked God to "make it known to her whether this was his work or not; and if not, to keep her from delusion." And God answered. When one of the Elders came to her and "told her her own thoughts just as they had passed through her mind," she was convinced that "this was the work of God, and that these people were his witnesses."[28]

Among the other members of Elizur Goodrich's extended family who were drawn to the Shakers was Daniel Goodrich Sr., who visited Ann Lee with several of his children. As Hannah remembered, "his family, at that time, had not got hold of much faith; some of them were still in stiff opposition; and one of his little girls, which he then carried with him, having by a fall, had her hip put out, was bowed together, and her leg began to perish, so that it was feared she would be a cripple." Daniel Goodrich "opened his trials and difficulties to Mother," and she called his children into the room and told them that faith and obedience would carry them even when signs and operations failed. She told them to purge sin from their family, and all would be gathered in. Then she took the lame girl on her lap, set her on her feet again, stroked her down her sides, and said, "Go home Daniel, and be faithful—This your child will become well." Goodrich's daughter healed and the family all joined the Shakers.[29] They needed no further proof that Ann Lee had divine powers.

Lucy and Elizur revealed in their own words that they were not deterred by Ann Lee's message about celibacy. Lucy testified that soon after opening the gospel at Watervliet, Mother Ann told married people, "You must forsake the marriage of the flesh, and travel out of it, in order to be married to the Lamb; which is to be married to Christ, or joined to the Lord in one spirit."[30] Elizur Goodrich recalled the same message more than thirty years later.

> Mother spoke of the root & foundation of sin, and plainly said, "It is lust." She said that in relation to the first man & woman, "They came together in the actual works of the flesh, & that was their fall and loss from God, & that has been the fall and loss of all mankind, ever since. I often see the dead in their agony and distress suffering for their doleful corruption committed through lust."[31]

Elizur Goodrich saw enough on his first visit with the Shakers to decide that he wanted to commit to them. "The first time I went to Watervliet to see Mother," Elizur recalled, "I received faith in the second appearing of Christ, confessed my sins, & received the power of the Holy Spirit." His conversion took place during a visit that lasted only a day or two.[32] His first act was confession, a prerequisite to membership. "Every sin of heart and life, though ever so secret," had to be disclosed. Confession bound him to the Shakers. He later said that Ann Lee's most important lesson was about confession. "You must confess and forsake all your sins," she taught, "right all your wrongs, take up a full cross against the world, flesh and devil, & for the future, do justice, love mercy & walk humbly with God."[33]

Lucy, however, was not persuaded, and Elizur remained "burdened for the soul of his beautiful young wife." He may also have wanted to avoid the trouble that would ensue with her and her family if he joined the society and she did not. Years later, Shakers remembered his quandary. "After Elizur Goodrich had embraced the testimony of the gospel, he opened his feelings to Mother [Ann] concerning Lucy Wright, to whom he had lately been married. He said her relations were a lofty high-minded people, and it was very doubtful to him whether she would believe and obey the gospel." Mother Ann mulled over the problem, then told him, "Take faith, Lucy may be gained to the gospel, and, if you gain her, it will be equal to gaining a nation." Joseph Meacham, the former New Light Baptist preacher who by then had joined the Shakers, considered Mother Ann's words a prophecy that Lucy would "stand in her lot, as the first Mother in Church relation."[34]

Elizur, however, doubted that Lucy would obey. He had cause for concern if Lucy followed him into a communal society that required obedience. Though Anglo-American common law made the husband head of the family, some men were unable to impose their will on their wives.[35] Lucy, who had "great firmness of mind," was among them.[36] Subsequent events would show that she had an air of authority and was adept at giving direction.

In July 1780, Mother Ann Lee was arrested on suspicion of aiding the enemy British, and Elizur visited her in jail in Poughkeepsie, taking along gifts that Lucy sent for her comfort. Once again, Elizur discussed his doubts about Lucy with Ann Lee. She gave him "much good instruction, and sent him away saying, 'Go home, Elizur, and love Lucy, as Christ loved his Church.'"[37] Ann Lee, always perceptive, would not have admonished Elizur Goodrich to love his wife unless she recognized an underlying problem for which the young husband needed counsel—and if that advice netted another convert, so much the better. Elizur went home to win over his wife.

Twice Lucy had not accompanied her husband to visit Ann Lee. She kept her distance from Elizur's new interest. Others said of her, "Lucy had a vein of cool, calculating prudence and discretion in her nature. Not rashly moved to hasty action, she deliberated, weighed and counseled with her good sense, before she moved to any course. From childhood she had been averse to anything outré, extreme or wanting in good taste."[38] Many people considered the Shakers radical; some called them deluded fanatics.[39] Lucy Wright Goodrich had to be convinced that they were neither. She appreciated evangelical worship, but she held back as her husband grew closer and closer to Mother Ann Lee and her followers. At the same time, he distanced himself from his wife, though he and Lucy continued housekeeping together, living amicably in their own home more as brother and sister than as husband and wife.[40]

Finally Lucy had to face the hard truth. Her marriage had lasted less than two years and her husband was devoting himself to the Shakers. She had to weigh her options and consider her alternatives.

She could have sought a divorce. If Elizur joined the Shakers and she did not, she might have been considered a deserted wife. Desertion was grounds enough to terminate a marriage in Massachusetts after the Revolution.[41] The state had already granted divorces to more than fifty women for just that reason. The state also dissolved marriages for sexual incapacity.[42] Petitioning for divorce, however, meant revealing uncomfortable personal details and perhaps becoming an object of gossip, pity, or derision. Women who sued for divorce had to expose themselves to public scrutiny. Moreover, divorce was expensive, and the process could drag on for years.[43]

With or without a divorce, Lucy Wright Goodrich had a more pressing need: economic support. She might have returned to her father's house or joined the family of a sibling, the most conventional choices. But Lucy's mother died before 1777, and when Lucy married, a stepmother ran her father's household, a likely disincentive for returning home.[44] Many New England households included spinsters or widows. But if Lucy had no children of her own, she had little assurance of familial care in her old age. At the time, towns took bids for housing the indigent, awarding contracts for paupers' care to the lowest bidders.

Lucy could have earned a living by teaching school or working at a trade.[45] Those jobs, however, did not guarantee economic security. In a society where marriage was almost universal, single women were often at the bottom of the socioeconomic scale. Though the cult of single blessedness was on the rise among New England women after 1780, Lucy was evidently not one of its proponents. She had married, after all, and did not intend to spend her life as a spinster or a dependent in her father's house.[46] When her husband joined the Shakers, however, he shut the door on their marriage. Lucy had no hope of resurrecting a marital relationship with a husband who preferred a celibate life. Nor could she remain in a foundering marriage.

Lucy's best alternative was the least conventional: following her husband into the Shakers' communal society. Her commitment to evangelical religion pulled her in this direction. Furthermore, the fact that the sect was led by a woman whose marriage had also ended gave Lucy a point of commonality with Ann Lee, whose interest in Lucy may well have been a draw. By joining the Shakers, Lucy would gain the socioeconomic support of a surrogate family who might prove more constant than her spouse. One door shut; another opened wide. So Lucy Goodrich stepped through the door that welcomed her into Shaker society and resumed her maiden name, symbolic of the dissolution of her marriage. According to Calvin Green, once she was convinced that Ann Lee's gospel was the truth, "she embraced it with all her heart and soul."[47]

By May 1781, Elizur and Lucy had broken up their household and contributed their assets (such as they were) to the Shakers. Lucy got rid of her "Babylonish stuff" (presumably including the sky-blue silk gown). She adopted habits of self-denial that she would advocate to the end of her days. She explained to a younger Believer, "I have naturally as particular eyes as any body else for I know and like to see fine things but I have always cross[ed my]self."[48]

As soon as Lucy shifted her commitment from her husband to her new religion, Mother Ann found it expedient to separate her and her husband.

She sent Elizur on the road as an itinerant Shaker preacher. Lucy moved to the Shaker community at Watervliet.[49]

Though Lucy Wright might have been tempted to blame her difficult decision on her "uncommonly continent" husband, she knew better than to harbor ill will toward him. Rancor could be destructive to the communal group, and Mother Ann often preached against such folly. Years later, Lucy remembered her saying:

> Hear ye my words, you that have hard feelings against one another, and yet think to keep the way of God! You are awfully mistaken; you cannot prosper. Though you may hang on for a while; yet you will certainly fall off, like withered branches; and when you drop into hell, these hard feelings will be like devouring worms to torment you. Remember my words! You can never enter the Kingdom of God with hardness against any one: for God is love: and if you love God, you will love one another.[50]

Lucy seems to have reconciled her frustrations over the disparity between the life she had anticipated and the life she now led. She followed Mother Ann's advice by setting aside regret and embracing profound change beyond anything she might have foreseen on her wintry wedding day. But she and Elizur did not immediately set aside their love.

Eunice Chapman described the Shakers' effort to "wean" Elizur and Lucy's "almost indelible affections from each other." Elizur was the greater challenge, however. According to the apostate Thomas Brown, "several gifts of mortification" were required to "separate the affections of Goodrich from his wife Lucy."[51] This comment, taken in context with his speedy conversion, suggests that Elizur was perhaps as inconstant a Shaker as he was a husband, quickly convinced but imperfectly committed.

Another story is equally revealing. When Elizur Goodrich became a traveling evangelist recruiting converts to Shakerism, he was persecuted by the world's people. To avoid harassment, he disguised himself by wearing a scarlet coat rather than his plain Shaker garment. When Ann Lee heard of his deception, she "reproved him sharply, telling him that he should never resort to deceptive measures, . . . that he should never counterfeit his profession."[52]

While Elizur was getting into trouble as a traveling minister, Lucy Wright worked with the Shaker sisters at Watervliet, where she inspired confidence and gained esteem through her diligence, faithfulness, and efficiency. In

Watervliet, as in Pittsfield, Lucy Wright became a leader among her peers. Ann Lee mentored the young woman accordingly.[53]

After Mother Ann died, Lucy Wright's responsibilities increased. By late 1788, the society's new leader Joseph Meacham had summoned Wright to New Lebanon, New York, established her as his female counterpart in the Ministry, and called her Mother Lucy. Together, they tackled the considerable task of bringing all things into Shaker order, reshaping the religious society, and gathering Believers into their own communal villages.[54] By the 1790s, a visitor wrote of the group, "I found them generally sincere in their profession, strictly moral, industrious as a hive of bees, and rigidly adhering to their tenets."[55] The Shakers by then were on a solid foundation, respected as "an honest, peaceable, industrious, thriving people."[56]

Lucy Wright and Joseph Meacham worked together for eight years, until Meacham's death in 1796. Shortly before he died, Meacham wrote to Lucy, calling her "one whom I esteem my Equal in order & Lot according to thy sex." He described their working relationship, aware of the temptations of their position and pleased that they had set a good example: "It was necessary that we should Support a greater measure of the union of the spirit and that we should Labour more to be mutual helps To Each other than any of the Rest of the members, Not for our own privit Good but for the Good of the Whole." God "hath kept us from all sin With Each other which hath Laid the foundation In & by us for the Gathering & Building of the Chh."[57] The fruit of their spiritual union was a church that would last more than two centuries.

An epilogue to the Wright-Goodrich marriage can be written in two more anecdotes. Elizur Goodrich spent years on the road as the Ministry's emissary, before and after the Shakers gathered into order.[58] By 1791, Joseph Meacham had brought Elizur to live as an Elder at New Lebanon. There Lucy and Elizur lived in closer proximity than they had for almost two decades. As a wife, Lucy had been subject to her husband, but as a Shaker, she outranked him, and she exercised her authority with confidence. After Meacham died, Lucy had to choose another Elder to promote to the Ministry, and she did not choose Elizur. Angell Matthewson wrote:

> Now her husband Elizur Goodrich is an Elder in the church, a man of decent deportment, a well-educated man, & had been a merchant before he embraced the faith—is one of the first talents in the whole community. It appears in justice that this lot ought to have fallen to him, but as the first Mother Ann Lee had broken down the marriage

covenant so it remains—it would be a reproach to the whole system for husband & wife to reside in the same house.

Matthewson conceded that Lucy Wright had the authority to "overlook" Elizur Goodrich, and he acknowledged that her candidate "understood spiritual gifts far better than a learned philosopher or historian,"[59] and presumably better than Elizur Goodrich.

Wright continued to impose her authority on her former husband. When the Ministry was considering collecting Believers' testimonies of Mother Ann Lee, Elizur Goodrich opposed the project, insisting that memories would not be equal to the task. Wright disagreed. She overruled him and sent Rufus Bishop to gather anecdotes.[60] That project, so valuable to posterity, would never have begun if Wright had shown the traditional deference to her husband.

And so the "uncommonly continent" bridegroom Elizur Goodrich lived a Shaker under the administration of his wife until he died in 1812 at age sixty-one.[61] No known documents record what he thought of their role reversal.

Lucy Wright proved to be a brilliant administrator with significant influence at every level of Shaker society. She survived the exit of disaffected young men in the 1790s and successfully sustained "petticoat government." Her long tenure as the Ministry's leader meant that she had ample opportunity to establish the principles of gender equality, as far as she was able to control it.[62] When she sent missionaries into the western wilderness, they founded new Shaker villages in Kentucky, Ohio, and Indiana, increasing the geographic range of Shakerism, as well as its membership. Lucy Wright remained "a pillar in the temple."[63]

Wright's true marriage—to the Shaker church—continued until her death in 1821. "A Mother in Israel has finished her course," one Shaker brother wrote. "Never was wisdom and Beauty more manifest than in her; clothed in righteousness and glory. She has left us; and all Zion feels the Shock."[64] Her biographer Calvin Green wrote, "I loved her with a filial love, for I revered her as my true Spiritual Mother."[65] Thus Lucy Wright was remembered for her motherhood in a way she surely had not anticipated on her wedding day in 1779.

3

Why Women Joined the
Shakers, 1780–1840

A practical salvation . . .

Lucy Wright joined the Shakers for the same reasons most other women did. According to D'Ann Campbell, these women sought a path to salvation and economic security. Some feared marriage or sexual intimacy or both.[1] Additional factors mattered, as well, and this chapter enlarges on Campbell's findings, drawing on my survey of forty-four New Lebanon Shaker sisters' testimonies.[2] Women were pulled into Shakerism by such factors as Ann Lee's charismatic personality, their sense of sin and disappointment in traditional denominations, their need for financial security, and the Shaker teachings about celibacy and the equality of the sexes. Other issues, including persecution or abuse, pushed women and girls away from the world's people.

At the outset, Ann Lee herself may have been the principal attraction, though women continued to join the Shakers after she died in 1784. About three-quarters of those who left testimonies were single women who joined in their late teens or twenties. Thankful Barce recalled that at age twenty-one, she saw Mother Ann as an angel of glory with a bright and shining countenance. Rachel Spencer recounted her conviction at age fifteen that Ann Lee was God's chosen representative on earth: "I really loved and feared her more than any person I ever saw." Hannah Cogswell was eighteen when she knew by God's revelation that Mother Ann was the second embodiment of Christ. "However incredible this may appear to an unbelieving world," she explained, "we know that we are not left in darkness and doubt concerning these things; they are as clear and certain to us as the light of the sun in a clear day."[3]

Older women converts were less effusive; life experience may have tempered their enthusiasm. Even so, Elizabeth Johnson, over forty when she met Ann Lee, recalled the effect on her when Mother Ann touched her arm: "Instantly I felt the power of God flow from her and run through my whole body. I was then convinced beyond a doubt that she had the power of God, and that I received it from her." When Mother Ann touched Thankful Barce, she, too, "instantly felt the power of God."[4]

In addition to drawing in converts and offering a focus for Believers' faith, Mother Ann provided an example as a female leader that empowered her female followers. One such follower, "a young, active girl," took a liberty that would never have been condoned in another church, condemning William Plumer when he got up to leave midway through a Shaker meeting in Canterbury, New Hampshire. He wrote that she "came whirling after me; she ran round me more than one hundred times, praying, singing, whining, crying, pointing and hissing, with her tongue out of her mouth."[5] Other evangelical religions permitted women's spiritual gifts, but they restricted church leadership to men, and would not have permitted a girl to publicly criticize an elite male. In the Judeo-Christian tradition, religion tried to keep women subservient, using the rationale that Eve's contribution to Adam's fall provoked God to give man the right to rule over woman. That tradition, however, may have been a reaction to earlier goddess worship, wherein women had both spiritual and political power.[6] A religion that worships a god, however, has one thing in common with one that worships a goddess; each favors mortal humans who are of the same sex as its deity.

The only way to reconcile the two sexes' religious cosmologies is to recognize both male and female. The opening hymn in the Shaker hymnal, *Millennial Praises*, first published in 1812, sets forth the Shaker view of God as both male and female: "This vast creation was not made / Without the fruitful Mother's aid." Other hymns refer to their view of a biune God.[7] Even today, Shakers refer to Father/Mother God in worship. Early Shakers balanced the interests of men and women in their view of a male (Jesus of Nazareth) and a female (Ann Lee) as the physical embodiment of the Christ spirit. Sister Anna Matthewson pointed out that few Christians would deny woman's agency in leading mankind into sin. "Why then," she reasoned, "should it be thought incredible that the agency of a woman should necessarily be first in leading the human race out of sin?"[8] Because a woman contributed to Adam's fall, balance could be restored through another woman's chastity.

For young women, the least powerful free adults in American society, Mother Ann's leadership was empowering, individually and collectively. Moreover, her successors in the Shaker Ministry, Joseph Meacham and Lucy Wright, consolidated the position of women as co-equal in the society, which provided continuing female role models as spiritual and temporal authorities—a sharp contrast to the world's example.

Many women joined the Shakers because they were convinced of their own sinfulness and disappointed with other churches' inability to combat sin. They had tried and rejected other denominations. The transition was not necessarily abrupt. New Lights, Baptists, Methodists, Congregationalists, and Presbyterians attended the 1779 revival, and many recalled that revival as a precursor to Ann Lee's preaching. They were open to the religious constructs that she used in her message and had already gathered together with others seeking community.[9]

The Shakers were a self-selected group of those willing to confess their sins. Thus, almost every individual who left a testimony revealed a finely honed sense of personal sin and the conviction that salvation was nonetheless attainable. Most attributed their search for religious perfection to their desire to live free of sin. Among those was Desire Sanford, who testified that when she confessed, she received "that strength & power over my carnal sinful passions, & over everything that had formerly brot condemnation upon me."[10] Thankful Barce was unmarried and pregnant when she came to the Shakers in 1779, but among the Shakers, she found acceptance and a home for herself and her son.[11] Mehitabel Farrington sought spiritual relief from sin, and Deborah Sackett said she had often felt the sting of guilt but knew not how to be saved. Martha Deming lost sleep over her sinful state, recalling, "I knew I had not the power that would keep me from sin. I felt under such condemnation that when I retired to bed at night, instead of sweet repose, I felt continual remorse of conscience for sin which I had not power to refrain from. I often promised God that if he would spare my life, I would try in future to abstain from sin." The attempt to bargain with God was futile; Deming felt no ease until she became a Shaker.[12]

Many sisters testified about how other churches failed them. Rhoda Chase sought protection from sin in Congregational and Baptist churches but received no help.[13] Chloe Tiffany's parents brought her up as a strict Baptist, but she felt that something was missing. As an adult, she tried several denominations before finding the Shakers.[14] Sarah Barker, a Presbyterian, was "troubled in mind" about her childhood misbehavior. "I was afraid to die lest I go to hell," she said. In adulthood, she gravitated to the Shakers, and after she confessed, she felt "releasement of soul" for the first time. "If salvation could have been obtaind from drunkards and harlots," she wrote, "I might have found it before I ever saw Mother [Ann]. For I saw enough of them in the world, & I knew what lives they lived."[15] Phebe Chase was a Congregationalist in good standing for six years, but, she testified, she grew in pride and arrogance, inclining more and more toward evil, even though her church thought her a good Christian. Her unease increased; she prayed but did not find deliverance until she confessed her sins to the Shakers. Other women had similar experiences. At age twenty, in 1775, Zeruah Moseley married Rufus Clark, a good Baptist, and they had three children in the next five years. Her conscience, however, bothered her as she "felt the nature of sin still growing stronger and stronger." Her "trouble and distress of mind" increased until she met the Shakers. Then, she recalled, "I felt myself as in the presence of God and saw my wicked life open before me as a book." A Shaker for the rest of her life, she never regretted her choice.[16] Among Believers, those women found salvation and peace of mind.

Balancing the Shakers' evangelical sense of sin was a sense of personal perfectibility; the two concepts maintained a dynamic tension that kept Believers working for salvation even though they were aware of their own imperfections. The Shakers' concept of sin may, in fact, require the concept of perfectibility to maintain equilibrium: Believers needed the possibility of grace (or at least measurable personal improvement) in order to make their war against sin worthwhile. Thus their awareness of sin was punishment for misdeeds; improvement compensated them for the struggle toward perfection, as it did for Elizabeth Johnson. Having confessed her sins, she was determined to quit them forever. "And in obedience to Mother's teaching," she wrote, "I found that power which enabled me to keep myself from all sin in my knowledge."[17] The phrase, "in my knowledge," gave her some leeway, but most Shaker sisters found what Anna Dodgson called "a practical salvation" based on self-denial.[18]

Supernatural experiences, which the Shakers called spiritual gifts, were another pull factor. Several sisters reported having a vision or feeling the power of God. Visions, whether Ann Lee's or the rank and file's, were interpreted, in keeping with passages in the Bible, as a foretelling of the millennium. In Joel 2:28–29, for instance, the prophet predicted that before the Lord arrived, God's spirit would be poured on all mankind; sons and daughters would prophesy; old men would dream dreams, and young men would see visions. Even lowly servants would receive the spirit of God. And in 1 Corinthians 12:10, the apostle Paul lists spiritual gifts, including the gifts of healing, prophecy, and tongues, all of them valid expressions of the spirit of God. For Shakers, those were not just stories from the mythic historical past; they were an ongoing and valued part of spiritual life. Ann Lee possessed those gifts, and so did some of her followers. In this sample of forty-four sisters' testimonies, sixteen (36 percent) had a vision or a prophetic or visionary dream, or they were overcome by the power of God. Several had those gifts of power even before they joined the Shakers. When Thankful Goodrich misbehaved, she testified, she saw a white hand (which she knew to be her deceased father's) stretched out over her and recognized his reproof.[19] Thankful Barce had a visionary dream of a shepherdess leading her flock, and when she met Ann Lee several years later, recognized her as the shepherdess. Lucy Wight, sick with a fever at age nineteen, had a vision of worshippers under the power of God, which prompted her to search for a way out of sin. When she visited the Shakers five years later, she recognized the people from her dream and found the answer to her prayers.[20] Rebecca Jackson also recognized the women she had dreamed about before she visited the Shakers.[21]

Sarah Barker was physically directed. When she heard of the Shakers, she set out for Albany on foot to visit them without a map or directions, but soon, she recalled, she and her companion received unexpected assistance.

> As the country was thinly inhabited, & we were entirely unacquainted with the roads which led in various directions, we were not sure of keeping in the right course. But we had not proceeded far before one of my hands was stretcht out by the power of God, & we followed its direction many miles, & when the power left my hand, we stopt & inquired the way. We were within six miles of Albany.[22]

Lucy Brown also reported an extraordinary experience, which she had at eighteen, soon after she joined the Shakers.

> Several weeks after I set out, as a number of young sisters sitting together were singing, I very unexpectedly saw a bright light, like a flash of lightning pass near my face, which seemed to set my body in motion and my tongue to speaking and singing in an unknown language for several hours. It carried my spirit above all earthly sensations and feelings, and filled my soul with comfort, happiness, love and thankfulness

to God that I had been called out from the world of sin and misery, and placed where I could receive the bread of heaven and waters of life to refresh my thirsty soul.

Shakers interpreted the gift of tongues as a sign that the speaker was filled with the holy spirit. Thus Lucy Brown, following Peter's instructions in 1 Corinthians 14, accepted her inspiration as a gift from God that confirmed her faith beyond all doubt.[23]

Hannah Chauncey was drawn to Shakerism by her unusual experience. Although brought up as a Presbyterian, she was not concerned with the state of her immortal soul until she was twenty-five. Then, after seeing her sister-in-law under the physical operation of a spiritual gift, trembling, "signed about," shaken so hard that "her hair was thrown every which way," Chauncey was struck with conviction. She knew she had to embrace Shakerism or forgo salvation. After she made her commitment, she testified, she saw the spirit of William Lee coming into meeting, the tears on his cheeks as plain as anything she had ever seen in her life.[24]

A later convert, Eliza Rayson, accompanied her husband into the society without making a wholehearted commitment. "An uncommonly natural minded person," she was for several weeks unable to shake off her unhappiness even though the sisters tried to ease her adjustment. Finally, after hearing a sharp testimony against sinful indulgence, conviction fastened upon her soul, she said, making her miserable. When she saw that she must make a sincere effort, the power of God came over her.[25] The experience was a turning point that bolstered her commitment. Like the other women who had had supernatural experiences, Rayson viewed her gift according to the New England Protestant tradition that a conversion experience confirms the individual's readiness for church membership.

Family was also an important factor in influencing women to join the Shakers, as D'Ann Campbell found. Most early Believers joined in family groups with parents, children, siblings, in-laws, or cousins. More than twenty of the Wells-Youngs family and at least twenty-five of the Goodrich family made the commitment.[26] An explanation for their coming in as families may be found in the recent identification of a gene that predisposes an individual to be religious. Because genes are passed from parent to child, familial perpetuation of religious belief is a matter of both nature and nurture.[27]

After Sarah Kibbee's father visited the Shakers, he returned home "with a strong desire that his family & friends would unite with him & set out to forsake the world & all evil." Family members did follow him, including Sarah.

The English immigrant John Mantle brought his wife and his four-year-old son and four-month-old daughter. Both children stayed in the society and "never expressed a wish to quit it." When Elizabeth Johnson's minister husband decided to join the Shakers, she and their children did, too.[28] About a quarter of the forty-four sisters surveyed were married women who joined with their husbands. Family ties also show up often in the records among those whose surnames differed. The Avery family became Shakers through the influence of Richard Bushnell, who was married to an Avery. The Youngs and Wells families were related, as were the King and Meacham, Bishop and Crosman, and Clark and Moseley families.[29] Two twentieth-century surveys of Christian church members found that the majority (from 75 to 90 percent) joined their churches because of the influence of family and friends. Less than 5 percent attributed their membership to evangelism.[30] This is not to suggest that evangelism did not touch Believers; it did—but the natural family had more influence, positive or negative. Furthermore, according to Metin Coşgel, those who joined with family were the most likely to persist as Shakers.[31] Kinship was important.

Economic support was tied to family, so those factors were intertwined. As we have already seen, married women whose husbands joined often followed their spouses into the society. Many women depended on male kin for financial support. Rural women rarely had much property and inflation robbed them as fast as assets accrued.[32] A visitor wrote:

> When fortune has frowned on the efforts of Enterprise and industry; where a wife and children have drunk the cup of suffering, a union with this family [Shakers] will secure an ample and luxurious support. When the widow has been left destitute, with the little ones crying for food, it is easy to conceive the motives which *might* bring her to such a society. Where the wife has been the victim of the vices and follies of a profligate husband, it is not difficult to imagine the reasons that would lead her to the peaceful dwellings of these people.[33]

A few married women refused to become Shakers when their husbands joined. Among them was Martha Youngs. She married Seth Youngs in about 1773, and after she had borne ten children, he joined the Shakers. Martha must have gone along at first, then decided to leave. Under coverture, a husband had legal authority over his wife and children; if he joined the Shakers and she did not, she had to fend for herself.[34] Thus, without the support of her husband or the adult children who became Shakers, Martha Youngs was indigent. The town of Schenectady supported her as a pauper.

Her caretaker, aware of the Shakers' prosperity, asked them for more money for her care, but they rejected the request. Her son Isaac Newton Youngs wrote the Elders' answer: "If my mother had chosen to remain with our society in years past, she might unquestionably have enjoyed every needful comfort thro' life as well as myself, without experiencing any distressing dependence on others."[35] The society supported Believers until they died; lifelong care was part of the Shaker covenant. But such care did not extend to family members like Martha who chose not to join.

Many people were drawn to the Shakers by their prosperity, and the Shakers recognized that some proselytes came because they were poor or alone. The world's people saw the Shakers as a refuge, as William Dean Howells put it, for "the poor, the bruised, and the hopeless." He wrote, "One whom the world could flatter no more, one broken in hope, or health, or fortune, could not do better than come hither." He advised his Shaker friends that "the disappointed, the poor, [and] the destitute" might be the best "field from which to reap."[36] Lucy Brown's friends and family in Berkshire County, Massachusetts, told her "it was those who were poor and had no home or parents that joined the Shakers." John Deming brought his family to the Shakers because he was in debt and did not know how to repay his creditors.[37] Polly Lawrence's father died at an early age. Later, her dying mother, "often embarrassed for means of support," told her children to go to the Shakers, and they did.[38]

During times of economic hardship, Shaker membership increased. In 1816, which came to be referred to as "the Year Without a Summer," the ground froze during the first week of June and July was so cold that food crops did not mature. Even the Shakers, who were competent farmers, felt the strain; Lucy Wright foresaw "a great scarcity."[39] Hundreds of people traveled only as far as the nearest Shaker community—and, fortunately, the Shakers had food enough to feed them. From 1810 to 1820, Watervliet grew more than 50 percent. New Lebanon Shaker village grew more than 20 percent, and the Hancock, Massachusetts, Shaker village, 70 percent. During that decade, the northeastern Shaker societies' population increased almost 40 percent.[40]

Fredrika Bremer noted that Believers "had sought for, and had found a haven amid the storms of life."[41] A Shaker village offered refuge to people of all classes. Shakers considered neither poverty nor wealth in accepting new proselytes. Zipporah Cory recalled, "Though I was a poor girl, and of poor parentage, yet I have never seen any difference made on that account; but I have always fared as well among Believers as the daughters of the rich."[42]

The Blake family illustrated several of the Shakers' attractions. Olive (Read) Harding Blake and her husband, Jacob Blake, eked out a living. Olive did weaving for pay and taught her daughter Rhoda, who was born in 1808, to wind bobbins for the weaver's shuttle. Rhoda Blake had fond memories of her father, who never struck his children; he spoke to them, and that was enough. Her mother's discipline, however, left bitter memories. With the proliferation of factories, the family's weaving business declined, and by 1814 Olive and the children were running an inn while Jacob farmed. Though the Blakes were Universalists, in 1816 they attended a Baptist revival, where they met Calvin Green and Morrel Baker, who drew them into Shakerism. In September 1817, as the Blakes were winding up their temporal affairs before moving to a Shaker village, Jacob fell off a load of hay and broke his neck. The widowed Olive Blake settled his estate, and in 1819, took her daughters, Rhoda and Hannah, to the Shakers.[43] Rhoda Blake loved her Shaker guardians, the office trustees Susannah Ellis and Molly Smith. They did not correct her in anger or use corporal punishment as her mother had done.[44] Their kind treatment won her over. For Blake, economic need was replaced by an emotional tie that held her in place.

Others found love among the Shakers. Betsy Crosman, whose admiration for Lucy Wright influenced her to join, recalled that Wright's religious advice "caused me to love her very much, & also to feel an anxious desire to become one of her people."[45] Crosman joined the Shakers not just because her kin joined but also because the society's female leader drew her affection. Zipporah Cory had "no natural relations with me." But, she said, "I have spiritual relations, elders, brethren and sisters, who are dearer to me than any of my natural kindred ever were."[46]

Salome Spencer was pushed to the Shakers by persecution and pulled by a miraculous gift of healing her mother received. After her parents, Phebe and Jabez Spencer, embraced Mother Ann's gospel, their neighbors tried to turn the children against the Shakers, even promising them homes if they would leave their parents. "Witchcraft & delusion! was the general cry," Salome recalled, but she resisted "the artful wiles of those pretending Christians who would gladly bewitch us away from our parents." Her decision to follow her parents into the society was affirmed by her mother's gift.[47] Rebecca Moseley was also moved by persecution to join the Shakers. She was with Ann Lee when a mob attacked the Shakers at New Lebanon in September 1783. "Instead of destroying the work of God among us, as intended," she

recalled, the attack "served only to increase it." The mob's wickedness bolstered Moseley's desire to shun worldly sin.[48]

Some women came to the Shakers to escape domestic violence. Prudence
Hammond, for instance, explained, "Having lost my mother in my childhood, I was placed by my father in a distant family, where I was much
abused." The man of the house hit her head so hard that the blow left her
deaf in one ear. Ann Lee healed her, and Hammond found a new home.[49]
Zipporah Cory tried to stifle her interest in the Shakers at first because
her father was opposed. Then Cory had a revelation. She saw her friend
Diana Martin united with Shakers in dance, and a scriptural reference from
Matthew 24:41 came into her mind, "Two women shall be grinding at the
mill; the one shall be taken and the other left." Cory recalled, "I felt as tho
I was left, sure enough." The next verse, "Therefore be on the alert, for you
do not know which day your Lord is coming," may have prompted Cory
to act. And so on her next visit she opened her mind to Ann Lee. When she
returned to her work spinning for a Quaker family, the power of God came
over her and brought her to her knees. "The family then discovered that I
was a Shaker," she remembered, "and all my acquaintance soon fell upon
me, to try to reclaim me, by their exhortations and warnings against delusion." Members of different denominations "beset" her "with persuasions
and flatteries" to join their churches. One Baptist deacon's harangue was
"very wearisome." She observed that he would not have worked so hard to
reclaim a prostitute as he was trying to divert her from living a sinless life
(and he admitted she was right). Cory returned home but found no peace
under her father's roof, either. She recalled, "There I found still greater
troubles to encounter. My father was like a mad man, and my oldest brother
was not much better. My father abused my mother very much, because of
her Shaker faith; and I was so persecuted by them that I really stood in
fear of my life. Many times, when I lay down at night, I did not expect to
see the light of another day." Alcohol fueled her father's rage; by Cory's
account, he was beyond reason. "All this persecution I suffered," Cory realized, "because I had set out to forsake sin and live a godly life." Finally she
found protection with Joseph Bennet's family in Cheshire, Massachusetts,
and stayed there until they were gathered into the New Lebanon Shaker
village in 1788.[50]

Other women suffered less dramatic persecution than Zipporah Cory's,
but some lacked the courage to join the Believers. At Shaker meeting, Elizabeth Williams received the power of God so powerfully that she could not

stand on her feet, yet she was unable to join the society because the man she worked for "was so opposed that [she] could not get sufficient strength to do so."[51] She was over twenty-five years old, but she had to support herself and lacked the nerve to challenge her employer.

Mary Andrews suffered from family opposition. As a girl in 1779, she attended a camp meeting "as an impartial spectator, with a rational and candid mind." She lost her detachment, however, after a Connecticut revival and returned home to tell her parents about the divine spirit. "While I was speaking," she recalled, "the power of God fell upon me in a remarkable manner. It struck me first upon my tongue, & extended through my head & over my whole body, & seemed to wash me from head to foot, like a shower of warm water." Her parents believed she had "the *megrims*" and tried to explain her behavior as the effect of an organic disorder. But Andrews knew better. When she heard of the Shakers, she was intrigued. She then read Valentine Rathbun's anti-Shaker pamphlet, and his description of Shaker worship attracted her. Her friends thought the Shakers were under the influence of witchcraft, and her family believed the Shakers had bewitched her. "To destroy the effects of this witchcraft," she remembered, "they sent for a doctor to bless me." They cut off her hair and nails and boiled them, "hoping thereby to *kill the old witch,* as they call'd Mother Ann." The charm did not work. They also tried bloodletting, and when that failed, they called an exorcist. Andrews recalled:

> They could not bleed the power of God out of my veins, not expel the faith of the gospel out of my soul, for the more they tried, the more it increast. At length an old man named Matthews who lived in the neighborhood said he could cast the Devil out of me, for he was a *seventh son.* He came & shook me & pulld & hauld me about in a very rough manner. The effect it produced was to make my arms and shoulders lame & excite disgust to their persecuting spirit.

The only effect of the exorcist's assault was to teach Andrews to keep her own counsel thereafter, saying nothing about her new faith. By late 1782, she had made a commitment to the Shakers, who treated her better than the world did.[52]

Eliza Barber married and "lived in the cares of the world" for four years but recalled, "It pleased God to cut short all my earthly prospects." Exactly what that meant, she did not explain, but she forsook Presbyterianism and became a Methodist. A sense of sin dogged her until she went to a camp meeting. On her second day there, she was kneeling in prayer when the power of God came over her. Later she was overcome at home, as well. In church, she was moved to testify against sin, but the Methodists did not appreciate her testimony. "Satan was soon enraged," she wrote, "& raised many to speak evil of me." A churchwoman harassed Barber until she screamed the woman out of the house. The Methodists thought she was crazy, and so did her mother. The Shakers, however, welcomed her and her children, and respected her as a visionist.[53]

These stories of persecution highlight the vulnerability that many women felt among the world's people. Issues of powerlessness suggest one con- clusion about Shakerism's appeal to women. For those who cannot gain power by other means, a closer alliance with an all-powerful God can be palliative.[54] The Shakers, however, provided an additional shield against powerlessness by institutionalizing equality of the sexes, including a God who was both female and male, and giving women power and authority equivalent to that of men. Jemima Bracket said of her Shaker life, "I have found peace and comfort which all the world cannot give nor take away."[55]

According to Suzanne Thurman, the Shakers provided a haven for women who wanted to avoid marriage or to escape abusive men.[56] Among the world's people, a married man, as head of the household, was allowed to physically chastise his family. His wife was subordinate and expected to be obedient as scripture such as 1 Peter 3:1–5 enjoined. The common-law "rule of thumb" allowed a husband to beat his wife, as long as he used a rod no thicker than his thumb.[57] It is not surprising that Zipporah Cory, for instance, preferred to join the Shakers rather than risk replicating her mother's victimization as a wife.

A final reason some women joined the Shakers was the tenet of celibacy, which had the effect of giving women authority over their own bodies while simultaneously denying access to men. For evangelicals who believed sex was sinful, a celibate communal group provided support for resisting temp- tation. Among Believers, discussion of sexuality was considered disorderly because it could lead to lustful thoughts and sensations, and so the topic was proscribed, except for secondhand accounts of Ann Lee's avoidance of marital sex.[58] Its absence from Shakers' written records, however, should not be construed as absence from Shaker women's life experience. An out- sider, Marianne Finch, described a conversation with a Shaker mother and daughter in a relative's Boston home. The daughter, Eleanor Hayes Wright, told Finch that nothing could induce her to return to her husband. After marrying him, she "never had a day's health or happiness"; his "sensual and selfish nature" inspired repugnance, rather than love, and she went to the

Shakers.[59] "Sensual" is the key word, and that allusion was more explicit than most. Outside of Shakerism, only singleness moderated the unequal power relations between women and men.[60]

Shaker celibacy worked much the same way. Shakerism combined an evangelical alliance with God and what may be women's oldest source of power: their control of sexuality and reproduction. Shaker sisters abstained by their own choice, and their religion supported that decision. By becoming a Shaker, a woman tapped into Ann Lee's power, which included the celibate woman's authority over her own body. By eliminating marriage and reducing the patriarchal authority that it gave men over women, Shakers reduced men's ability to rule women. Because Shaker sisters were acknowledged as equal partners in Shaker villages, rather than subordinates in the world's families, they had more power than most worldly women had. Among Believers, men vowed self-denial, humility and obedience just as women did. Moreover, both sexes had to strive for reciprocity not only to maintain their union as a group but also because each sex needed the other if all were to prosper. This is not to suggest that nineteenth-century Shaker women and men shared a twenty-first-century view of gender equality, but it does point up the truth of the eighteenth-century poet Susanna Wright's assessment of women's rights; she wrote that a man "only rules those who of choice obey."[61] Shaker sisters could obey Shaker brethren, or not. If they chose to resist men's decisions, the brethren had to negotiate a compromise. Thus equality was an important pull factor for women—and may have been correspondingly unimportant (or even alarming) for men.

Every society maintains a dynamic tension between the sexes. Among the world's people, the disadvantages of marriage convinced many women in the nineteenth century to remain single. Living apart, often under male government, worldly women lacked the strength of the organized group. But among Shakers, as Susan Starr Sered points out, Shaker women lived in close proximity with "lifelong and multifaceted commitments to one another," so they were able to use their religion to serve their collective interests.[62] By working together, women can resist patriarchy more effectively than individuals can do separately.

Moreover, because union and consensus were so important to the Shakers, the sisters had more influence than organization charts and theological treatises might suggest. Sisters believed they were equal to brethren. Their perception was their reality. In addition, brethren had been socialized to support that equality whether they truly believed in it or not. Furthermore,

Shaker sisters could draw on one another for support if brothers tried to subordinate them.

That reality, however, may not have been the same at all Shaker villages. Though Joseph Meacham and Lucy Wright established the ideal of equality of the sexes, they could go no further with that concept than their followers would.[63] Scholars have not yet made a comprehensive effort to compare the situation of sisters at different villages to determine how much they differed and in what respects.

After joining the Shakers, women avoided the drawbacks of spinster-hood, which could include poverty, dependency, and loneliness.[64] Shaker-ism offered better-than-average food, housing, working conditions, medical care, lifetime care, opportunities for leadership, and a path to salvation. Furthermore, a Shaker woman had no fear of assault by an abusive parent, husband, or employer. She also had the support of her sisters in the faith.

More women than men were happy as Believers; a higher percentage of Shaker-raised girls stayed Shakers. Elder Seth Youngs Wells attributed girls' persistence to their better manners and morals, but that was not the whole story.[65] Women's testimonies show the hazards girls faced among the world's people, as well as the loving homes they found with the Shakers.

4

Shaker Girlhood

An honorable and upright life . . .

A SHAKER GIRL'S LIFE WAS BUILT ON A FOUNDATION OF conformity—generally safe, peaceful, and predictable. Children were expected to conform to adults' expectations in work, school, and worship. But sometimes parents who were not Believers tried to take their daughters away from the Shakers. Forced to decide where they would be better treated, some girls chose to stay with the Shakers. Among them were Betty and Phebe Lane. After their father, Prime Lane, a free African American, indentured the girls to the Shakers at Watervliet, New York, he had second thoughts and sued to void their indentures in 1811. Because slavery was still legal in New York, he argued that they were his property. When he lost his case in court, Lane and his wife, Hannah, invaded the Shaker village, grabbed Betty, and dragged her down the street. By "resolute and violent struggles," Betty Lane freed herself and returned to the Shakers' protection. Betty and Phebe Lane remained Believers until they died.[1]

Other parental efforts at removal were equally unsuccessful. Rufus Bishop described an event in 1833: "Mariah Webster was kidnapped by her mother, but after having her clothes torn made her escape."[2] In 1849, Enoch Haskins entered the Shaker village at Enfield, Connecticut, to remove his daughter Jane. He "clinched" her, but she fought her way free with Shakers' help.[3] In another case, "violence was used" when a father grabbed one of his three daughters, but the other two got away. The Shakers "made out to keep the other two girls who were crying with fear of being taken."[4] A lot was at stake in those assaults. Shakers' best prospects for perpetuating their society were the youth who would become the next generation of converts.

The most interesting aspect of these abduction attempts is that so many girls conformed not to parental expectations but to the Shakers'. Communal groups such as the Shakers require conformity, which has two gendered components. Compared with boys, girls are typically more responsive to social cues about proper behavior.[5] Furthermore, children who spend more time with same-sex peers experience "stronger pressures to conform to gender-related behaviors" than children who spend less time with peers of the same sex. Psychologists suggest that peers "play the role of gender 'enforcers,' who monitor and maintain gender boundaries by conveying information about the correct behavior for girls and boys and about the consequences likely to occur if gender boundaries are violated."[6] Shaker-raised girls spent virtually every waking hour with other girls and women, who policed community mores.[7] Thus, older sisters trained girls in conformity, and girls promoted it among their peers. This does not mean that Shaker girls were raised to be passive; on the contrary, some fought—and won—brawls with their parents for the privilege of remaining Shakers.

Parents were often forced by circumstance to take their children to the Shakers. Some children arrived when their parents joined the society; others were left at the nearest Shaker village. "Poverty, illegitimacy, and sickness," Edward Deming Andrews and Faith Andrews point out, "produced waifs and strays and a need that the Shaker communities, like the monasteries of old, felt it their Christian duty to fill."[8] In the 1830s, ten-year-old bobbin doffers in textile mills contributed to their families' support, but when unemployment was high, neither children nor adults could find work.[9] During the economic panic of 1837, Shaker indentures surged as desperate parents signed over children they could not afford to feed. At Watervliet, the youngest was two years old, perhaps just weaned.[10] Aurelia Phillips of Shaftsbury, Vermont, was seventeen when she came to the Canaan Shakers with her infant daughter, Jane, in April 1838. Two months later she, went away, one Shaker reported, "we know not where," leaving her baby behind.[11] In February 1854, a deaconess wrote that George Clyne of Sand Lake, New York, had brought his four children ages two to nine to New Lebanon. "They were barefoot, and indecently clothed," she noted—in weather raw and cold with snow, rain, ice, and a stiff wind. She added, "We will just mention by the way . . . that grain of all kinds, is at present very high; wheat from 12 to 14 $ per barrel & other kinds accordingly. The poor children say they have lived upon potatoes & Jonnycake."[12] Some children came to the Shakers because of the loss or disability of a parent. Polly Lawrence was an orphan who went to the Shakers at her dying mother's request.[13] One father brought three children to New Lebanon because his alcoholic wife did not care for them while he worked.[14] The move to the Shakers could be a relief. Rhoda Blake said her mother had "that nature which is stronger in some, than in others, to fight, destroy, or inflict pain." By contrast, Blake recalled that her Shaker guardians, Susannah Ellis and Molly Smith, cared for her tenderly. She "turned around them like the staff tree around the oak."[15]

A legal indenture was no guarantee that a child would stay with the Shakers, and sometimes Believers had to take extraordinary measures to retain custody and reduce conflict with nonbelieving parents. When William Pillow Sr. tried to void his son's indenture, the Shakers moved William Jr. to Hancock, then to Tyringham and Enfield in an effort to keep the boy hidden from his father, who finally tracked him down and seized him.[16] Eliza Danes ran away from her husband on Long Island and in January 1849 gave birth to twin boys at the Hancock Shakers' South Family. Danes remained with the Shakers, but when census takers enumerated Believers, neither she nor the boys were listed—until 1870, when the boys would have been of legal age.[17]

The quickest intake of a child occurred when someone anonymously left a baby, presumably born out of wedlock, on the Shakers' doorstep and hurried away.[18] Legitimate parents, in contrast, might visit the Shakers and stay a while, sizing up the situation before signing an indenture that would bind a child to the society. The visit gave Shakers a chance to assess both adults and children. If either seemed too troublesome, they were sent away.[19] Contentious spouses caused trouble. A Hancock Eldress wrote, "Susan Erving had a falling out with her husband & left him & come here with three little children expecting we should take her & them, because we had already taken five of her children, but this we could not do without the concent of the man, neither did we think it would be of any use."[20]

Some children were indentured for a term that ended when they reached legal age, with very specific legal documents signed by parents and Shaker trustees. Shakers were careful to take only children whose parents or guardians had legal authority to bind them out: a married woman lacked that authority, but a widow, an unmarried mother, or a father could do so. In the indenture agreement, a parent agreed not to interfere with a child's upbringing; Shakers promised to provide schooling as well as training in work appropriate to the child's age and sex.[21]

Some children do not seem to have been indentured; perhaps they were left with the Shakers at a time when a trustee was absent, and the agreement was not executed. In 1834, for instance, several children at the Canaan

Upper Family were listed as "not yet bound," but Believers nonetheless considered them "as belonging to the family."[22] In 1855, the stepfather of Margarette McGloughlin retrieved her from the New Lebanon Second Order. "Having no security of the child," the deaconess wrote, "she was obliged to go, tho' much against her feelings." It seems possible, then, that children could be left unindentured with the Shakers, even when a parent did not join the society. In other cases, Shakers noted arrivals and subsequent departures without mentioning a legal agreement. Ellen Mercer left her three girls, ages four, seven, and twelve, at the Second Order in 1857. Seven months later, she returned for them. "Ellen takes her children on foot & alone," the deaconess wrote. Neither entry notes an indenture or a protest against the girls' departure, suggesting that the Shakers felt they did not have a claim on the children. Furthermore, an indenture was not necessarily upheld by both parties. In 1860, Sarah Hastings signed an indenture to bind her daughters Henriette and Fanny at the New Lebanon Second Order. Hastings lived at the North Family for two weeks, then returned to Albany with her two little girls. No fuss was recorded; the indentures were voided without involving the law.[23] The Hastings family may have been in the village for a probationary period, during which the contract could be set aside unilaterally or by mutual consent.

Many Shaker-raised girls had kin in the same village who helped them adjust to their new home. At Watervliet, Catherine Ann Slater was bereft when she first arrived, but her sister eased her transition into their new home.[24] From 1835 to 1870, about 60 percent of the New Lebanon Church Family's girls under age fourteen had a sibling there.[25] They lived with their biological sisters, went to school or worked with them, played with them, and received emotional support from them, as well.

Polly Reed adjusted readily, but she was something of an anomaly. She made her own decision to join the Shakers at age seven, when two missionaries visited her family in Herkimer County, New York. With her parents' blessing and a new pair of shoes, she set out with the brethren and walked almost seventy miles through the snow to start a new life. Calvin Green wrote, "I thot she was about the bravest, & most spunky little one I ever saw & one worth having."[26]

A minor, strictly speaking, was not a party to her indenture, which was a contract executed between adults. Nonetheless, a child could affect the outcome of the agreement by misbehaving. In 1856, for instance, the New Lebanon Second Order returned Leanora Baker to her mother. She was "a very refractory & troublesome girl . . . determined not to reform . . .

extremely obstinate, & unwilling to go away: it seemed to be her element to be contrary!"[27]

Baker was the rare girl expelled for her bad attitude; expulsion for cause was more typical of boys.[28] Girls were more willing to conform to Shaker expectations. That gender difference is still noted among children today. Girls are outwardly more compliant and less trouble than boys as early as preschool.[29] Thus, some Shaker rules were designed to deal only with boys' misbehavior. At Sabbathday Lake in the early twentieth century, boys sat in front in the meetinghouse where adults could keep an eye on them, while girls were trusted to behave and sat in back.[30] Seth Youngs Wells wrote that because more girls chose to become Shakers, "we may infer that immorality is not so prevalent among them."[31] Girls' conformity promoted their persistence in Shaker villages, while boys were more likely to leave.

Lizzie Horton conformed to Shaker expectations. She wrote of her 1881 move to the Canterbury village. "When a very little girl I was placed with the Shakers by a kind father who wished me protected from the sins of the world. He knew that with this people I should find a good home, receive an education and be taught to live an honorable and upright life." By age thirteen, Lizzie had decided to remain a Believer. She "never regretted the day nor the working of the good spirit" that brought her there.[32]

In their new home, girls lived and worked in groups just as women did. In 1840, the New Lebanon Church Family formed a separate Girls' Order at the East House.[33] Two caretakers, Zillah Potter, age thirty-one, and Rhoda Wilson, age thirty, were assigned to oversee fourteen girls. From 1840 to 1870, the Girls' Order housed from eight to twenty girls between the ages of three and fifteen.[34] Some caretakers did not relish the job. After twenty-one-year-old Amy Reed moved to the East House in 1841 to help seventeen-year-old Harriet Goodwin with seven young girls, she was "sad & sorrowful."[35] Reed's objection may not have been to the new job but to the move away from a favored roommate or union meeting partner—a "particular affection" that might have necessitated the move.[36] Though Reed and Goodwin were young, they had adult responsibilities. Reed's maturity as a Shaker showed in her acceptance of her assignment; she conformed to expectations just as she expected her young charges to do.

Year-round, according to Isaac Newton Youngs, New Lebanon's girls spent most of their time at work "under the particular watch of their caretakers, at sewing, knitting & spinning &c.—being sent here and there occasionally." They did kitchen work and mended their own clothes. As an afterthought, Youngs noted that "the girls, both in the First and Second Order, employ a part of their time at the proper season of the year at learning to *spin,* as that is an important duty of life." The New Lebanon Second Order girls spent more time cleaning roots, because that was the family's business. Later Youngs must have realized that he had underreported the girls' duties and added that they made paper and cloth seed bags, braided palm leaf, and embroidered initials on clothes and handkerchiefs.[37] Despite those additions, however, Youngs minimized the girls' productive labor. Even a brother as conscientious as Youngs may not have realized how much work Shaker sisters did, much less girls, because he seldom worked with them.[38]

Shaker-raised girls' writings provide a better record of the work they did. Lucinda Day entered the Tyringham, Massachusetts, village in 1843 when she was thirteen and stayed until her mid-thirties. "We were always busy," she recalled. Because girls' indentures specified that they were to be instructed in housewifery, Day learned to make textiles from the raw wool or flax through every stage of manufacture to the finished garment. She assisted older sisters in "cooking, washing, ironing, milking, making butter, cheese [and] sewing, besides the knitting of our stockings and sox." Girls rotated through kitchen work every four weeks, as did women.[39] "S. P." wrote of her work setting and clearing the tables for meals. She was told to move no more than six plates or four cups at a time. "When we clear off a table the food should be taken off first," she wrote. After that, the girls removed dirty dishes, brushed off crumbs, washed tables, swept the floor, and set the tables for the next meal. Girls did that work three times a day.[40] Several girls ran errands for kitchen sisters year-round.[41] They helped do laundry, as well. Frances Carr learned to iron on flat work. Trudy Reno Sherburne had a child-sized ironing table, where she enjoyed doing up small pieces, such as handkerchiefs and table napkins.[42]

Girls did outdoor work, as well. In summer, they helped in the medical garden.[43] Anna P. Carll, who grew up in the village at Canterbury, New Hampshire, picked berries and grapes and collected potatoes. She called apple-picking "exhilarating." She climbed the highest ladder to the top to see the view and felt she was monarch of all she surveyed. She also worked long evenings boiling cider, husking corn, or cutting apples for sauce or drying, while a sister read aloud.[44]

At work, girls were under the supervision of an older sister. In 1860, Isaac Newton Youngs noted that the girls did "many kinds of little jobs, going here & there to help the older sisters when wanted."[45] After Nathaniel Hawthorne visited the Hancock Shakers on August 8, 1851, he wrote, "In the great house, we saw an old woman—a round, fat, cheerful little old sister—and two girls, from nine to twelve years old."[46] Adults oversaw children to make the best possible use of their time. "I have seen a ninety-year-old woman sit in a rocking chair spinning with a tiny six-year-old tot on the platform beside her, also spinning," Julia Johnson remembered. The elderly sisters were probably not the girls' caretakers. Because some jobs such as spinning or knitting were best taught one-on-one, girls were farmed out one or two at a time for lessons; they could not have spent all their time in the same group with their caretaker. Based on an account by the apostate Hervey Elkins, Judith Graham claims that children seldom mingled with adults other than caretakers, teachers, and an occasional apprenticeship mentor, but girls were probably not segregated as much as she suggests. Other memoirs show girls working with several sisters, including an Eldress, deaconess, nurse, and cook, as well as their caretaker. A girl might work in a kitchen, a laundry, a garden, an ironing room, a seed shop, a weavers' shop, and a spin shop, supervised in each location by a different sister. But when girls did "gang" labor, taking part in spinning bees or picking up kindling, they probably worked under their caretaker's direction, as they did when mending on Saturday mornings.[47]

In letters to the *Shaker Manifesto,* ten-year-old girls wrote about their knitting and sewing, but they did not realize the scope of their contribution to village profits when they made goods for sale.[48] In 1859, the New Lebanon First Order's fifteen girls wove 340 yards of edging and braided 592 yards, probably for hats or bonnets. They knitted 30 silk "head nets," sewed 170 cushion bags, and made 90,000 seed bags. They spent a hundred girl-days making shagging, fifteen picking hair, and twelve pressing bonnets. Deaconess Betsy Crosman wrote that they also made "many more items for home use" and commended caretakers and girls for their industry.[49]

As Shaker businesses expanded and contracted, girls' output changed to meet the demand for labor. In 1865, for instance, the New Lebanon girls' sale work included 16,600 paper seed bags, 49 cotton seed bags, 280 "tomatoe mareno cushions," 1,820 velvet cushions, 86 yards of palm leaf braid, 15 quarts of butternut and walnut meats shelled, and days spent picking dandelion seed. Two years later, with their caretakers Elizabeth Cantrell and Robena Gothra, the girls made 6,680 cushions and 286,200 paper seed bags. In 1868, they made another 200,000 paper seed bags and 114 cloth seed bags, reducing work on other products.[50] Their labor was not unusual. In the nineteenth century, children were expected to work at whatever they were physically capable of doing. The daily stint of work was common for worldly children, too; idleness was "a cardinal sin" in some families.[51] Among the Shakers, every skill that a girl mastered and every job she completed showed her conformity as well as her diligence.

"Work before play" was the rule. Girls had to earn their keep. According to Eleanor Brooks Fairs, an orphan who grew up in the Watervliet South Family, each child had an assigned stint of work to finish before she could play.[52] Julia Johnson recalled that in winter, all rose before dawn and wallowed through snowdrifts to the dairy house to spin. "Eight or ten would spin at a time. The stints were two 'runs' a day for wool and one 'run' for tow." At one village, if a girl had not completed her stint of work, she had only dry bread for her next meal. Sisters meted out other work-related punishments, as well. Martha Hulings had to stay home from an outing on a beautiful day because she had not finished her knitting. "I hadn't done my daily stint," she wrote. "You accomplished a prescribed amount of the odious knitting before you did any playing—in this case, hiking. So there I sat. All alone with the needles filled with bright red yarn and the unfinished part of what was supposed to be a sweater trailing beneath them."[53] Another Shaker-raised girl recalled knitting so many socks that she wondered whether she was supplying the rest of the world. But after a day spent weaving Shaker bonnets or making and trimming table mats, an hour of knitting in the evening "seemed more like rest than work."[54] Learning a good work ethic was part of a Shaker girl's upbringing. Jobs as mundane as braiding trim, knitting socks, or pasting seed bags were lessons in careful and precise production, satisfaction in a job well done, even perfectionism. Those who turned out high-quality products were an asset to their village.

Some girls, however, lacked aptitude for the jobs they were assigned. Hulings, for instance, thought it was a great day when Eldress Anna Case started teaching her how to knit. "It looked easy and I was eager," she wrote. "But it wasn't easy. I worked too tightly, I split stitches, and dropped them." Knitting was supposed to be "a smooth rhythmic operation," but to Hulings, it was "painfully hard labor" that reduced her to tears. Hulings was not lazy; she worked six days a week. She enjoyed dairy and kitchen work and did chores willingly. "I did not always do them right or well," she recalled, "and when this happened I was simply told to do them over again. There was no yelling or nagging. To do a thing right was considered only reasonable and logical," and so, except for the knitting, she learned to do things right. Into old age, she remembered Sister Freida Sipple's advice, "All that you do, do with all your might."[55]

Girls also learned more complicated jobs, such as washing clothes, a Monday chore. Laundry required heavy labor even after the process was partly mechanized. Sister Frances Carr writes that girls over age ten helped by putting wet wash through the wringer and hanging it outside to dry. Laundry work could be hazardous. In August 1815, fifteen-year-old Olive Wheeler was scalded when a wash house boiler exploded. Wheeler survived, but her co-workers died.[56] The wash house had other dangers, including water-powered machinery that "milled" the clothes. After a Monday wash day, the Watervliet scribe wrote that ten-year-old Augusta Latimore "was killed this morning, at ½ past 6, by having her clothes caught on the Shaft of the Wash-Mill. Her back & neck were both broken, and her body very much bruised."[57] In an era of child labor when machinery lacked safety mechanisms now taken for granted, industrial maimings were common for children as well as adults.

Little girls did not work all day. Seven-year-old Hattie of the west Pittsfield Shakers, for instance, wrote, "Tomorrow is Monday and I think I shall help iron some clothes in the forenoon, and in the afternoon all the little girls will have a play time."[58] After a girl finished her daily stint of work, her time was her own. But Shaker villages' expectations of children evidently varied. Playing at Watervliet's North Family, Trudy Reno Sherburne heard a visiting Eldress say to Sister Ella Winship, "Well, if she were in our family she'd be working." In retrospect, Sherburne recognized that she had been spoiled, perhaps because she was the only small child in the family.[59]

Children's caretakers, however, did punish willful misbehavior, though most Shaker punishment was less severe than that of the world's people. In 1815, Seth Youngs Wells wrote guidelines to regulate discipline. For many children, he said, gentle admonition was sufficient.[60] Memoirs by Shaker-raised girls reveal that corporal punishment was rare. In 1888, the editors of the *Shaker Manifesto* reprinted an article advocating not striking children unless absolutely necessary, never in anger, and only on the one or two portions of anatomy "which may be struck with comparative safety." They added that children "trained from early infancy to habits of obedience" rarely need whippings after age five or six. Martha Hulings recalled spankings with a hand or a switch, but more often, she had to sit in the corner or go without dessert.[61] By 1900, some villages may have abandoned the "chastening rod" except as a metaphor. Shakers had to temper discipline with love if they were to retain children as adult Believers.

Girls' memoirs also show that some sisters fostered them with affection. Sister Frances Carr loved second Eldress Jennie Mathers and later, Mildred Barker, as well; both became friends and mentors.[62] Anna Dodgson, who served the New Lebanon First Order as both girls' caretaker and schoolteacher, loved her students, and they loved her in return.[63] In 1886, a visitor wrote that Sister Polly, the girls' caretaker (probably at New Lebanon's North Family), said, "God help parents in the flesh if they love their children more than I have loved these!"[64] Shaker sisters shared kind words and hugs. Eleanor Brooks Fairs recalled "no shortage of affection" at Watervliet, where, according to another memoir, Catherine Ann Slater loved Sister Mariah Gillette. Trudy Reno Sherburne recalled her time there as the happiest years of her life. Moreover, the sisters encouraged girls to think for themselves and express their opinions. Fairs believed that Shaker children "probably had more freedom than children had in private homes."[65]

The occasional caretaker, however, was ill-suited to her work. Frances Carr and her peers did not care for her first teacher or the girls' caretaker at Sabbathday Lake Shaker village, and when authority figures did not win children's affection, those children were unlikely to persist as Shakers in adulthood. Fortunately for Carr, other sisters took an interest in her so she did not lack for affection.[66] At Watervliet, Catherine Slater reported physical cruelty from Sister Nancy Wells, the younger girls' caretaker, and Martha Hulings told of a Watervliet caretaker leaving an injured girl to suffer in the snow for hours without help—intentional negligence that Sister Mary Dahm, the village nurse, found reprehensible.[67] Evidently a few Shaker sisters took out their frustrations on their charges—a human failing that many parents would recognize. Nevertheless, among Believers, an injured girl had alternatives; she could turn to another authority figure for help, if necessary.

Girls' schooling was another opportunity for fostering conformity, and by all accounts, it worked admirably. Beginning in 1820, New York State school inspectors examined the New Lebanon Shaker school once or twice a year and found that it met or exceeded public school standards.[68] From the 1820s into the 1860s, Sarah Bates, Polly Reed, and Anna Dodgson taught the girls for a four-month term, from late April or early May until late August or early September.[69] Discipline was probably mild; school accounts included "prize books and rewards," candy, confectionaries, sugar plums, raisins, and other treats.[70]

Several sources suggest that Shaker schoolgirls were well-behaved. In "The Scholar's Soliloquy," a Shaker schoolgirl says: "I'm always happy when I do / Just as I'm taught the whole day thro'. . . . When I remember what I'm taught, / And do exactly as I aught, / I'm happy then, because I see / My teachers are well pleased with me. . . . If I'm obedient 'twill repay / Their kindness, as they often say."[71]

The world's people often visited Shaker schools during the summer tourist season, when girls were in class. (In the nineteenth century, boys attended school in winter.) In 1847, Jeremiah Hacker called the New Lebanon girls' school one of the most orderly he had ever seen. Sarah Bates, "an excellent teacher," and one assistant had thirty pupils from age four to sixteen. The girls, he reported, "take delight in obeying their teachers, and in striving to make each other happy." He found that obedience was prompt and cheerful.

> The rod is never used. . . . All were as busy as bees, and appeared as cheerful and happy as if they were at play; their studies were amusement to them. Little girls six or seven years of age had their slates "writing composition" or cyphering, while older ones were engaged in some other study, and I had never seen children of the same age further advanced in their studies than these, and certainly I never saw any that had a better understanding. . . . When I asked them a question they could give me the "why and wherefore" [and] . . . they understood what they had studied.[72]

Hacker's assessment of the New Lebanon Shaker school was typical. In 1848, Lewis Gaylord Clark visited the girls' school. The children, he reported, were "evidently happy and certainly healthy," and the visitors "heard exercises in composition, geography and astronomy which would have done no discredit to any similar school." The New Lebanon and Hancock schools were "excellent, in all respects."[73] In 1850, John W. Barber wrote of "hearty, rosy-cheeked, and contented children, from eight to fifteen years of age," who had "a very creditable examination in the various branches of astronomy, grammar, reading, spelling, arithmetic, &c., and gave us the most satisfactory proof that they are not trained up in ignorance."[74] A bemused *Harper's* editor ran a story about a visitor to a Shaker school who was encouraged to see for himself how competent the children were.

> At the insistence of the head instructress our Eastern friend called out a little girl who possessed a face indicative of more than ordinary intelligence, to go through her paces in spelling. "Will you oblige me by spelling the word *feeling*?" was the first question. "*F-two-e-l-i-n-g*," replied the child, without a moment's hesitation. "Try again, my dear," answered the examiner, with a shake of the head. The pupil spelled the word over again, in precisely the same manner as at first. With a dissatisfied expression of countenance the disappointed visitor was about calling for the "next," when, before he could do so, the instructress

interposed with, "Nay, friend, perhaps our system of spelling is not familiar to thee. Under no circumstances do we consent to *doubling any thing here.*[75]

In 1886, Herrick Kenyon commended the children under instruction in the New Lebanon schoolhouse.

> The young scholars were remarkable for their erect, graceful attitudes and modest demeanor; the government over them being mild, gentle, and beneficent, which generally produces willing obedience to what is required, the practical exercise of gentle manners being early inculcated; while churlishness, moroseness, all rough, unfeeling behavior, uncivil deportment, all mischievous and evil propensities, are carefully watched against and reproved, and the greatest pains taken to lead them into the practical exercise of truth, honesty, kindness, benevolence, and every moral virtue; obedience to their instructors, respect to parents and superiors, reverence to the aged, kindness and civility to all, being strictly enjoined.

He concluded with the observation that Shaker "teachers are not laboring for pecuniary compensation, but for conscience' sake, for the good of those entrusted to them."[76] What he did not say was that Shakers hoped to be the beneficiaries of the virtues they taught. If girls conformed to Shaker expectations, they would persist as Believers in adulthood.

Shaker schools changed as their society did, and not only because Believers had to adjust children's education to maintain state accreditation and to compete with the world's schools. At a Watervliet school in 1879, Charles Dudley Warner found a teacher, Mary Nelson, directing a play about women's rights, and again, the visitor was amused by the incongruity of the scene.

> And then we had a little comedy acted, out of the reading-book, by half a dozen girls, one of them disguised as an old lady in a Shaker bonnet, two of them shouldering brooms as representatives of martial women's rights, and all taking their parts in perfect gravity, without the least, even perfunctory, sense of humor, but with a sweet sincerity to duty, and wholly oblivious of all the worldliness, the love, the satire on strong-mindedness contained in the play.[77]

Schoolgirls imbibed feminism along with Shakerism—not surprising, given Shaker gender equality. In this, too, they conformed to sisters' expectations.

In August 1854, Polly Reed took her schoolgirls on an outing, starting at the tannery, where they were weighed. They walked through the seed and botanical gardens, where Harriet Goodwin and Elizabeth Sidle sang to them, then hiked to the burying ground to look at the graves. They were "much satisfied" with the ramble. In July 1857, schoolgirls from the First and the Second Orders joined for a special tour of the village, then went to the orchard to sing and read aloud.[78] In 1856, twelve-year-old Amelia Calver wrote a poem about a four-hour hike up the mountain by thirty girls and their teachers. The girls ran free, played in the stream till they were soaked, then snacked on crackers, cheese, and cake.[79]

Toys were conspicuously absent from early nineteenth-century Shaker girls' recreation. In Ann Lee's day, play was discouraged, and some Shaker communities were slow to relinquish those early customs.[80] At Watervliet in 1839, for instance, the sisters told Catherine Ann Slater that she had to give up dolls and toys as "vanities." A rebellious girl, Slater fashioned a replacement doll from a corncob, a chestnut shell, and a bit of muslin. Others risked reprimand by rolling a handkerchief into the shape of a doll. Slater made mud pies, played house with clamshell plates and acorn-top cups, and raced dandelions down the creek. "These were happy days," she recalled. Her stay at Watervliet included organized recreation, as well. A picnic was a special treat, even though the girls were accompanied by elderly sisters who "stalked solemnly along as if they were marching out to dig their own graves."[81] Occasionally there were mishaps. After a kindly brother made skis for one girl, she injured herself on her first outing. At Canterbury, another girl sledded into a wall, breaking her nose.[82]

By the end of the nineteenth century, some Shaker villages had relaxed prohibitions against toys. At Watervliet, Trudy Reno Sherburne recalled, sisters permitted girls to retain stuffed bears or pull-toys, which had to stay in their rooms while the girls worked. A stuffed bear, however, was known to make a quick flight outdoors through an open window so he could accompany his owner on an excursion normally forbidden to bears. The new century brought other innovations, as well. Each summer, the girls went to a park, which required a trolley ride—a high point of the day. Girls enjoyed traditional fun, too, picking chestnuts on a fall day and later roasting the nuts. In winter, Watervliet's girls sledded or had an occasional sleigh ride. Some evenings they popped corn or made taffy. One Christmas, the family had a "spider's web" for gift giving. Throughout the house, adults hid presents with strings attached. Each child found a string with her name on it and followed the string to her gift's hiding place—an exciting hunt in a big dwelling. Gifts were things they had made, or something special they had been given during the year and saved to pass along to a favorite person. Christmas day often included music and recitations.[83]

Maple sugaring marked the end of a long winter spent mostly indoors. At New Lebanon Shaker village in early April 1857, Isaac Newton Youngs wrote that the girls "went down to the sap-woods to have a spree at boiling some sap," adding that there was "some animation" in the excursion.[84] At Canterbury, Anna Carll recalled that on such an outing, girls had "entire freedom from unnecessary restraint" and ran wild, performing gymnastics, climbing trees to collect spruce gum, picking wintergreen berries where snow had melted, and singing around the open fireplace.[85] Another girl related that they "broke loose."

> This was the one day in the whole long year when we were allowed to scream, and scream we did with all our might. I think I can safely say that a more comprehensive collection of whoops, shrieks, and catcalls was never heard in a civilized land. Later I learned that the elders used to notify the neighbors the day before that they might not be startled by the fearful noises. . . . A kind-hearted brother put up swings for us, and on this happy day we were also permitted to jump rope, an amusement absolutely prohibited at all other times. Our caretaker made maple candy for us, while we searched in sheltered spots for clean, unmelted patches of snow in order to have "stick-chop." Altogether it was a day long to be remembered in our repressed lives.[86]

Sometimes the Eldresses took the little girls to the sugar camp and boiled sap for the treat of maple wax. The New Lebanon Second Order called it a "holly day in the sap woods." A First Order brother wrote, "Sisters having a season of recreation in the sap woods, making maple sugar, swinging, &c."[87]

In warmer seasons when the weather was good, a special treat was to "ride out," without a work assignment. With an older brother to drive the horses, Zillah Potter and seven girls went for a ride in August 1838.[88] According to two memoirs, girls had such an outing only once a year. They woke on that special day "in a state of wild exultation." Getting through the usual morning routine of dressing, chores, and breakfast was a trial, but as soon as the girls were packed into the wagon with lunch baskets and caretakers, they started singing. After lunch, they were allowed to remove shoes and stockings to wade in a stream. At the end of the day, one girl rode home thinking "how many weary days of 'being good'" lay between her and the next ride.[89]

Because children joined adults in most of their daily activities, sisters gave attention to the transition from childhood to adult responsibilities. In 1835, Betsy Bates wrote, "It is thought best by us, to have the girls have tea twice a day when they are in the kitchen, after they begin to work for a hand; and once a day when they are out of the kitchen, so if they share like the Sisters at their meals, they may feel obligated to act like women in their work."[90] Evidently some girls were slow to adopt a mature work ethic. The Hancock Shaker schoolmistress commented in 1860, "When they get to be 14–15, it is harder to teach them."[91]

Saturday afternoons were devoted to confession. The girls' caretaker read the church orders, perhaps concentrating on violations, while each girl sat and considered her sins. Then the caretaker went into the next room and called them in one at a time to confess. "Everyone was expected to have something to tell, either about herself or about some of her companions, and she who said the most was considered the most truthful." Confessions could take all afternoon. The girls had their own religious meeting after supper, singing and marching around their room, ending with testimonies of their intentions for self-improvement. When everyone had spoken, they said their prayers and went to bed.[92]

At Hancock, older children attended adults' family worship on Saturday evening. Near the end of the meeting, after an hour or more of spiritual labor that worked the group up to "white heat," the Elder reprimanded misbehavior.

> Now is the time for the elders to improve the occasion, to strike the iron while it is hot; for they know that the people when wrought up to the present high state of exultation, will submit to and accept criticism which at other times they would not listen to without resentment. Frequent, keen and incisive are their remarks, which go straight home to the parties intended, without mentioning names. If one has been idle, or lost his temper, if there has been jealousy, evil-speaking, backbiting, tattling. If there have been symptoms of affection for one of the opposite sex, or of going to the world, if one has come into the house without cleaning his shoes, or has been careless about his clothes, or shown vanity in the way in which he combed his hair; if a child has fondled the cat, or been disrespectful and disobedient—in short, every infraction of order and discipline, serious or trivial, is stringently animadverted upon, and invariably seconded and supported by the older part, the deacons, nurses, care-takers and burden-bearers.[93]

This exercise was not unique to Hancock. At New Lebanon in 1820, Isaac Newton Youngs wrote that they heard a piece of writing that "set forth the evil passions . . . which lead souls astray, and showed the effects & working the passions separately, such as anger, malice, envy, backbiting, unreconciliation, pride, lust &c." He added, "It was pretty plain & pointed, and tho' I believe [the] writing was not intended to point to any one in particular I thot likely some might think *you mean me now*! & not relish quite as well."[94] Individuals like Youngs may have resented having their shortcomings publicly exposed, but criticism was a lesson in humility, and a good Believer humbled himself or herself to the gift. Persisting as a Shaker meant learning from mistakes. One who conformed avoided humiliation.

When a girl reached mid-adolescence she left school and moved into adult quarters. Village scribes marked some of those moves in the official records: "Abigail Hathaway left girls' order & went to NE garret, No. 28," or "Margarette E. Falkenburg moved from the girls' order, into No. 4."[95] These older girls were scattered among chambers headed by mature women. In 1840, for instance, room Number 12 housed three sisters over age forty, five in their twenties, and two in their late teens. Number 14 had only one girl in her teens; her roommates ranged in age from twenty-two to fifty-eight. Number 16 housed two girls in their teens with sisters aged twenty-one to forty-eight.[96] By scattering the young sisters among older ones, Shakers discouraged cliques and provided mature oversight.

Some girls left the Shakers when their indentures ended. By age eighteen, a girl was considered an adult and was expected to have mastered all necessary skills, including textile manufacturing, sewing, knitting, laundering, cooking, dairying, and perhaps bonnet making. Several of those skills might have been useful for earning money among the world's people. By eighteen, then, if a girl left the society, she was thoroughly trained in housewifery, except for one skill: money management. As a Shaker, she might never have learned how to shop or trade for goods; she had no opportunity to negotiate a price or wages. She did not know how to budget her money because she had none; she might never have handled cash or engaged in any business transaction. Catherine Ann Slater pointed out, "Our education in Wisdom's Valley did not seem to be practical for the world." This gap in preparation for adult life was not limited to girls. When one male seceder left the society, he "knew little of business" and was "totally ignorant of the value of coins."[97] The apostate Julia Johnson wrote of "the heavy burden" of self-support. Outside of the communal society, she found "isolated life" difficult. Shakers brought up children with the same lack of financial preparation many of them had been brought up with themselves.[98] Though well fitted to live as Believers, where financial life was controlled by deacons, deaconesses, and trustees, Shaker-raised youth were not fully prepared to manage their own finances among the world's people.

Shaker-raised girls who stayed in the society, however, found good lives as Believers. "The girls mostly stay," a Believer in the 1880s said, then added, "the boys as often as not run away." Seth Youngs Wells attributed the gender difference to girls' better manners and morals; in his judgment, girls were more willing (than boys) to conform to Shaker mores.[99] Scholars suggest, however, that Believers with low earning potential, such as girls, were more likely to stay, while those with higher potential earnings, such as boys trained in lucrative trades, were more likely to leave.[100] My sense, however, is that girls did not base their decision to stay or leave on their earning potential. Unless they became deaconesses, or had lived a long time among the world's people before coming to the Shakers, they had little understanding of the economics of self-support. Moreover, as the testimonies discussed in Chapter 3 reveal, sisters often mentioned their affection for other sisters; thus, for girls, love and the security of Shaker life may have been more important than money.

The disparity between boys and girls in persistence as Believers contributed to the growing feminization of Shaker villages. Shaker women were in the majority after 1800. By 1900, Hancock Shaker village housed forty-three Believers—and only two of them were men.[101] As the number of men dwindled, women again became the public face of Shakerism, regendering the society's image so that it mirrored its origin in Ann Lee.

Outsiders looked at sisters in consternation, baffled at their apparent contentment. Parents, confounded that their children did not want to leave, continued to try to kidnap their offspring. Without understanding the benefits of communal life or equality of the sexes, the world's people gave short shrift to the girls and women who chose to wear the Shaker cap.

5

Chastity and the Shaker Cap

At about age fourteen, they begin to wear caps.

IN APRIL 1851, JOHN IRVING RETURNED TO THE HANCOCK, Massachusetts, Shaker village to remove his daughters with the help of a sympathetic sheriff. But the effort deteriorated when fourteen-year-old Justina and ten-year-old Elizabeth resisted. As Irving and the sheriff carried them away, one observer wrote, "Their bitter cries was enough to melt the hardest heart." The Shakers took immediate legal action, and the sheriff brought the girls back that afternoon. When they returned, Justina's Shaker cap was in her hands, not on her head. Her father had torn it off.[1]

Justina had tried to protect her cap. It was more than a head covering; it symbolized her commitment to a life of virgin purity.[2] John Irving surely knew that. One might suppose that his daughter's resistance humiliated him and that he took out his anger on the symbol of the Shakers who were her new (and preferred) family. The Shakers also had the benefit of Justina's labor—a loss for a family that may have needed the wages she could earn in a textile mill. Justina's "bitter cries" are more easily understood; her father dragged her away bodily when she did not want to go, and he tore off her cap and tried to burn it. No wonder she preferred the peace and safety she had found among the Shakers.[3]

From this story of a girl's head covering, we can begin to piece together a religious view of clothing in this communal society. In and of itself, a woman's cap is a minor article of apparel with little significance. But when the cap is invested with religious significance as a prescribed covering for a woman's head, it becomes an emblem of faith.[4]

According to anthropologists, the visible representation of the body is a template for expressing identity.[5] In a communal group, identity is collective, as well as individual. A Shaker sister's cap was an eloquent form of nonverbal communication, a sort of social insulation separating insiders from outsiders. If a Believer deviated from the norm, peers would rally to restore conformity, because a religious group manages deviance in dress at a "minute" level, particularly for women.[6] Thus we might infer that the sisters repaired or replaced Justina's cap as soon as she returned to the Hancock Shaker village.

Margaret C. Reynolds, an ethnographer who studied Pennsylvania's Old Order River Brethren, wrote that dress and other ritual traditions "do more than reflect values. They are essential to *perpetuating* those values."[7] Comparing worldly values to Shaker virtue, Sister Emily Smith wrote,

How oft I have looked on the gaily dressed crowd
While their bearing bespoke they were haughty and proud,
And breathed forth in silence my thanks unto God
For a way to escape from the path I once trod.
As adorning without nor yet graces within
Can e'er beautify those who're living in sin.[8]

Shaker costume showed the wearer's purity "without and within," her modesty, humility, and celibacy, as well as her obedience to group standards.

The sisters' uniform head covering diverged from mainstream tradition. Worldly women's best caps and bonnets, worn only to church, served no more purpose than to show off the wearer's fashion sense. (Some women actually stayed home from church because their millinery was subpar.)[9] In August 1878, for instance, a visitor at Shaker Sabbath listed women visitors' luxurious accouterments: velours, satins, silks, flowers, ribbons, plumes, feathers, and jewelry.[10] Prescriptive authors recognized churchwomen's misguided attention to fashion and chided them not to "interrupt a train of pious thought," by "watching for the entrance of friends, spying out new bonnets."[11] Because church was where Christians showed off their best outfits, the sight of rank upon rank of Shaker sisters dressed alike, with identical caps, was startling to visitors accustomed to Sabbath displays of idiosyncratic female dress. Worldly women's efforts to upstage their peers stood in sharp contrast to Shakers' uniformly humble and modest attire. Nineteenth-century lithographs of the Shakers show the difference.[12]

Uniform garments, including head covering, emphasize the bonds between women who dress alike. Because religious women's costume is a repository of social standards, their garments' total meaning exceeds the sum of the parts. The cap was an emblem of a Shaker woman's commitment to her religion.[13] One sister said, "None but the saints could wear their caps; for they came in a gift to Mother Ann."[14]

Furthermore, uniform dress "simultaneously *separates* women from men while creating *cohesion* among women."[15] Shaker garments highlighted the differences between the sexes, who were equal in status, though not in dress. In the nineteenth century, sisters wore layers of fabric that obscured their figures year-round, while in hot weather men wore only a one-layer frock over trousers. When women's clothing is markedly more modest than men's, that difference, according to sociologists, represents a patriarchal attempt to control women's sexuality.[16]

The religious history of women's head covering began long before the Shakers, with the apostle Paul's first letter to the Corinthians 11, which stipulates that a woman must cover her head when she prays. Many Christians adopted that practice, and because pious women were prayerful night and day, they covered their heads during all their waking hours. In that traditional view, head covering also symbolizes women's subjection to men.[17] Those customs came to North America with female immigrants from England in the 1600s. Although women's caps varied in style and quality, most married or affianced Anglo-American women wore caps in public. The folk tradition was that those without caps were "in the market for marriage."[18] As a sociocultural marker in the eighteenth and nineteenth centuries, Shaker sisters' caps signaled that their wearers had already made a commitment— not to a husband but to a life of virgin purity.[19]

According to Sherry Ortner, an object of cultural importance will have five markers if it is a "key symbol." The group will say it is important. They will not be indifferent about it. The object appears in different contexts, including symbolic domains. It requires elaboration or interpretation. Cultural restrictions are placed on it, including rules about its use or misuse.[20] All of those criteria apply to the Shaker cap. Ann Lee required sisters to wear the cap, and they adhered to her instruction long after she was gone. The cap aroused debate and dissension a century after Ann Lee died. Caps appear in Shaker journals, poetry, art, and photographs. Newcomers had to be taught rules of cap wear, and sisters devoted a great deal of time to working on caps.

By 1784, Ann Lee had revised the mainstream tradition of women's caps. She said, "When your daughters are grown so large that men will lust after them, you must put caps on their heads." Ann Lee institutionalized the "cap of purity," detaching it from the Christian standard that showed women's subordination to men and redefining it as a symbol of celibacy.[21] Scholars believe the cap tradition was rooted in the patriarchy's attempt to control women's sexuality.[22] However, Ann Lee's words show that it was men's sexuality—not women's—that required control.

Judeo-Christian tradition hearkens back to the temptation of Eve and the subsequent fall of Adam. This account reveals the early Church's fear of women's sexual influence over men. Some religions still attempt to undermine women's power by hiding the female form. Many devout women support those views by willingly following dress codes; others dress accordingly because they fear the consequences of violating the norm. But when women have to cover themselves more than men do, their garments testify to cultural recognition of men's weakness in sexual self-control. If men could control themselves, or exert sufficient control over one another, then women would not have to cover up more than men do. In terms of gender, covering women to reduce men's lust is a curious thing. Given the twenty-first century's understanding of personal responsibility, it seems absurd to make women responsible for men's heterosexual behavior. However, worldwide religions do just that.

Mother Ann Lee's successor, Lucy Wright, supported that concept. She told Shaker sisters that they had the greater responsibility for self-control.[23] A later Elder was more candid. Among the Shakers, he wrote, caps were intended to "screen young females from the temptations and trials of males as suitors."[24] In this worldview, then, head covering and modest dress symbolized women's self-government as a substitute for men's self-discipline and was thought to offer protection against male sexual aggression.

Among the Shakers, head-covering customs evolved during the nineteenth century. Typically, little girls went bareheaded until about age ten. From age ten to fourteen, a girl's hair was "drawn into one braid and turned up the back of the head and fastened." A black net covered her hair.[25] Net and cap customs, however, could vary from village to village.[26] An undated Shaker note says that seven-year-old girls had to wear hair nets to meeting. At age eight, they began wearing cloth caps to meeting, and at age twelve, wore cloth caps every day. Those rules could be adjusted for girls who were "very large" for their age.[27]

The shift in headgear did not necessarily take place at a particular age.[28] A girl's physical development signaled that she had met Ann Lee's criterion of being "grown so large" that men would lust after her. At Hancock Shaker village, Justina Irving had passed that point by age fourteen. Among the

New Lebanon, New York, Shakers, so many of the girls between the ages of thirteen and sixteen were capped that the occasional uncapped girl was conspicuous.[29] Margarette Falkenburg had her cap by age thirteen, Mariah Lapsley and Letsy Ann Bennett at fifteen, and Abigail Hathaway at sixteen.[30] Sometimes a girl's first wearing of a cap was marked in the village journal. At Shirley, for instance, a scribe wrote, "Martha went to Meeting with a cap on."[31] At New Lebanon, Eldress Betsy Bates noted that Clarissa Fay felt "very shamed" when she put on her Shaker cap.[32] Shame seems an odd reaction, unless the cap marked a girl's first menses, a very personal life passage that a modest girl might have felt uncomfortable about revealing publicly.[33]

The acquisition of a girl's first cap, as Beverly Gordon and Peggy Reynolds point out in separate studies, was a rite of passage, a material symbol of a girl's transition from childhood to maturity. Shakers may not have had a capping ceremony beyond an older sister's presentation of the cap to a girl, perhaps with instruction in cap making and care, but the occasion was significant nonetheless. When the girl put on her cap, she consecrated herself to God and signaled her obedience to group standards. Her choice to conform was reinforced by older sisters' approval.[34]

Around the time a girl received her first cap, as a general rule, she stopped going to school, left the Girls' Order, and moved into the adults' dwelling, where she took on grown-up responsibilities. But these changes were not necessarily simultaneous; one photograph of Canaan, New York, Shaker schoolgirls shows a capped girl still in school.[35]

Before the 1890s, once a girl put on a cap, she wore one as long as she remained a Shaker. The cap was one of the first garments a Shaker sister donned in the morning and the last she took off at night. Putting on the cap "was anything but simple." She had to comb her hair, pull it straight back, and twist it into a knot, sometimes braiding it first. She secured that mass of hair with pins or a bar and wrapped it in a crocheted netting (called pegging) that she tightened with a string that ran around the edge. Finally, she put on the cap and secured it with pins. It was a "tedious procedure."[36] But older girls were so accustomed to wearing this symbol of modesty that removing the cap in public was shocking. According to Catherine Slater, a Shaker girl was mortified to be seen without her cap.[37]

The cap was so much an emblem of Shakerism that when girls left the Shakers, the cap was the first thing they shed. Catherine Slater wrote, "I did not wear again the heavy worsted fillet or cap," and, she added, "both head and brow felt the grateful relief."[38] (The fillet was worn like a headband to which the cap was anchored with pins.) Mary Briggs wrote that she left the Tyringham Shakers because she "detested" their headgear, but her subsequent marriage shows that she had an additional reason for leaving.[39] When fifteen-year-old Eliza Van Houten left the Shakers "to enjoy the flesh," she did not take along her cap of purity.[40] In 1837, a visitor recorded a singular event at New Lebanon Sabbath worship. "A girl of seventeen," he noted, "threw up her handkerchief into the air, tore off her cap, and required the care of two or three of the older women to hold her down."[41]

Shaker women spent a great deal of time making and maintaining caps. Unseemly pride in cap making was to be avoided, however, since the cap was meant to be an emblem of humility as well as chastity. Thankful Goodrich recalled a chiding she received from Mother Lucy Wright: "One time I was making caps, Mother Lucy came into the room, & sat down by me to see me work. She said, 'Thankful, if I should take as much pains, & feel as much about the caps as you do, it would be sin in me. It seems to me that you think every stitch you take must be perfect enough to enter the Kingdom of Heaven. I cannot feel as you do about these things. . . . I am willing that you should do your work well, but do not set your heart & fancy too much upon these things, so that you cannot heed the gifts & power of God, which will never fail.'" Undaunted, Goodrich retorted with the words of Father Joseph Meacham, who warned Believers to beware the spirit that says you do not *have* to be neat and must finish it off quickly.[42]

Good cap makers helped others. A few sisters made caps for girls about to receive their first one. At Harvard, Eliza Babbitt made thirteen girls' caps in early 1856.[43] In 1842, Eldress Annie Williams of the New Lebanon Second Order reported, "This week twelve sisters make 29 shirts and finish 32 caps." Another time, she said, they finished 70 caps in four days. In 1850, at the Canaan gathering order, Minerva Reynolds and Marcia Bullard went to the lower family to help with cap making.[44] Sewing bees may have been necessary because some sisters lacked the necessary steadiness, eyesight, or patience to make caps of thin material. At these gatherings they could set up a production line where every sister could do what she did best and expert cap makers could coach those who were less skilled and experienced. At Harvard, Olive Chandler wrote, "Emily [Hall] is a nice cap maker" and showed her appreciation by asking Hall to fit her with a cap.[45]

Once made, caps required time and effort to keep them neat and clean. Each sister owned from nine to sixteen caps, including old ones worn for dirty jobs such as spring cleaning or painting.[46] A sister may have changed her cap several times a day, depending on her duties. Eunice Chapman wrote that Shaker sisters changed their caps four or five times in one day.[47] If a sister began her day in an old cap for milking, then changed to a clean one for breakfast, put on another "dirty-work" cap for gardening or the messy job of breaking tow, which filled the air with fibrous dust, and later donned the clean one for dinner, she would have changed caps three times before noon. The Believers' emphasis on cleanliness suggests that sisters would never have worn soiled caps to meals.

Only a few sisters were skilled at mending, washing, bleaching, and ironing the finest fabrics. The most adept ironers did caps, which were so fragile they could be easily ruined by unsteady hands or scorched with an overheated iron. At Canaan in 1852, Elizabeth Garvey, Nancy Wilson, and Minerva Reynolds, who were entrusted with ironing fine linen caps, were always looking for ways to improve their cap care.[48] At New Lebanon, Betsy Bates wrote in 1835: "I iron caps they are starched without tallow in the starch for the first time. . . . I have done some for the Ministry & journey Caps before, I think we shall like it."[49] Caps required a lot of attention. In the 1850s, Olive Hatch spent entire days making, mending, starching, and ironing caps—more than thirty on one occasion. She also taught cap making to other sisters.[50]

As Shaker society evolved, so did the Shaker cap. In 1790, visitors noticed that the Shaker sisters' caps were "tight" and fit "close" to the head; thus they used less fabric than the typical revolutionary-era mobcap.[51] The sisters may have conserved cloth by scanting their caps in the early years when their society was just getting established. Rebecca Clark, who was gathered in at Hancock in 1791, recalled, "We manufactured all of our own clothing for many years; even our caps and handkerchiefs we spun and wove for a number of years."[52] Only the best spinsters could produce thread fine enough for caps and handkerchiefs.

The sisters wore a uniform "head-dress" as early as 1795.[53] The first uniform caps were made of homespun linen. The front or forepiece was four inches wide, with a narrow border of thinner material.[54] The New Lebanon Shaker historian Isaac Newton Youngs described them about 1800:

> For the head-dress they wore fine lawn or linen caps; they were formed by plaiting and gathering, so as to fit to the head behind, being strait before, with a border about an inch wide, with open work, so as not to obstruct the sight sidewise. There was a wide hem behind, in which

was inserted tape-like strings, that were bro't up over the head, & down again, & tied behind. The cap was also secured to the fillet by a pin. Also there were tape strings at the lower part before, that might be tied under the chin.[55]

Around 1806, the sisters adopted imported muslin for caps, relieving them of the necessity of weaving fine linen.[56] By 1814, sisters in Kentucky were wearing what one visitor described as a uniform "long-eared white cap, pinned or tied neatly under the chin."[57] In May 1817, the sweltering western sisters were happy to hear that Mother Lucy Wright was wearing thinner caps in summertime and asked for a full-sized copy of the pattern.[58] In 1819, Shaker sisters revised their design again.

> The crowns were made larger and cut in the form of a half circle. On the circling side was a wide hem, in which was inserted a tape string (as in the former caps,) by which to draw up the cap. The foreside of the cap was a straight piece, about three inches wide, and fifteen or sixteen inches long, on one side of which was set a border of leno, or open work, as on the former caps, and the other side was set to the straight-side of the crown, without any gathering. These caps were ironed out flat and smooth, and then drawn up by the tape, to fit the head.[59]

In 1826, Anne Royall, a visitor, described the sisters' caps as "very fine," adding, "I have never seen any thing that combined so much taste and beauty."[60]

Other changes followed. Betsy Bates refers to a "Holy border," which she had not "sot on" before 1835, but it is hard to know whether she meant open work or something divinely inspired.[61] Charles Daubeny, a visitor in September 1837, observed "a very neat and brilliantly-white muslin cap, on which it would appear that all their arts of embellishment had been concentrated."[62] The "embellishment" may have been the lappets hanging from each side of the cap's front. In July 1838, James Silk Buckingham wrote of a sister's "cap of clear muslin, fitting closely to the face, with long descending lappets."[63] Those lappets seem to have disappeared before August 1856, when Benson Lossing visited New Lebanon and sketched the sisters.[64]

In 1863, Polly Reed wrote that Betsy Bates "has been making some improvements. The long strings that have formerly been put up over the head are left off entirely."[65] Watervliet sisters wrote a long poem to thank the Ministry for simplifying the caps and included ironing instructions for the new design.

With all great wads of fillet / We thankfully dispense
For surely they look bungling / And injure common sense.
The head more neatly fitted / To make a shorter strap
And thus prevent the friction / Of collar neck and cap.
The cap maintains more firmly / The place for it designed
Eleven inches length of tape / Will meet and tie behind
The string is stitched on slanting / Quite near its usual place
And half an inch of front hem / Puts on a finished grace.
. . . .
To iron them compl[etely] / The starch must not be thick
And by the Lebanon manner / We do them neat and quick.
As usual crimp the casing / On right side or on wrong
Then lay the pleats up straitly / And bow them down always
Nor think the cap is finished / Till to the head it lays.
And if they're rightly ironed / The front pleat will be small
Which makes them look more comely / And not inclined to fall.[66]

The changes reduced the amount of fabric needed—an important consider-
ation when prices were high during the Civil War—and made the cap more
attractive, less itchy, and more likely to stay put.

It is worth noting that sisters were not permitted to individuate their caps
with idiosyncratic decoration—though some may have tried. A thirty-three-
page poem on Shaker beliefs, dated September 1847, says: "God's people
must have oneness; / Each form and fashion must subject / To one united
quorum. / Not every one as they would like / Have bonnet, hat or raiment, /
Nor introduce for fancy's sake, / A fashion, style or garment."[67] The altera-
tions in design, the "Holy border," and the poem prohibiting new fashions
"for fancy's sake" show that the sisters had an ongoing dialogue about their
clothing, which suggests tension between tradition and desire for change.

Because the symbolism of religious costume is so loaded, that tension
often plays out in challenges to dress standards.[68] Furthermore, because gender is socially constructed, gendered norms such as Shaker caps change in
response to such challenges—and the sisters did challenge the cap throughout the nineteenth century, as their efforts at improvement show.

A significant challenge arose in 1869 when Groveland Eldress Polly Lee
asked the New Lebanon Ministry to eliminate caps. The "tiny, frail, and
independent" Eldress Polly Lee may have been unusually candid, because
the Ministry overreacted; the draft of their answer was fifteen pages long. In
short, the Ministry felt that this particular change would not be beneficial.

Ministry Elder Giles Avery responded to the sisters' cap complaints. He said that if "Believers all felt union in it," then they might consider a change in cap wearing. He reminded Eldress Polly that modesty required covering a woman's charms. Without caps, worldly women took too much pride in dressing their hair in "fantastical arrangements." Avery added that "exposing the neck &c" had "evil effects" on men. "It is one of nature's resorts to attract a lover," he said. Furthermore, he added, Mother Ann tried to prevent the "influences of sexual passion so prominent in worldly life." Avery admitted that some sisters took inappropriate pride in their caps—but the Ministry felt that "entire nudity" would be worse. The Ministry did not favor change, even though some sisters felt they were sacrificing comfort, convenience, principle, or health "to a fashion, a custom, or a superstition." They had to wear caps.[69]

Polly Lee's request would have been unthinkable only a few decades earlier. But hers was not the only challenge to cap standards that reveals the ongoing tension between tradition and innovation. Lace was another. The Millennial Laws banned "lace for cap borders," an indication that the issue had been raised before the 1845 laws were revised. However, though lace was "utterly forbidden," the Ministry could permit such things if they were not "superfluously wrought."[70] Lace could be one of the fripperies that plain dress eliminates along with "Babylonish" luxuries. But the lace does not require a labor-intensive (and therefore expensive and fancy) pattern; lace can be a simple open-weave fabric with small holes between the threads, as in grenadine or bobbinet. The Ministry allowed the use of this fabric in 1870. A Harvard Believer wrote, "Sisters petition for lace caps and their petition is granted to wear them at home."[71]

The following year, the Ministry promoted lace caps. In December 1871, the New Lebanon Church Family deaconess Betsy Crosman wrote, "Lace caps have been introduced, we have all had one. Made by the Ministry." The new caps omitted "chin strings" and the tapes that passed over the head, so they were less confining.[72] In 1872 and 1873, Polly Reed and her helpers made nine hundred lace caps for the eastern Shaker societies' sisters—a monumental undertaking.[73] By making the caps themselves, the Ministry sisters such as Eldress Polly made a metaphorical gift into a physical one that promoted union, a basic Shaker virtue; thus, the new uniform caps strengthened their society while accommodating the sisters' desire for change.

Change was inevitable. By 1870, nearly all of the first generation of Believers were gone. Shaker feminism was well entrenched, and sisters were not subordinated to brothers. Believers were ahead of most of the world's people in recognizing that women should have the same privileges as men, including the right to vote.[74] To sisters who wanted to put their equal rights ideology to practical use, the question may have been: "Why must we cover our heads every waking minute, when brethren do not?" But the society's customs meant that caps could not be shed immediately, so the sisters did the next best thing: they made caps translucent—a step toward making them disappear entirely.

Even outsiders noticed the minimalist new cap. In 1878, a visitor wrote that the New Lebanon Shaker sisters wore a "would-be cap of transparent net stretched on a wire frame." In 1880, a visitor to the Canterbury, New Hampshire, Shakers commented on the sisters' "cap-like bonnet of stiffened illusion, or blonde, made over a wire frame."[75] In 1885, another visitor identified the cap's fabric as white bobbinet.[76]

This cap was lighter weight and cooler, but it was barely a covering at all. Some women who wear plain dress say that because the Bible says a woman's hair should be "covered," the cap must be opaque; a translucent cap does not qualify. As Shaker photographs show, ears and hair were clearly visible through the net. Furthermore, the net cap lacked strings. Women of the Old Order River Brethren, who wear plain dress, have a saying, "When the strings go, everything goes." To them, cap strings are significant; when devout women relax their standard of dress, their most fundamental beliefs are at risk.[77]

The Shaker church was in trouble well before then. Members' persistence halved after 1830, and membership dropped from 1840 on.[78] Statistical studies confirm that among noncelibate denominations, growth rates correlate strongly with "strictness." The liberal mainstream denominations' share of the churchgoing population has declined since the American Revolution, while stricter churches' "demands for complete loyalty, unwavering belief, and rigid adherence to a distinctive lifestyle" have promoted the growth of conservative religion. According to one analyst, "Strict churches proclaim an exclusive truth—a closed, comprehensive, and eternal doctrine. They demand adherence to a distinctive faith, morality, and lifestyle. They condemn deviance, shun dissenters, and repudiate the outside world. They frequently embrace 'eccentric traits,' such as distinctive diet, dress, or speech, that invite ridicule, isolation, and persecution."[79] According to this definition, Shakers had a strict church.

However, the majority of persisting Believers were women, and the society had to accommodate them. Stringless caps were just one sign of change. The late nineteenth-century Ministry and the new generation of Believers gradually repositioned their society. As Elder Henry Blinn pointed out, "Medieval customs and habits were eminently proper in that age, but as the earth or world moves, the people must move with it or be left in the rear. To stop this onward progress would be like attempting to stop the wheels of time." By adopting dress reform, promoting vegetarianism, and working for pacifism and women's rights, they moved with the times. Thus, Shakers adapted their customs to be "more in accordance with the light of to-day."[80]

Well before 1890, most women among the world's people had discarded caps as relics of bygone days, no longer needed to symbolize subordination, marital status, or modesty. The Shakers did likewise. In 1895, the Ministry shared a gift that made caps optional for sisters under age thirty. Most sisters "gladly accepted the relief," though Canterbury, New Hampshire, and Alfred and New Gloucester, Maine, retained the older custom longer.[81] The textile historian Beverly Gordon's statement that Shaker sisters wore caps at all times is illustrated, ironically, by a photograph of three New Lebanon sisters sewing, not one of them wearing a cap.[82] Increasing individuality was visible evidence that Shakerism could adjust to meet members' demands.

After 1895, the "cap of purity" declined as a key symbol for Believers. Abandoning the cap meant that the sisters gave up the symbol of their historic responsibility for controlling men's lust. They no longer needed head covering to represent women's self-government as a substitute for men's self-discipline. On one hand, the declining numbers and increasing age of persisting brethren may have been a factor in caplessness. On the other hand, Believers realized that with or without the cap, some individuals had the gift to stay chaste, humble, and obedient to communal standards, while others did not. Persisting Shakers focused on the substance of godliness, not the outmoded symbol. Among the Shakers, men could and did control themselves—or they had to leave. Shakers required self-discipline. Their example shows that if a society has the will to do so, it can influence men to live up to the same standards of chastity demanded of women. The Shakers also allowed for differences of opinion: women who preferred the cap continued to wear caps among their capless peers. The cap's long history of change shows that Shaker women had the power to alter their utopia, even if it meant setting aside one of Ann Lee's earliest teachings—her admonition to cap girls as soon as they were old enough for men to lust after them.

Daguerrotype of two young Shaker sisters. These two sisters are wearing white lawn kerchiefs, and palm-leaf bonnets over their caps, dressed for an outing, perhaps in the 1840s or 1850s. Note also the mitts on one sister's hands. Location and photographer unknown. Collection of Michele Clement.

"Shakers (their mode of worship)." Lithograph by Kellogg and Comstock, circa 1850. Collection of Hancock Shaker Village.

Visitors' images of Shaker dance showed little differentiation in sisters' appearance; the artists individuated the men more than the women. Visitor accounts also describe African American Believers — a reminder that Shakers welcomed people of color into their ranks. Regardless of their other gendered differences, Shaker women and men marching or dancing in worship engaged in the same activity, in the same way, neither sex exalted over the other, and their songs praised a God who was both Mother and Father.

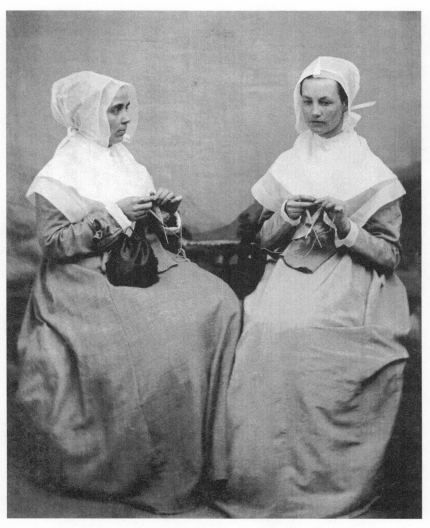

Tintype of Shaker women, probably in the 1860s. Photographer unknown. Communal Societies Collection, Hamilton College.

Though the provenance of this tintype is unknown, these two women were identified as Shakers, based on evidence provided by their costumes, including identical garments, lawn caps, and kerchiefs, as well as their propensity for documenting their labor. Women of the world's people usually wore their fanciest apparel and rarely dressed alike for the photographer. In addition, the sister on the right strongly resembles Watervliet Sister Anna Caroline Ulrich, who died in 1871. Identification clues provided by Steve Paterwic, Brother Arnold Hadd, Magda Gabor-Hotchkiss, and M. Stephen Miller, "An Early Shaker Tintype," Shakers World *(1996): 4–6.*

New Lebanon Church Family Second Order sisters Sarah Jane Rea (middle) and Eliza Avery (right) in the finishing room where extracts were labeled. [Benson J. Lossing], "The Shakers," Harper's New Monthly Magazine, *July 1857.*

This may be the earliest image of Shaker sisters at work and is one of the few Church Family interiors.

OPPOSITE PAGE, BELOW   *Canaan Shaker school. Photo by James Irving, Troy, N.Y. Collection of Hancock Shaker Village.*

In August 1869, a sister noted that a photographer visited to take pictures, but she did not identify the individual. (Canaan Upper Family Sister's Journal [1866–74], August 1869, LC 3:46.) The girls in this stereopticon of the late 1860s may include Emeline and Lydia Forester, Almira Hull, Adelaide Sherman, Maria Schultz, and Charlotte Tremper, according to Magda Gabor-Hotchkiss in Shaker Image, *197. Canaan's schoolteachers included Betsy Stone (1813–after 1855), who came to Canaan from the New Lebanon North Family in April 1852 to run the girls' school, Emily Sears (1803–1890), who taught in 1871, and Emily Offord (1848–1896), identified as the teacher in the 1880 census. (Canaan Upper Family Deaconess's Journal [1850–53], April 1852, LC 3:39; Canaan Upper Family Sister's Journal, August 1871, LC 3:46.)*

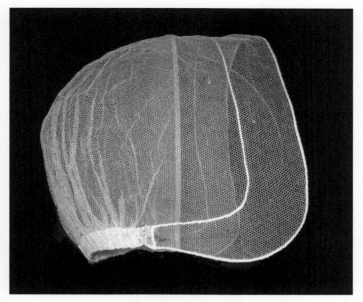

Shaker sister's net cap, probably made between 1870 and 1890.
Cap in collection of Shaker Museum and Library; photo by
author.

Joseph Becker, Shaker kitchen, *Frank Leslie's Illustrated Newspaper,* September *1873. Collection of Hancock Shaker Village.*

Publicity such as this was important for illustrating Shaker modernity. This is perhaps the most detailed of the few early interior views of the New Lebanon Church Family. The artist's attention to the many conveniences of this kitchen suggests a cook's understanding of the work involved in preparing meals for a very large family. Betsy Crosman (1804–1892) became the First Order's junior deaconess in 1837 and was promoted to the first position in 1839. She served until 1872, training Matilda Reed (1817–1902), Julia Ann Scott (1839–1919), and Anna Dodgson (1818–1897) as her successors. (Records Book No. 2, NYPL 2.6, pp. 44–47, 388.)

New Lebanon Church Family meetinghouse. Stereo view by James Irving, before 1875. Communal Societies Collection, Hamilton College.

During the summer tourist season in the nineteenth century, several hundred visitors typically thronged the Mount Lebanon meetinghouse at Sunday worship. Men entered at the door on the left; women on the right. On occasion the street was lined with visitors' vehicles for half a mile. Some mentioned the Shaker amenities for visitors, including a place to water their horses. According to Steve Paterwic, the building partly visible at the left of the photo may have been the wood house that burned in the great fire of February 1875.

Sisters climbing into the wagon for an outing, Enfield, N.H. Detail from stereo view by E. T. Brigham, Lebanon, N.H., between 1860 and 1880. Communal Societies Collection, Hamilton College.

When sisters went to town or on picking expeditions to distant locations, or when deaconesses traveled to the tourist resorts to sell their wares, they were generally accompanied by brethren who drove and wrangled the horses. The platform helped sisters get into the high wagon without help.

OPPOSITE PAGE, ABOVE   *Anna Dodgson (1818–1897). Photo by Joseph N. McDonald and Edwin S. Sterry, Albany, N.Y., circa 1882. Communal Societies Collection, Hamilton College.*

In addition to being a visionist in the 1840s, Anna Dodgson was a Mount Lebanon Church Family schoolteacher from 1856 to 1866, and served as a deaconess from 1872 to 1887.

OPPOSITE PAGE, BELOW   *Shaker sisters labeling and packing extracts, from an 1885 almanac. Collection of Hancock Shaker Village.*

This resembles a "bee" or work party, which was one of the ways sisters' indoor hand labor was organized. The extract business has been generally attributed to the brethren, but the sisters gathered, dried, and sorted the roots and herbs for processing into extracts, then bottled, packaged, and labeled the final product. In 1855, according to visitor Benson J. Lossing, the Church Family used 75 tons of herbs and roots in manufacturing medicinal preparations, which required a great deal of women's work.

Sister Mary working in the Canterbury, N.H., garden, with "help." Stereo view by W. G. C. Kimball, Concord, N.H., between 1868 and 1890. Communal Societies Collection, Hamilton College.

In addition to the indoor jobs for which Shaker sisters are better known, they did outdoor work such as gardening, harvesting food crops for home use and for sale, stacking firewood, and cleaning up dooryards.

Bert Geer Phillips, "Where Luscious Blackberries Grow," published in Demorest's Family Magazine, *September 1894, 646. Collection of Hancock Shaker Village.*

From April through November, Shaker women and girls gathered hundreds of varieties of wild foods, as well as medicinal roots and herbs. Some produce was consumed fresh or preserved for home use. They sorted, dried, and packaged the rest for sale as their contribution to the brethren's extract and medicinal herb businesses. According to Lesley Herzberg, these sisters probably lived at Mount Lebanon.

Mary Hazard (1811–1899), Emma Neal (1847–1943), and Augusta Stone (1836–1908), perhaps in the Mount Lebanon Church Family Office, 1889. Hancock Shaker Village copy of Shaker Museum and Library original.

Deaconesses such as these managed the sisters' temporal affairs, made work assignments, tracked rotations through the kitchen, ran manufacturing operations such as the palm leaf bonnet and fancy goods businesses, dealt with the brethren's demands for sisters' labor, and made sure that the family was clean, fed, and clothed.

Unidentified sister using a knitting machine for flat work, perhaps in the second floor north room of the Canterbury, N.H., Church Family laundry in the 1890s, according to Canterbury Shaker Village curator Renee Fox. Photographer unknown. Communal Societies Collection, Hamilton College.

Knitting machines were among the many labor-saving devices that sisters used and brothers maintained. Enfield, N.H., Shakers had four knitting machines as early as 1850, for knitting flannel drawers to sell. (June Sprigg, By Shaker Hands [Hanover, N.H.: University Press of New England, 1990], 185–86.) By 1894, the Canterbury Shakers used machines such as this for making sweaters to sell. ("Canterbury, N. H.," Shaker Manifesto 24.7 [1894]: 168.)

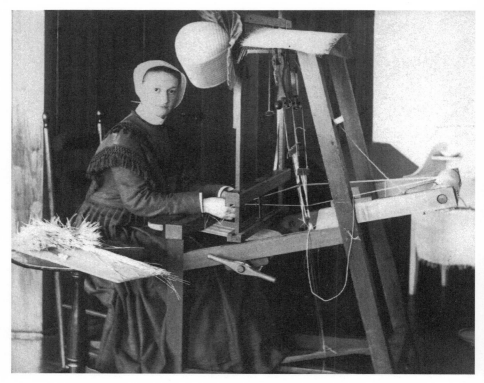

*Bertha Mansfield (1862–left in 1898) weaving palm leaf at Canterbury, N.H.,
1885–1890. Photographer unknown. Collection of Hancock Shaker Village.*

*Woven palm leaf was the basis of the deaconesses' bonnet business, which
peaked in the late 1830s but sparked additional ideas for fancy goods in the
decades that followed.*

Mount Lebanon North Family laundry ironing room, 1895. Photo by James E. West, Hoosick Falls, N.Y. Collection of Hancock Shaker Village.

Adults are Rosetta Stephens (1860–1948), Daniel Offord (1843–1911) (operating the press), two unknown sisters, Sarah Burger (1855–1933), and Martha Anderson (1844–1897). Identifications provided by Magda Gabor-Hotchkiss in Elmer R. Pearson and Julia Neal, The Shaker Image, 2nd ed. (Pittsfield, Mass.: Hancock Shaker Village, 1995), 64 and 194.

Sisters sewing at Mount Lebanon Church Family circa 1900. Hancock Shaker Village copy of original at Shaker Museum and Library.

The tailoring counter suggests that the location was a tailoress's shop, where sisters needed good light and space for laying out fabric to be cut into garment pieces; the treadle sewing machine was a great labor-saver in sewing long straight seams in cloaks and skirts. The sister at the right may have been reading to the other two while they worked.

Mount Lebanon North Family store interior. Postcard by H. M. Gillette, Lebanon Springs, N.Y., 1901–1918. Collection of Hancock Shaker Village.

Note the sale goods. Racks of Shaker photographs and postcards brought income into village coffers, as well as serving as marketing tools. Sisters made many of the other items sold, including feather dusters, bonnets, baskets, knitwear, fancy goods, and on one low shelf, perhaps at a little girl's eye level, dolls in Shaker dress.

Jessie Evans (1867–1937) in her traveling gear, East Canterbury, N.H. Photo by Kimball. Communal Societies Collection, Hamilton College.

Sisters were not confined indoors unless they were ill or otherwise physically incapacitated, and their wardrobes show that they went out dressed for the weather. Jessie Evans's garments included gloves, cape or coat, and overskirt.

Mount Lebanon North Family sisters, perhaps in May 1902. Photographer unknown. Collection of Hancock Shaker Village.

The North Family was known for literary efforts by sisters as well as brethren. Pictured here are at least nine published authors and poets. STANDING: *Agnes Lee (1846–1910), Leila Taylor (1854–1923), Martha Burger (1853–1926), Ruth Barry (1823–1903), Anna White (1831–1910).* SEATED: *Cecilia DeVere (1836–1912), Maria Blow (1821–1906), Sarah Burger (1855–1933) on ground in front and Annie Rosetta Stephens (1860–1948) seated behind her, Eliza Rayson (1834–1908), Mazella Gallup (c1851–1944), Fanny Tyson (1836–1918).*

Watervliet North Family Shakers circa 1912 in front of their dwelling. Photo by P. S. Goodfellow, Niskayuna, N.Y. Communal Societies Collection, Hamilton College.

FRONT: *Tippy (dog owned by Jennie Wells), Elder Josiah Barker (1847–1921), Eldress Lavinia Dutcher (1830–1923), Eldress Polly Lee (1820–1916), Sister Jennie Wells (1878–1956).* BACK: *Esther Relyea, Irene Coburn, Sister Agnes Stebbins, Sister Ella Winship (1857–1941). Identifications provided by Steve Paterwic.*

This Shaker family's demographics may have been typical in the early twentieth century. Their experience as Believers was also characteristic of their time: several were former residents of Groveland, which closed in 1905, and they had to move again after the Watervliet North Family closed in 1919. Jennie Wells later lived at Mount Lebanon and Hancock, as well.

*Watervliet Shaker nurse Mary Dahm (1883–1965) and Maggie Caldwell
(1867–left 1921). Postcard circa 1913–1920. Collection of Hancock
Shaker Village.*

*Mary Dahm and her natural sister Grace (1874–1958) were born in
Kinderhook, N.Y., and came to the Shakers in 1887. According to
Magda Gabor-Hotchkiss, Mary was trained as a registered nurse, a
useful occupation in a village with an aging population, and also served
as trustee, gardener, basket maker, and poultry-raiser. After Watervliet
closed in 1938, they moved to Mount Lebanon, and when that community also closed in 1947, they went to the Hancock Church Family.*

Part 2

Work and Worship

6

The World's Views of Shaker
Sisters, 1782–1865

*More the appearance of celestial beings than
earthly inhabitants . . .*

SHAKERS DEPENDED ON THE OUTSIDE WORLD FOR NEW
members, so they welcomed visitors, despite the inconveniences of
hosting the world's people. During the tourist season, from July into October, a visit to the Shakers made a nice excursion from Lebanon Springs. In
August 1836, Eldress Asenath Clark noted, "A great crowd of spectators attended the public meeting to day—perhaps as many as ever came at any one
time."[1] Sometimes rumors boosted attendance. In 1837, a Ministry sister
wrote, "In consequence of a flying report that Mother Ann was to appear
in our Meetinghouse to day and introduce matrimony into the Society, the
inhabitants from many miles round flocked to the Meeting to be spectators
of such an extraordinary event. Their carriages lined our street to a considerable extent north & south, on each side, and great was the throng of
wonder-mongers to witness the wonderful scene." Believers met as usual.
The scribe concluded, "The multitude who came to feast their eyes on some
new wonder, returned home to sup on disappointed curiosity."[2] Both the
rumor and the world's response to it showed just how much celibacy cap-
tivated public attention.

Public worship could be a trial—so much so that some Believers resisted
going. In August 1833, Betsy Bates wrote that the Ministry "want the
Church should go at this season of the year when there is so many of the
world attends to the public meeting."[3] In May 1835, Semantha Fairbanks

reported, "We have a short meeting this forenoon and are informed that we are to attend meeting to the meeting house in general thro' the summer, and not to be heard complaining and telling what a cross it is but to go cheerfully and labor for a gift of God."[4] The New Lebanon Church Family preferred to worship without spectators, and the Elders' admonition reflected the tribulations of summer, when the world's people overran the meetinghouse, flaunting their wealth and showing disrespect for Believers.[5] A few visitors recognized the problem. One wrote, "The condescensions of fashionable people who visit Mount Lebanon, parading their silks and jewels before its simple folk and exhibiting such well bred amusement at their ways and appearance as might be in place in visiting a poor-house or a menagerie, have made entirely excusable the reluctance of many of the Shakers to be pitied and patronized."[6] Because as many as six hundred spectators attended New Lebanon Shaker Sabbath, thoughtless disruption by even a small number could ruin the experience for the rest.[7] Worse yet, some of those visitors later ridiculed Shakers in published accounts.

One of the best ways to visit a place in bygone times is to read a visitor account. Many travelers kept journals with vivid descriptions that are useful in studying groups such as the Shakers. These accounts, however, come with a caveat: visitors were neither authorities on the Shakers nor impartial observers. Most authors had preconceptions that biased their views. Many derided evangelical religion in general, and Shaker worship in particular. Most who wrote about Believers were men, and they often ignored Shaker women and children. Visitors assumed that Believers followed traditional gender roles, and in some respects, that was true. Sisters cooked, sewed, kept house, manufactured textiles, and did laundry, while Shaker men farmed or worked in trades. But Shaker women also wielded power in ways that outsiders did not see until late in the nineteenth century.

The material benefits of Shaker life were visible to visitors from the road through the village. Believers' communities were more attractive and more prosperous than those of their neighbors. Daniel Moseley recalled of his first visits to the Shakers' Watervliet farm in the 1780s, "I was brought up in New-England, among good farmers; but such neatness and good economy as was here displayed in the wilderness I never saw before."[8] As a Believer, he was naturally biased, but outsiders corroborated his opinion. The New Lebanon Shaker village was "a very paradise."[9] In 1819, Benjamin Silliman wrote, "The utmost neatness is conspicuous in their fields, gardens, court yards, out houses, and in the very road; not a weed, not a spot of filth, or any nuisance is suffered to exist." Silliman had not seen such neatness anywhere else in the United States.[10] What most visitors did not realize was that Shaker order was based on the teachings of Ann Lee, who insisted on thrift and cleanliness.[11]

A few outsiders recognized that Shaker sisters kept the village neat and clean. A Polish visitor, Julian Niemcewicz, spoke with an apostate who worked at a New Lebanon inn. She told him, "The women work no less than the men." They did "ceaseless laundry" because, "Cleanliness is one of the tenets of this society." When the sisters went to Sabbath services, Niemcewicz added, "One cannot look enough at the fineness and whiteness of their linen." Nonetheless, he thought their religion absurd.[12] Visitors often praised Shakers' temporal success and then disparaged their religious beliefs without understanding the link between the two.

On weekdays, visitors could easily relate to what they saw, even feel comfortable with the familiarity of a Shaker village. At work, sisters resembled either businesswomen, running the Trustees' Office store and making goods for sale, or farmwives engaged in the usual domestic responsibilities of cooking, cleaning, laundering, dairying, and sewing. Visitors could see the benefits of sisters' work—the spotless rooms, clean dooryards, brilliantly white linen—and could also sample the products of the sisters' labor, taking dinner or tea, tasting their excellent meals, and purchasing food, seeds, cloth, or fancy goods.[13]

Those who visited only on Sunday, however, had a different view of Shaker society. The Shakers did not sell goods, give tours, or wait on visitors on the Sabbath, a day of rest, but they did welcome outsiders to their morning services in the meetinghouse. Sunday visitors, with time or inclination to make just one visit, saw Believers only at worship.

Anne Royall was one of the few who visited on both a weekday and the Sabbath. She was also one of the few worldly visitors who complimented the sisters and credited the Shakers' social equality as well as their temporal success. Shaker sisters particularly impressed her. She arrived on a Saturday, on foot and exhausted. The sisters, however, rushed to her aid, and invited her in for refreshments. Royall recalled one sister's kindness.

> She immediately asked me to walk into a cool parlor, addressing me in the sweetest and softest accents. Seeing I was fatigued, after communicating to her my motives in visiting their village, she told me to wait till she prepared a cup of coffee and refreshments, and she would send a message to the elders in the mean time, and apprise them of my visit. In a very short time, every delicacy was spread before me, and sweeter

butter, I never tasted; every thing, however, corresponded; and the kindness, sweetness of manner with which I was pressed to eat and drink,
was altogether fascinating.

Such charity was good business because visitors were potential proselytes—
and Shaker women could be delightfully hospitable. After refreshments,
the sisters took Royall to meet the Elders and "Miss Betsey," an Eldress she
admired.

The female elder was a native of Massachusetts, and of course the be-
nevolence of her state shone in her countenance. She was a female of
good education; unaffected in her manners and conversation, affability
and sweetness itself. She was a tall and elegant figure, and very handsomely featured; after shaking hands with all of them, she invited me
with a smile, to be seated until I recovered a little, and she would walk
with me over the village.

During the tour, Royall made a point of learning about the status of
women in Shaker society. "The drudgery of the house is consigned to a
certain number of females," she wrote, "who perform their work cheerfully, and are held in no subordination whatever." Most visitors overlooked
Shaker women's equality to men, and criticized the policy of celibacy without noting the system's benefits.

Like other weekday visitors, Royall spent time in the village store. "The
females make fancy goods in a superior style of taste and elegance," she
wrote. She thought they sold their manufactures below cost, but she probably did not factor in the Shakers' lack of wages. "Every stranger who visits
them, generally buys something as a remuneration for the trouble they give,"
she noted. The sisters treated her to tea before she departed.

Royall returned for Shaker Sabbath. Finding the services solemn and
interesting, she took the trouble to learn the significance of their hand movements. "They do not let their arms hang by their side," she wrote, "that
part, from the elbow down, is held at a right angle with the upper part, and
during the exercise of dancing, they are continually moving their hands (or
shaking them rather) up and down, which means shaking off the sins of the
world." Royall also appreciated the sisters' appearance. "The females have
more the appearance of celestial beings than earthly inhabitants, being the
very picture of grace and modesty," she wrote.[14]

Other outsiders enjoyed tours of the New Lebanon Shaker village. In
August 1818, for instance, Eliza Williams Bridgham noted that "not a speck

of dirt [was] to be seen in their dominions, even the roads were exactly so." She admired the stone walkways, probably recognizing that sidewalks cut down on mud tracked indoors. She praised sisters' work at their assigned tasks, weaving and making cheese and butter. Other sisters sewed or did housework so that no one was burdened with drudgery. Shaker sisters' housekeeping was exemplary. "We viewed one establishment throughout, & you can form no idea of the neatness of every thing; even their floors have a kind of polish on them, exactly like varnish." She also admired the conveniences and "complete order" in their kitchen.[15]

When Bridgham attended their Sabbath services the following day, her tone changed. She began gently enough with the sisters' entrance.

> The women, dressed in long white robes, square book muslin hand-kerchiefs folded square, & pinned exactly alike—their hair combed straight back, with white muslin caps—their bonnets the same color as the men's hats; their shoes black cloth—with heels, about two inches high!! as they entered, two & two, they hung up their handkerchiefs, also white, with a dark-blue edge, sat down, & clasped their hands, exactly similar.

Demonstrating their beliefs about union and order, Shakers carefully staged their public Sabbath performance. But because Bridgham knew nothing of Shaker history or belief, she did not know what to expect and did not understand the significance of such aspects as the sisters' uniform dress and their "exactly similar" hand positions. She thought an Elder who preached did so "handsomely." Of "their exercises, though solemn," she said, however, "I could not realize were devoted to God & when the dances began, it actually appeared more like a Theatre than the house of the Lord!" She had heard that Shaker worship continued as long as "the Spirit moves," but she was startled at what followed the preaching.

> Then the men & women all sang a long hymn, there seemed no tune, but a kind of Methodistical cant. They really sang as it were from the bottom of their souls & made such a screaming, that few of us were fortunate enough to escape without the headache; then commenced dancing, in a kind of figure. All stood in rows on the floor, & they be-gan dancing, forward and back, then forward & turning, then a kind of shuffle balance, then singing & dancing again.[16]

Julia Mayo Cabell visited the Shakers on both Saturday and Sunday. She enjoyed the workday at New Lebanon. After carefully examining the sisters, she described their work clothing in detail: white muslin kerchiefs and caps, dark-colored gowns, and black stuff shoes with old-fashioned high heels. She also noted that they "turned their hair back from the forehead and tucked it up behind." The sisters welcomed her and showed her around the village.

> We were received with much hospitality, and treated with delicious cider, bread and butter, cheese and milk. They showed us their whole establishment, the dairy, the cheese-room, the dining-room, kitchen and chambers, and we were surprised at the numerous ingenious contrivances they had for saving labor, and rendering themselves comfortable.
>
> In their depository, or store, they had for sale boxes, brooms, sieves, brushes, silver pens, pincushions and various other articles, but no baskets, much to our disappointment, for we wished to have purchased some; they told us they had been in such demand, that from a large supply, not one was left! Their work, of every description, was uncommonly neat and substantial, so we consoled ourselves with mats and wooden spoons. In consequence of a shower, we were detained among these singular beings for several hours; at length we got off, probably as much to their satisfaction as our own.

Cabell appreciated the sisters' hospitality and admired their cooking, housekeeping, and sale goods. She envied their labor-saving devices. Her approval, however, ended on Sunday, when she and several carriages full of friends returned for Shaker Sabbath. "The service lasted upwards of two hours, and was well worth a journey to witness," Cabell wrote. To that point, she was pleased with everything she had seen outside and inside the meetinghouse. "But what fantastic ceremonies did we witness within!" she added, "None that inspired either devotion or respect."

She noted that between the exercises, "an old man advanced towards us, and requested that there might be neither whispering nor laughing among the strangers, at the manner in which they were about to worship God." And she described the dance in detail.

> [The worshipers] sung, with loud and harsh voices, a monotonous tune, and danced with all their might for at least fifteen minutes; then, with the skill of experienced soldiers, they arranged themselves four abreast, (males and females always in distinct columns,) and marched round and round, till their bones must certainly have ached. They held their arms up from the elbow, and let their hands droop from the wrist,

looking for all the world like a flock of penguins;—sometimes they prayed, sometimes they loudly clapped their hands and sung—yet, did they make less noise than another set, who stood with joined hands, as if going to dance a reel in the centre of the church, and almost stunned us with their vociferations. We rejoiced when the commotion was over and the moment of departure arrived, and did not fail to hasten ours.

Cabell compared Shakers to flightless birds and complained about the music. She did not understand the significance of Shaker dance or their arrangement of the men in a corps opposite the women, the worshipers' hand motions, or their separation in the meetinghouse. Despite the hours Cabell spent among the Shakers, she had learned little about the society. She neither saw nor appreciated the sisters' authority. She concluded, "It was painful to behold our fellow creatures under the influence of such absurd fanaticism!"[17]

Such criticism was not unusual. A survey of visitor accounts from 1782 to 1865 shows that most authors visited Shaker villages only on the Sabbath and primarily as tourists seeking novel entertainment. Most of them did not speak to a Believer or read a Shaker publication, so they gleaned no information beyond their superficial impressions. And some were rude enough to laugh or talk during the services.

Visitors may have had an additional reason for disliking Shaker worship, perhaps allowing offense to bias their accounts. One preaching Elder addressed his worldly audience thus: "All other Churches of the world are totally corrupt, and as ignorant of the will of God as the brute beasts. Should I explain the scriptures from Genesis to Revelations, as to mystical implications of the prophecies, the labor would be lost, for want of capacity in the world to understand spiritual things, thro' their sins, lusts, and false learning."[18]

Most visitor accounts were written by men, whose commentaries from 1780 to 1890 outnumber women's by about four to one, reflecting the gendered opportunities of the nineteenth century. Among the male authors were artists, agricultural reformers, authors of popular fiction, Congregational ministers, lawyers, merchants, politicians, college professors, physicians, a sailor-poet, slave-owning Southern aristocrats, New York editors and other journalists, a variety of utopians, and several neighbors of the Shakers. Most identifiable visitors were members of the educated elite.

The women who wrote visitor accounts were also a diverse group: a divorced actress, mill operatives, English authors, a Southerner, a housewife, a marriageable Yankee girl, and widows and spinsters who supported themselves through writing. Spas such as Lebanon Springs served as a "marriage market," and some summer visitors angled for husbands there.[19] Most male visitors had minds closed to the possible benefits of celibacy, but female visitors' comments show a rough correlation between marital status and favorable opinion. Most of the unmarried women, such as Anne Royall, found Shaker sisters admirable.

Married women visitors, in contrast, disparaged Shaker sisters. Margaret Hall wrote, "The women are the ugliest set of females I ever saw [and] . . . their particularly unbecoming dress . . . make[s] them look as ugly as art can possibly devise."[20] Worldly women did not share the values that the Shaker sisters' modest dress suggested by concealing, rather than revealing, their figures. Nor did visitors understand that sisters' uniform dress exemplified Shaker values such as celibacy, humility, and union. Among the Shakers, no one's clothing was better than that of her peers—a concept incomprehensible to married elite women who flaunted their possessions.

Most visitors were either members of the leisure class who could afford to vacation in the Berkshires or journalists who wrote for that audience. Genteel women, by the mid-nineteenth century, were expected to be pious, passive, and domestic, according to the cult of true womanhood. To them, Shaker Sabbath was shocking. Sisters' performances in public worship were anything but passive.[21] The most disrespectful visitor accounts, however, show that sisters were leaders in worship from Shakerism's earliest days.

In the 1780s, William Plumer wrote about Shakers' "wild and extravagant" Sabbath: "Near the centre of the room stood two young women, one of them very handsome, who whirled round and round for the space of fifteen minutes, nearly as fast as the rim of a spinning-wheel in quick motion." After a break, he wrote, "the young lady who was the principal whirler walked into the middle of the room and began to dance. All the men and women soon joined her, —dancing, singing, whirling, shouting, clapping their hands, shaking and trembling." When the young sister began to shake again, she told Plumer that her shaking was not voluntary; she was acted upon by "a supernatural impulse." His response was to test her. When she was whirling, he grabbed her and held her immobile, despite her protests. Plumer, a young man of the worldly elite, felt entitled to experiment with the young sister. His disrespect was obvious. His description, however, showed that Shaker women led some parts of worship.[22]

Shaker women's equality, not to mention their leadership, was a threat to the Christian social order, which was based on the doctrine of subordination of women from St. Paul. Thus, many visitors, who might have made cutting remarks about both men and women, derided the sisters while ignoring the brethren on the other side of the meetinghouse. In August 1790, for instance, Elkanah Watson wrote, "Among the women were some tall oaks, some shriveled dwarfs, and some young saplings. Their white capped heads of various heights, bobbing up and down in the mazes of the dance, had a queer and ridiculous appearance."[23]

Occasionally an early tourist, such as François-Alexandre-Frédéric, duc de la Rochefoucauld-Liancourt, who visited New Lebanon Shaker worship in the late 1790s, recorded impressions of Shaker sisters without harsh judgment. Liancourt wrote, "The women wore a long white gown, a blue petticoat, an apron of the same cloth of which the men's pantaloons were made, a large, square, well plaited handkerchief, and a plain cap, tied under the chin." Each carried a blue and white handkerchief. Their singing voices were "tolerably melodious." After several dances, executed "with a precision and exactness, which would do honour to the best disciplined regiment," he wrote, "two women appear, each furnished with a broom, and sweep first the place occupied by the men, who draw up in close order, to make room for the sweepers, and then that occupied by the women."[24] He appreciated their performance but did not realize the significance of the sisters' and brethren's positions in worship, which exemplified their equality, or their choreographed movements, which showed their union.

Julian Niemcewicz, who visited a Shaker community in 1798, also missed the significance of what he described. He noted that six men and six women formed a choir to lead the singing and that the best singer set the pitch.[25] But he understood neither the Shakers' reason for standardizing the performance nor their visible efforts to balance gender roles. Furthermore, Shaker Sabbath was shaped during this period by Lucy Wright, whose leadership went unrecognized by most visitors.[26]

Other visitor reports reveal that, unlike women in most Christian churches, Shaker sisters felt free to address the congregation if the spirit moved them. At a Watervliet service in July 1838, for instance, when the congregation sang, "Come, Holy Angels, quickly come, / And bring your purifying fire; / Consume our lusts, in every home, / And root out every foul desire," a few spectators gave each other significant looks. After the song, a brother addressed the visitors. He said that many outsiders alleged that Shakers did not live lives of purity, but that was untrue. He said that they avoided temptation to stay pure. When he finished, an older sister spoke, adding her rebuke to the visitors for their skepticism. She said she had been forty years a Shaker but had never felt inspired to speak in public before. "Now, however, she felt it her duty to unloose her tongue, and declare that [the visitors'] aspersions upon their purity were altogether unwarranted." The other sisters responded with loud "acclamations and clapping."[27]

The stage star Fanny Kemble. a visitor in 1853, admired Believers' business acumen and their prosperity. "They are perfectly moral and exemplary in their lives and conduct, wonderfully industrious, miraculously clean and neat, and incredibly shrewd, thrifty and money-making," she wrote. But her admiration ended there. She went on to say:

> Their dress is hideous, and their worship . . . consists of a fearful species of dancing, in which the whole number of them engage, going round and round their vast hall or temple of prayer, shaking their hands like the paws of a dog sitting up to beg, and singing a deplorable psalm-tune in brisk jig time. The women without a single hair escaping beneath their hideous caps, mounted upon very high-heeled shoes, and every one of them with a white handkerchief folded napkin-fashion and hanging over her arm. In summer they all dress in white, and what with their pale, immovable countenances, their ghost-like figures, and ghastly, mad spiritual dance, they looked like the nuns in "Robert the Devil," condemned, for their sins in the flesh, to post-mortem decency and asceticism, to look ugly, and to dance like ill-taught bears. The whole exhibition was at once so frightful and so ludicrous, that I very nearly went off into hysterics.[28]

Despite her familiarity with public performance, Kemble seems to have deliberately ignored the careful staging of Shaker Sabbath and the Shakers' well-rehearsed choreography in what seems to have been an effort calculated to appeal to skeptical upper-class readers—those who could afford to buy her books or pay to attend her performances.

Charles Daubeny, in contrast to Kemble, had no need to bolster his own position by criticizing women. His description of New Lebanon sisters in worship on September 10, 1837, is a good baseline for comparison with later changes.

> The women were dressed in one uniform costume, consisting of a loose flowing bedgown, (as we should call it) concealing the figure and extending down to the feet; and of a white linen shawl covering the neck and bosom. Each female held in her hand a large white napkin, which

was in frequent requisition during the course of the subsequent exercises. On entering the room they took off and deposited on a peg a
plain straw bonnet, and then displayed upon their head a very neat and
brilliantly-white muslin cap, on which it would appear that all their arts
of embellishment had been concentrated. Their shoes had immoderately
high heels, like those used by our grandmothers. As to person, they were
in general thin, and in every instance that I remarked, excepting in one,
(who was probably a new convert,) their faces were pale and devoid of
colour, so that sitting as they did with their arms crossed before them,
on their respective benches, almost motionless, during the half-hour
preceding the commencement of the ceremonies, they looked like so
many statues.

The sisters looked ghostly. "As each group, of the women especially, approached me, it looked like a succession of as many spectres, so cadaverous
and unearthly was their general aspect," Daubeny wrote. Other visitors had
made similar comments since 1794.[29] Some thought the sisters were pale
because of celibates' lack of love; passion might have put a bloom in their
cheeks. But Daubeny speculated further.

> I am aware that rumors exist respecting the women, to which the pale-
> ness and unhealthiness of their complexions may seem to lend some
> countenance, but I believe there is nothing to corroborate any such
> suspicions, and it may be suggested, that any practices, which should
> be sufficiently prevalent amongst them, to prevent the natural conse-
> quences of illicit connexions from taking place, could hardly escape
> detection for any long period, and would thus, before this time, have
> brought about the downfall of the institution.

Evidently Daubeny had heard but rejected rumors that Shaker sisters were
sexually active and used abortifacients that made them look ill. He added,
"There is, indeed, some truth in the remark that the women themselves are
antidotes to the tender passion, but the sallow and withered appearance
they present seems to have arisen from their continuing as members of the
society; for certainly some of the fresh converts look more like beings of
flesh and blood."[30]

Daubeny observed that the women were full participants in spiritual
labor and that some performed solo as the spirit moved them. At a time
when women of the world's people did not speak in public, their actions

were startling.[31] One sister knelt, Daubeny wrote, and "went on without intermission bowing her head and body nearly to the ground, like a Chinese mandarin." Another sister turned her attention to the visitors.

> Towards the close of the service, when all present had become excited to their highest pitch, one or two of them began to address their exhortations more directly to the strangers; and a woman in particular moving several times to and fro, among the ladies' benches, with an air and manner like that of another Pythoness, went on exclaiming:—"The end of the world is at hand—the word of God is to be preached to kindred tongues and peoples—yea, to kindred peoples and tongues—by the despised society of Shakers—by the poor despised Shakers."[32]

The sister's description of Shakers as "despised" repeats a dichotomy familiar to Believers: the righteous Shakers versus the world's people. Moreover, Shaker sisters showed initiative by exhorting their visitors.

Daubeny recorded another sister's assertiveness in another anecdote. A young Georgia man among the spectators "fixed his eyes pretty intently" on a beautiful young Shaker sister. An Elder announced that a sister was upset, and that the person bothering her ought to leave. The visitor made no move to go. Finally, "a sort of scene ensued." The Shaker sister rushed up to her tormenter and exclaimed, "Eschew devil! Eschew devil!" Only then did the young man depart.[33] The episode resembled Plumer's experience half a century earlier. Some worldly men thought they could distract sisters—but the sisters proved them wrong. A sister could expel a visitor from the meetinghouse—evidence of Shaker women's authority. That authority was not limited to New Lebanon. At Shirley in 1831, a sister reprimanded visitors who laughed at Shaker worship. A bystander described her "bold and taunting language, and acrimonious deportment," but her rebuke quelled the disturbance.[34]

Sisters had new outlets for their spiritual expression during the Era of Manifestations, which began at Watervliet in 1837 with an outburst of religious enthusiasm. Over the next year, inspiration spread through the society, reaching New Lebanon in April 1838. The Era of Manifestations brought more spontaneous expressions of the spirit, including songs, dances, marches, bowing, jerking, turning, and speaking in tongues.[35]

Elite Protestants, such as Fanny Appleton Longfellow, found Shaker sisters' physical operations disturbing rather than inspirational. Longfellow described the sisters at worship in 1839.

Very gradually Shakeress after Shakeress opened noiselessly their side door, glided on tiptoe noiselessly, across the beautiful floor, to their respective pegs, hung thereon their white shawls, fichus, and straw bonnets (which resembled *en masse* huge hornets' nests), then sat down, as joined dolls do, upon the wall benches, handkerchief straight across lap and hands folded over, turning not an eyelash to the right or left, like so many draped sphinxes or corpses set on end. The little girls copying so well the same rigid repose—so unlike the fidgetiness of youth—is a horrible sight, as if they were under a spell.

Longfellow's distaste increased as the Shakers went through their worship exercises.

But no witch's Sabbath, no bacchanal procession could be more unearthly, revolting, oppressive, and bewildering. The machinery of their stereotyped steps, plunging on in this way so long without rest, the constrained attitude forward, the spasmodic jumps and twists of the neck, and the ghastly visages of the women in their corpse-like caps, the waving of so many shrill voices, and the rigid expression of their faces combined to form a spectacle as piteous as disgusting, fit only for the dancing hall of the lower regions or the creation of a nightmare.

She described the actions of one woman "whose horrible contortions will haunt me forever."

She wrenched her head nearly over her shoulder on one side and the other, and then jerked it nearly to her knee with a regularity of manner for such an immense time that I thought I should have rushed out for relief, as my eye saw always this dreadful figure. I supposed at first it was St. Vitus dance, or a fit, but she stopped at the end and varied it by spinning like a dervish, twisting her arms round her head like snakes. Shrouded in such a dress, and carried to such a pitch, it was the most frightful human gesticulation ever perpetrated. Doubtless they regard her as a saint, for I saw a faint imitation of it in others.[36]

Longfellow admired only one Shaker sister, a "tall girl with a fine profile, who seemed to curl her lip in some scorn at this insane mummery and waved her hands very languidly."[37] Like many visitors, Longfellow knew so little about the Shakers that she dwelled on surface appearances. She did not understand the symbolism of their choreography, the benefits of physical movement, or the Shakers' desire to move as one in the dance. She could not comprehend spiritual enthusiasm; nor did she appreciate a mode of worship that allowed women to act spontaneously as the spirit moved them.

Other visitors described sisters' increased enthusiasm in the late 1830s. At Watervliet Shaker worship during the Era of Manifestations, James Silk Buckingham wrote, "The females became perfectly ungovernable."[38] One visitor saw several sisters who "appeared to be thrown into violent hystericks," and one girl restrained by older women. At a service another visitor attended, three sisters had to escort an incoherent fourth woman out of the meetinghouse.[39] Whether she was deranged or inspired, her peers deemed her behavior inappropriate for public worship. In 1842, the Shakers closed their worship to the public.[40] When they reopened Sabbath services several years later, Shaker gifts had moderated, though some sisters remained inspired.

Visitors continued, however, to write disrespectful accounts of what they observed. One from the 1840s described the sisters as "a swarm of saints who had just alighted for a little rest." They clapped their hands and stamped their feet "in strange unison with the music," continuing for about an hour "until the perspiration streamed from their faces and the women looked quite rosy and intelligent." Meanwhile, a brother spun like a top. Then,

> not wishing to see the arduous enterprises achieved exclusively by the other sex, a short, fat woman, about fifty years of age, stepped forth and followed suit. She held out about ten minutes and then began to totter and stagger, her head rolled from side to side, her face became distorted, her muscles twitched, and she dropped into the hands of her sisters, thoroughly intoxicated and apparently unconscious. A few moments however sufficed to revive her sufficiently to enable her to stand; she resumed her place with the singers.[41]

Even as the sight of Shakers' enthusiastic worship repelled the world's people, it also attracted them, and when Believers did not turn, visitors were disappointed and reported that spontaneous spiritual gifts had ended.[42] After 1860, public worship was relatively sedate, and the world's criticism abated with Shakers' public inspiration.[43] Today, Shakers' public worship combines prepared messages, scripture reading, singing, testimony, and a profound spirituality that can bring tears to a visitor's eyes.

Several conclusions can be drawn from visitors' critiques of Shaker sisters. Outsiders admired sisters at their temporal labor, where they resembled hardworking farmwives and businesswomen among the world's people.

Celibate sisters' rejection of marriage, sexuality, and childbearing (which also meant rejection of men's authority over women), however, was the antithesis of what the world's people held dear. Equality of the sexes was based on celibacy, but most visitors did not understand that. Moreover, sisters' physical enthusiasm in worship aroused newcomers' antipathy. The sisters' rejection of marital subordination, their equality with men, their assertiveness, and their spiritual gifts violated Pauline standards that most Christian denominations followed. Visitors expected men to rule women, and among the Shakers, they did not.

The radical nature of Shakerism began with celibacy, which established women's equality, and extended to women's leadership, whether temporal or spiritual. Thus Shaker celibacy threatened the status quo. Because the elite particularly profited from the status quo, they defended their own position by attacking the Shaker alternative. Most visitors, however, did not recognize Believers' gender equality, even when they shared anecdotes that showed sisters' authority.

7

Work, Reciprocity, Equality, and Union

In perfect union . . .

S CHOLARS' UNDERSTANDING OF MEN AND WOMEN LIVING
as Shakers includes the "fact" that the sexes were separated. They draw
that conclusion from two sources: the society's Millennial Laws and visitors'
reports. The Millennial Laws were designed to maintain physical distance
between men and women. Brothers and sisters were not supposed to be
alone together, work together without the Elders' permission, or visit each
other's rooms and shops unnecessarily.[1] In addition, many visitor accounts
mention Shaker separation of the sexes. Visitors, however, often overstated
the facts. In 1792, for instance, an outsider wrote, "They do not speak nor
look at each other . . . they neither talk, walk, nor sleep together."[2] She was
correct only in the last respect.

As a practical matter, celibacy required separation but not to the extent
that it impaired the society's functioning. D'Ann Campbell points out that
no one has examined the extent to which the sexes were separated.[3] Most
scholars focus on separation, without noticing that brothers and sisters
often worked in each other's company. In fact, Shakers could not achieve
their goal of union without working together.

A few outsiders realized that the sexes were not entirely separated. An
early nineteenth-century visitor noted that their mixing was "much less restricted than is generally supposed."[4] At Watervliet, a visitor wrote in 1824,
"The women sleep on the one side of the house and the men at the other but
they have continual opportunities of talking to one another, meeting very

often with each other."[5] The Millennial Laws allowed latitude within the bounds of propriety. With the Elders' permission, men and women could work together or visit each other's shops. Isaac Newton Youngs, for instance, recorded many occasions when he instructed tailoresses or spoke with Eldresses.[6] Shaker men and women attended union meetings, which brought them together several times a week to socialize.[7] Male and female singers met in the evenings to practice or teach new songs, as when, according to two journal reports, Isaac Newton Youngs, Luther Copley, Henry De-Witt, Sarah Bates, Joanna Kitchel, Rachel Sampson, and Mary Ann Mantle went to the North house to sing.[8]

Brethren and sisters had a joint interest in their society, as farmers and farmwives had a joint interest in their farms. In both cases, a good working partnership, including a sense of reciprocity or mutual support, contributed to their success. Sisters kept brethren fed and clothed; in return, brothers tried to lighten the sisters' workload. That reciprocity contributed to Shaker union.

Isaac Newton Youngs, the tailor who was also the New Lebanon Shakers' historian, said that union between the sexes existed only "in embryo" before 1792 but that Joseph Meacham and Lucy Wright promoted it.[9] Union depended on equality of the sexes, though Shaker men were not necessarily fully invested in women's equality. Many brothers grew up among the world's people, where men reaped the benefits of patriarchy, and when some brothers joined the Shakers, they did not leave behind the idea of male dominance. Meacham and Wright's partnership, however, was a model for all Believers. In 1796, Meacham praised Wright as his equal, acknowledging that her responsibilities were not limited to women's traditional work but extended to leading their religious society of several thousand members.[10] Their version of equality of the sexes meant that sisters were authorities "in their lot," just as brethren were authorities in theirs. Where their responsibilities overlapped, they worked together to achieve the desired result.

Believers sought to perfect their utopian society by institutionalizing equality of the sexes, acting in the common interest and negotiating and compromising from positions of relative equality. Wright's words suggest that for some, it must have been difficult. She preached, "There is a daily duty to do; that is, for the Brethren to be kind to the Brethren, Sisters kind to the Sisters, and Brethren and Sisters kind to each other."[11]

Communal life, however, generated friction between men and women. At the New Lebanon North Family, for instance, issues involving the installation of a new water system provoked a sister, Cecilia DeVere, to deride brethren in verse. Her poem "Our Water Works" is criticism disguised as humor. As light entertainment, her poem did not threaten Shaker union. Women have long incorporated such strategies of coding information to covertly express ideas that men might not appreciate, sometimes exclaiming simply, "Men!" or "Boys will be boys." Devere used trivialization.[12]

Her poem begins by playing to a stereotype of women, who sat "demurely mute" while brethren discussed renovations. Devere then played against a stereotype of men in an effort to defuse her covert message: the brothers installing the system did not know what they were doing. "It seemed to uninstructed minds," she wrote, "that brethren must be playing / With instruments of various kinds, but lo! they were surveying." Probably it was the dirt that set DeVere off. The brethren tore up the village digging trenches that were still open months later. Brothers came late to meals and tracked mud into the dwelling. When the brethren installed the indoor plumbing, they descended through a flue and emerged "dressed in soot."[13] The dirt and disruption annoyed the sisters who prepared the food, cleaned the floors, and did the laundry. The sisters' housekeeping was otherwise exemplary. Sisters kept their dwellings spotless because Ann Lee believed that good spirits would not dwell where there was dirt.[14] Visitors to Shaker villages invariably complimented their cleanliness, neatness, and shining floors.[15] The waterworks renovation, however, was a mess from spring into fall. The sisters coped with the dirt, knowing that the new water system would be a boon when it was finished.

Most of the time, brothers were helpful to sisters. As part of their cultural mandate to lighten sisters' workload, brethren did favors for the women who lived across the hall. Sisters' work—cooking, dairying, and laundry, assigned in rotation—involved brethren in many ways.[16] Food was a case in point. In a society where food was the only acceptable sensual pleasure, meals were important to morale. A typical breakfast at the New Lebanon Church Family included rye-and-Indian bread, wheat bread, tea, milk, potatoes, meat, butter, applesauce, apple pie, pickles, salt, and water.[17] A visitor described a meal of ham, potatoes, squash, kidney beans, preserved fruit, beets, white and brown wheat bread, Indian pudding, pie, and "by far the finest butter" he had ever tasted.[18] After a special treat of maple syrup, a brother offered this accolade: "We thank the Sisters for their care / Who feast us on such luscious fare / Now we'll be thankful every one / For the sweets from Lebanon."[19] Shaker products, especially cheese, were known for their high quality, and Believers' perfectionism extended to food.[20] Isaac Newton Youngs appreciated the dairy sisters' herb cheese so much that he extolled it in verse: "Look if you please / On yonder cheese / Flowers so fine I see / Leaves of sage / Set by a gauge / For superfluity. / I'm sure such cheese makers / Cannot be Shakers / Who for their fancies please / Spend all their time / While in their prime / To finify cheese."[21] Youngs, like other brethren, appreciated good food, and the kitchen sisters tried to feed the brethren well. Shaker cooks were so competitive about their cooking that Mother Lucy Wright suggested in 1816 that the sisters "leave off striving to excel each other in making good victuals."[22] Nonetheless, a "winter Shaker" at Watervliet observed, "One brother sometimes eulogized a sister whom he thought to be the best cook, and who could make the best 'Johnny cake.'"[23]

Kitchen sisters processed tons of food, much of it raised by the brethren. After brothers butchered livestock, sisters tried fat into lard and chopped hundreds of pounds of meat for sausage.[24] Men, women, and children picked apples together every fall in a "general turnout" at New Lebanon. In 1839, Benjamin Gates shook apple and pear trees for the sisters who were gathering fruit for drying.[25] Each apple had to be peeled, cored, and sliced before it went into the kiln to dry.[26] Sometimes brethren helped the kitchen sisters in the evening, cutting apples or pumpkins for drying, or picking over beans.[27]

Maple products sweetened Shaker food. Brethren did the heavy labor of gathering sap. Some years, they had so much sap that they ran out of containers. A deaconess wrote in 1857, "Every sugar tree of the Shaker valley is pouring forth praise in liquid streams to the old tin pans, iron bound buckets . . . whey tubs, cider barrels, molasses hogsheads, & so on." Every container was "filled to over flowing save the Brethren! they come home empty!"[28] Sisters fed brethren so they could work; brethren tapped trees and hauled sap—eleven thousand gallons of it in March and April of that year.[29] At New Lebanon, the sisters usually boiled the sap into syrup, but in 1854, the brethren offered to boil it at the extract building, to save the sisters time and labor. Deaconess Betsy Crosman responded gratefully, "We all feel great union" with the offer.[30]

Brethren helped kitchen sisters generally much more than men helped women among the world's people, where many farmwives were overworked. In 1845, for instance, a farmwife complained in *Massachusetts Ploughman* that farmers viewed their wives only as domestic beasts of burden, much the same way they viewed their horses or oxen.[31] A Shaker sister did not share that fate because in a Shaker village some of the work traditionally done by farmwives was done by men, for women's benefit.

At New Lebanon, Joel Turner did the baking and other cooking chores from 1787 to 1790, as did Samuel Bennet and Daniel Wood. After 1790, however, sisters did all of the Church Family's cooking, and brethren found other ways to ease the cooks' workload.[32] Brothers made the cooking fires and did the heavy labor of butchering animals and cutting meat.[33] The brethren also piped water to the dwelling, dairy, and laundry, and installed boilers, stoves, drying racks, and other conveniences. A visitor wrote in 1818 that the kitchen had "two large marble sinks, & ovens, & boilers, &c. innumerable."[34] New Lebanon sisters had conveniences that most farm-wives lacked, including a pump that brought water indoors. Many worldly farms lacked indoor plumbing well into the twentieth century. Built-in coun-ters, a big stove, drying racks—all those things were installed by brethren for sisters' convenience. Even the windows in Shaker kitchens eased sisters' work. In 1835, an English visitor, Andrew Bell, noted of the kitchen, "None in London could exceed theirs in neatness of equipment."[35] Another visitor, Hester Pool, concluded in 1888: "The Brethren have devised unheard-of comforts for the indoor workers, and the visitor leaves with the feeling of pity for the housewife who does her cooking in the ordinary way. Here every step tells, every movement counts."[36] Lucy Ann Hammond, a visit-ing Harvard Shaker sister accustomed to well-appointed kitchens, was im-pressed by New Lebanon's. "They had the most convenient kitchen I was ever in," she wrote.[37] The Shaker kitchen was a visible result of reciprocity.

Brethren supported the sisters' butter and cheese production by building a dairy near the barns, supplying running water, milking cows in winter, and providing sieves, scoops, measures, oval boxes, buckets, barrels, and vermin-proof containers. Many of those jobs brought men into the kitchen and dairy. Thus, even in workplaces that were gendered female, men were present. Shaker meals depended on the joint efforts of men and women—farmers, coopers, mechanics, deacons, deaconesses, dairy sisters, and cooks—and every member of the village benefited from their cooperation.

Some brethren, however, did little to lighten the load, among them one brother, immortalized in the poem "The Slug," who disrupted sisters' cook-ing: "Kitchen sisters ev'ry where / Know how to please him to a hair. / Some-times his errand they can guess, / If not, he can his wants express; / Nor from old Slug can they get free / Without a cake or dish of tea." By going alone to the kitchen, presumably without an Elder's permission, the brother was disorderly. Other verses describe his laziness, as well as his gluttony.[38] The sisters accommodated him, nonetheless; refusing him would have impeded union, even though a Shaker kitchen was a busy place where a snacking slacker did not belong.

Laundry was another job done by the sisters but facilitated by the brethren. On wash days, a brother built fires to heat water. Brethren put in stone sinks, boilers, and other conveniences. They built or bought labor-saving innovations, such as water-powered washing machines, a wringer for squeezing water out of the wash (or the more expensive "centrifugal dryer"), hoists to lift laundry into the attic for drying, and indoor drying racks.[39] Brothers installed special stoves for heating irons, as well. Sisters did the washing, ironing, and folding, but a brother was there to tend machinery or operate the clothes press.[40] When sisters needed clothes pins, two diligent brothers produced more than thirty-five hundred.[41]

Among the world's people in the nineteenth century, indoor plumbing and mechanical assistance for farm women were unusual. Many women had to carry water in buckets from a well, stream, or river that might have been as much as a quarter or half a mile from the house. Farmers who installed running water typically ran the pipes into the barn, rather than the house.[42] Because worldly farmers privileged men over women, they improved the outdoor facilities men used, but rarely installed anything to ease women's work. The resulting overwork wore out farmwives.[43] A nineteenth-century article suggests that the "most intelligent" of the rising generation of girls preferred not to marry farmers because they remembered their worn-out mothers.[44] Many Shaker women, on the other hand, had water piped into their kitchens by 1830.[45]

This is not to suggest that every Shaker community reached the ideal. At Canaan, New York, the brethren were remiss in providing conveniences for the sisters. The female author of a Canaan journal pointed out how the brethren's mismanagement afflicted women in that family. Those sisters had no wash house for years; they did laundry in the kitchen at night after supper. They also lacked indoor drying space until 1838. "For ten long years the sisters had stretched their lines from one apple tree to another to hang the clothes for drying," she said. "Sometimes a whole week would elapse before the weather would be suitable to put the clothes out and often would they have to wade through deep snow to put up their lines."[46] Most of the Canaan brethren lacked a sense of reciprocity.

One New Lebanon sister commended a brother's help. Deaconess Betsy Crosman wrote in 1854, "Our new counter was . . . set up in ample order, done by David Rowley, a complete workman." Crosman rarely complimented anyone, so that was high praise, coming from her.[47] Several years earlier she had complained, "Cut sage at the end of the lane (with dull knives & not a friend to sharpen them)." Usually a brother, perhaps the deacon who was her union meeting partner, would have done such a favor, but hers did not. The next year, she wrote, "Deacon Stephen sick & more helpless than usual."[48]

A more serious gap in reciprocity occurred in 1853 after several tailoring apprentices left the Shakers. At New Lebanon, sisters had always sewn brothers' shirts and frocks, while the tailor brothers and their apprentices made the men's heavy outerwear. When the apprentices left, Isaac Newton Youngs was overwhelmed with work. Lacking male assistance, he had to ask for the tailoresses' help. Youngs was in a good position to expect reciprocity: he taught tailoresses how to cut out garments, built counters with drawers, and did other favors for them.[49]

The tailoresses, however, balked at the extra work. The deacons had Youngs buy sewing machines to speed the sisters' stitching, but the sisters remained adamant. They believed that once they started making the brethren's outerwear, it would become their permanent responsibility. The disagreement seesawed back and forth for months. Pressured by the Elders and deacons, the tailoresses finally agreed to help, but they complained. "They feel as tho' they are already drove out of reason with their work," Youngs wrote, "& to think of taking the burden of the tayloring, that properly belongs to the brethren, feels more than they can patiently bear." The tailoresses showed "party spirit" when they resisted filling the men's labor gap. To preserve union, deaconess Betsy Crosman reassigned several sisters from other departments to tailoring.[50]

In 1835 Eldress Betsy Bates wrote in her journal about another instance when Believers foresaw the potential for trouble and compromised to avert conflict between the sexes and promote union.

> The Brethren want to set up making their own Hats & they want the north room second loft in the hatters' shop where the Sisters comb . . . & the Sisters will want it soon to hatchel in & card too. But the Sisters have agreed to put off their work four weeks from this very day. . . . For the Brethren tell us, let them have it now 4 weeks, if we will, we may have it till we get through our work in the Fall. Then and hereafter, the Brethren can do their work in the Winter . . . & get it all out of the way before we want to go there in the Spring. & if we will try to get along this year & next, they will build us a new shop or add on some of our other buildings next year & year after.[51]

Sisters maintained union through careful negotiation, and Bates recorded their agreement to forestall future questions about the sisters' concessions or the brethren's promise. The brethren did provide a new workroom in 1836.[52] If brethren had dominated sisters, the men would have simply issued an edict and the women would have had to acquiesce. Among the Shakers, however, equality gave the sisters bargaining power, and reciprocity gave each sex incentive to accommodate the other.

The cooperation between brothers and sisters in making baskets provides another example of how Believers worked together to promote union. In 1813, New Lebanon sisters began making baskets for sale. The business thrived. In 1835, seven sisters made eight hundred baskets to sell and sixty for home use.[53] By the 1840s, they had diversified to sell broomcorn brushes, bonnets, and fancy goods.[54] Brothers purchased raw materials, cut and split wood for poplarware and baskets, turned handles, made the oval boxes that sisters finished as sewing kits, and occasionally prepared palm leaf. Women and girls assembled the final products.[55] Moreover, as Suzanne Thurman points out, the sisters' sale goods boosted Shakers' cash flow during the summer months when seed sales were low. Everyone recognized the significance of the sisters' economic contributions.[56]

In the spirit of reciprocity, sisters contributed to brethren's businesses, too. Sisters wove tape and seated the chairs brethren made. Sisters sorted and washed herbs and roots, prepared and bottled medicine. In one day, sisters filled fifteen hundred vials of pulverized sage, savory, marjoram, and thyme, then pasted labels on, sealed, and packed them in boxes.[57] Women and girls also harvested seeds, pasted envelopes, and filled them for sale. In 1839, the sisters put up 154,450 bags of seed.[58] As these facts show, the brethren's lucrative chair, seed, and herb businesses rested on a foundation of women's labor. Without reciprocity between the sexes, those businesses would have failed. Union depended on cooperation, and so did economic prosperity.

Most sisters worked at textile production, which also benefited from brethren's assistance. In January 1840, the primary employment of almost two-thirds of women in the New Lebanon Church Family involved textiles: combing, spinning, quilling, weaving, knitting, working with cloth and yarn, mending, covering buttons, making cloth shoes, sewing, and tailoring.[59] Even Sister Dolly Sexton, at age one hundred, rose in the morning before five and did her daily stint of sewing.[60] After Harvard sister Tabitha Babbit died at age seventy-four, a scribe called her "a remarkably useful woman—& very industrious. . . . [S]he has practiced knitting without light, sitting up in her bed, before time of rising!"[61] She probably had more than she could do during daylight hours because she knitted footings for boys, who were notoriously hard on their clothes.[62]

Spinning was one of the Shaker sisters' most time-consuming textile jobs. In Proverbs 31, spinning symbolizes women's industriousness. The distaff, a spinning implement, came to represent all women's work, and the word *distaff* became a synonym for feminine because women spun miles of thread. Among early Believers, as among the world's people, "spinsters" supported themselves by spinning for other families.[63] Shaker brethren facilitated sisters' textile production by building the great wheels, foot wheels, reels, and swifts that made spinning, measuring, and winding more efficient. Brethren helped in smaller ways, as well, making sisters' tools. Isaac Newton Youngs made knitting needles. A brother turned a lovely glove mender for Lucy Smith and inscribed her name on it.[64] Sisters made garments, gloves, mittens, socks, and footings for the brothers and for sale. Thus they supported one another. Brothers also spent some evenings winding yarn, sewing, knitting, or making hooks and eyes. Occasionally, everyone stayed in the dining room after supper, working at the tables while someone read aloud.[65]

Even the sisters' caps showed collaboration between men and women. Sisters made the caps, but brothers sharpened scissors and constructed equipment and tools, including looms for weaving fabric or cap strings, and bodkins for pulling strings through casings.[66] Other handcrafts show similar collaboration. For the sisters' palm leaf bonnets, for instance, brethren made leaf-splitters, wooden patterns, and bonnet molds, as well as small looms for weaving palm leaf.

Shakers were quick to adopt improvements in textile manufacture. When the New Lebanon Church Family First Order built a rinsing box for cleaning wool in 1850, the Second Order used it, too. A deaconess wrote, "Continue wool washing with much satisfaction, & expedition. We consider it the greatest improvement, both in usefulness & ease, that ever graced the rugged path of female labor."[67] Other stages of textile work also benefited from men's cooperation. When a village got a spinning jenny, the sisters undoubtedly rejoiced at its speed. The jenny lightened sisters' work, but it also increased brothers' labor, because at first the mechanics were hard-pressed to keep the jenny running.[68] At the Enfield, New Hampshire, Shaker village, sisters ran knitting machines, but brethren probably maintained them.[69] At some villages, however, Shaker men did not adopt mechanical improvements as fast as women wanted them. Canterbury deacons, for instance, refused to buy a sewing machine until the sisters earned enough money to defray the expense.[70] And Harvard sister Lucy Ann Hammond's comment about the New Lebanon kitchen, cited earlier, shows that Harvard's kitchen was less thoughtfully laid out and equipped than New Lebanon's.

Though brethren did most of the New Lebanon Church Family's heavy labor, sisters (like other farm women) did much more outdoor work than the stereotypical nineteenth-century domestic ideal would suggest.[71] Shaker sisters often worked outside in the company of men. From April to November, sisters gathered wild foods. At times, so many were out picking that they were, in Sister Elizabeth Lovegrove's words, "scattered from Dan to Bersheba."[72] Gathering was serious business. New Lebanon sisters collected dozens of species of plants, seeds, nuts, and berries to use at home and to sell. In June, the sisters gathered elder flowers, red root, masterwort, and skunk cabbage. July brought more species to maturity and the sisters picked dandelions, yellow willow, burdock, crosswort, meadowsweet, raspberries, and whortleberries. In August they picked frostwort, pond lily roots, spice bush leaves, and spruce seedlings; in September, stromonium leaves, dock root, elderberries, silk grass, culver roots, cranberries, blackberries, and lobelia; in October, butternuts, walnuts, barberry, and buckthorn berries; and into November, sisters collected beech nuts and sassafras twigs. From spring into fall, they gathered Labrador tea and wintergreen berries.[73] The sisters also picked currants and grapes, sometime prying up fallen fruit frozen to the ground. Betsy Crosman collected a bushel and a half of strawberries in one day.[74] The brethren helped with transportation on trips beyond their village, driving the wagon and wrangling horses.

Sisters did other outdoor work, as well. At New Lebanon in 1830, Lucy Ann Hammond spent most of her days visiting and working indoors. In good weather, she worked outside, spending one afternoon picking apples and a morning piling firewood. Other sisters' days were similar. In 1838, Isaac Newton Youngs noted that the sisters did "a great deal out of doors—such as helping clear up the brush in the orchards &c."[75] The "&c" included raising eight acres of table vegetables, which had to be cooked or processed for storage.[76] In some of those jobs, women and girls worked alongside men and boys.

Sisters were a Shaker village's reserve labor force for heavy jobs. After a flood carried away New Lebanon's dam, carding mill, and two shops in 1814, Mother Lucy Wright asked the sisters to help with the cleanup. Even though the damage had been done primarily to brothers' workplaces, the sisters joined the effort and worked "like a band of strong men."[77] Women's heavy work shows the Shakers' flexibility in the sexual division of labor, as

Suzanne Thurman has documented for the Harvard and Shirley Shakers.[78] The village depended on sisters for whatever work they could physically do, indoors or out.

Occasionally a sister had the initiative to tackle even heavier jobs. When Lucy Wright asked the Canaan brethren to remove a building, they did not immediately act on her request. According to one sister's memoir, most brothers in that family were lazy and did not fully respect Wright's authority to command their labor. Impatient with the brethren's procrastination, Wright stepped beyond gender norms to start the job herself. Her enterprise shamed the brothers into doing the work.[79] This incident also shows how sisters' equality might bring them additional responsibilities. If brethren were not up to the task, sisters had to step in.

It is worth noting, however, that if both sexes had felt they were completely equal in all things, the Canaan brethren might have stood back and let Wright finish the job. Such standoffishness would have been impolitic, at best. If women in a celibate society did not need men's help to do heavy labor, perhaps the sisters would have decided they did not need men at all. The brothers surely realized that they had to step in, and quickly, not only to save face among their worldly neighbors but also to preserve their own status and traditional gender roles. Men could not risk becoming superfluous.

The work Shaker sisters did alongside brethren shows how celibacy, equality, and reciprocity contributed to union between the sexes. Celibacy promoted equality because neither men nor women were treated as chattel or servants or as though they were incompetent. Both sexes had the same rights in Shaker society; they governed, and were governed, by consensus and compromise, which gave each sex power over the other in their joint enterprise. Shakers could not have equality without reciprocity in their work lives. That reciprocity was essential to union.

Shaker sisters' work was vital to feeding and clothing Believers and in supporting the community economically. As Susan Starr Sered points out, "When women have an important subsistence role, women are perceived as 'cosmically' powerful."[80] Among the Shakers, the sisters' contributions were as important as the brethren's. But the sisters' equality did not grow out of their labor; their equality originated in their religious ideology, which put women and men on an equal footing. Certainly no one believed that brethren and sisters were exactly alike; their gender boundaries, though flexible, were fairly clear. Thus, Joseph Meacham praised Lucy Wright as his equal *in her lot,* according to her sex. The Shakers recognized that women owned their share of the society. The sisters' "lot" was, however, whatever they wanted or needed it to be, and it could range from cooking, sewing, and housework to entrepreneurship and building demolition. Lucy Wright's lot included leading the society for more than two decades. The brethren supported the sisters in those activities, not always promptly or willingly, but because their society's ideals and their own well-being required it.

In villages where brethren did not support sisters as their equals, sisters could rise up against them and make them look ridiculous. The ideology of equality was foreign to many converts, who arrived in Shaker society burdened with the gender mores of the world's people. Newcomers had to work at equality, just as they had to work at celibacy. Some never quite succeeded, and they remained in the lower orders because they had not shown sufficient travel in the faith. Others moved up in the church hierarchy, perhaps ultimately reaching the New Lebanon Church Family which, despite the progress of its members, occasionally suffered from unresolved issues of gender and power.

Union and reciprocity demanded cooperation, and sisters were equal to brethren, not their subordinates. Equality in status and reciprocity in work were necessary for the "perfect union" that sisters and brethren believed made a Shaker village into heaven on earth.

8

Gendered Conflict among the Shakers

A man that the sisters have turned out doors is not fit to be on consecrated ground.

MOST OF THE TIME, SHAKER MEN AND WOMEN WORKED together amicably enough to maintain union and reciprocity. Both sexes knew their responsibilities. A note written by Philemon Stewart shows one aspect of their division of labor in 1834.

> Our good Sisters have rallied forth from their shops this afternoon to clean the road and dooryard. And it is a fact they have caused the street and matters around our buildings to wear a very different aspect. They seem now to smile in good order, instead of groaning in confusion, that is as far as the Sisters have been able to make them so. Tis true there are some broken gates and fastenings &c that very much need repairing, but this comes in the Brethren's line.[1]

Exemplary housekeepers, sisters cleaned up outdoors, as well as in; brethren performed mechanical repairs—or should have done so. And evidently the brothers sometimes ran behind the sisters' timetable.

Even among Believers with the best intentions, things sometimes went awry. By 1845, the revised Millennial Laws acknowledged that conflicts arose between individuals and stipulated that brethren and sisters should attempt reconciliation only with the Elders' permission.[2] We might infer that the Elders wanted to know of all disputes and to be part of their resolution, if only to reconcile parties and forestall repeat episodes. Irreconciliation had to be addressed to keep resentment from damaging Shaker union.

Some conflicts were just between women. In one instance, which Polly Reed described in 1872, a problem arose between two Second Order Eldresses. Contrary to Shaker values, junior Eldress Adaline Sears was "too haughty & unsubdued," and senior Eldress Hannah Agnew was jealous of her. Moreover, Agnew had "not so much of the real Elder as they would be glad to have her."[3] Besides the poor example these two prominent and responsible sisters set, there would have been a concern that the disputants might draw others into the fray.

More dangerous than personal disputes, however, were issues, often rooted in traditional gender roles, that disrupted union between the sexes. Ann Lee may have avoided an early gendered conflict when she assured her followers that she recognized the divinity of Jesus of Nazareth and compared herself to a wife who was in charge when the husband was gone. She did not suggest that she was Jesus' subordinate but rather a partner who shared authority. By walking a very fine line, she assured potential converts of both sexes that she respected what each could bring into the communal group. Mother Ann's reasoning was enough to convince Joseph Meacham to become a Shaker—a fateful decision, for he and Lucy Wright would work to institutionalize equality of the sexes in Shakerism, as far as that was possible.[4]

As with all communal groups, Shaker villages had individuals with differing interests, diverse viewpoints, and varying levels of commitment. Many Elders and Eldresses did not work together as well as Meacham and Wright did. When Molly Goodrich, presumably an exemplary Believer, first arrived in the west, she "sometimes would rise against" the Elders. She did not automatically accept the authority of those to whom she was supposedly subject. And later, when she was an Eldress paired to lead with Benjamin Seth Youngs, they tested each other. David Darrow wondered how their partnership would work. Molly Goodrich did not accept a man's authority; she clearly considered herself Youngs's equal, not his subordinate. "I do not know yet," Darrow wrote, "whether they have settled it to know which shall be the Elder to bear rule—have the lead," an indication that he did not assume that Youngs would be the dominant one. Molly Goodrich and Benjamin Seth Youngs overcame their early differences, however, to establish a working partnership.[5] Evidently both individuals had strengths, and the Ministry let them work out the details without assuming the primacy of the male.

The Shaker model of equality of the sexes required men to have faith in women; every man who joined the society had to adjust his thinking and act accordingly. This, then, was a fundamental strength of Shakerism: the possibility that a woman could assume leadership over her male partner. Whether most Eldresses did so or not was irrelevant; as long as the example existed among living Shakers, sisters had role models in addition to Ann Lee and Lucy Wright. Moreover, brethren (who might have been otherwise dubious) had role models in Elders such as Ebenezer Bishop, who said, "Some have not much faith in women, but I have a good deal I confess!"[6]

To preserve their society, Shakers promoted union as a fundamental ideal. But human nature was the serpent in their Eden. Even when Elders and Eldresses worked well together, issues such as work, food, gossip, leadership, and children's indentures could stir antagonism between men and women.

After Joseph Meacham died in 1796, Lucy Wright was the acknowledged head of the Ministry, but her leadership provoked gendered conflict. A female helpmate serving alongside an established male leader such as Joseph Meacham was acceptable to the brethren, but a strong-willed woman who dominated the Ministry was not. As a result, a vocal minority of men protested "petticoat government" and left the society. They evidently had what a Shaker poem calls "the great male sense so prone to man in nature."[7] Presumably, persisting brethren tolerated female rule, supported equality of the sexes, or had a greater need to remain in community and were wise enough to keep their objections to themselves.

Wright faced another challenge in 1815 and 1816. Elder John Barns, head of the Maine Shakers, criticized her leadership. New Lebanon brethren, however, rebutted Barns with the observation that "petticoat-government and breeches-government both belonged to the flesh" and had no part in Shaker society.[8] The Barns conflict may have been behind Isaac Newton Youngs's 1816 report of the New Lebanon Elders warning Believers not to discuss "being placed in order, brother & sister in an equality." By then, he wrote, no Shaker communities except Watervliet and New Lebanon fully supported equality.[9] It is hard to know, today, just how equality of the sexes played out at villages far from New Lebanon—and how Elders' resentment of female leaders may have affected sisters in those faraway locations. A close reading of Shaker journals, however, turns up occasional clues.

Sometimes the traditional division of labor was a source of friction. Because Shaker men and women had different jobs, assigned by sex, their work relationships had the potential for significant conflict. We have already seen one such example, when Lucy Wright began the project of dismantling a building after the brethren procrastinated too long. Another occurred in the 1870s when Watervliet and New Lebanon sisters united in refusing to milk the cows. Traditionally, sisters milked during the season when cows produced the most milk and when brothers' outdoor labor was most taxing, from April to November. By the 1870s, however, the shortage of capable young sisters meant that the less able were called into service, and finally, rank and file sisters balked. Sarcastic journal entries by sisters and brethren reveal an un-Shaker-like contentiousness. Union suffered until, after numerous meetings to settle the issue, the sisters prevailed. Order was restored by regendering the job of milking to make it a male responsibility.[10]

When brothers did not behave according to Shaker prescriptions, they lost sisters' respect—and that was nowhere more evident than at Canaan. The Canaan gathering order, which held new members until they were deemed acceptable for a higher order, was a poor example of Shaker union. The anonymous female author of a Lower Family memoir lived there for twenty-five years, none too happily. She wrote that the earliest brothers in the order were unreliable workers, adding, "During the first ten years they would certainly have failed had it not been for the exertion of the sisters." "This the sisters were fully aware of," she wrote, "and the effect was not salutary. It had a tendency to create a sort of independence and rather overbearing spirit, (of which there is a plenty in human nature) that when the scum was cast off and replaced with respectable brethren, it was injurious to the union of the family." That fundamental difference in outlook between the family's brethren and sisters provoked years of conflict. For example, the scribe said, their buildings were constructed by "uninterested parties whose only object was to get the work done without any reference to the future." She added, "The sisters shop was built unwillingly to appease the feelings of the sisters who felt that they had done enough to entitle them to a comfortable place to work in; then who can wonder that the buildings are no better." The situation did not improve. She wrote:

> Ten years had passed and the family were not better off than when they first moved here. In fact they were not as well off for nothing was finished that had been begun and they were in debt. Besides the many misfortunes attending, the family was almost constantly changing members. In the fall they would fill up with lazy men who only wanted an easy home during the winter. In the spring they would be off and of course must go with clothes no matter how ragged they were when they came.

The sisters were thus forced to make clothing for a succession of "winter Shakers" who did not adequately repay their efforts. Elders James Farnham and Thomas Estes, as well as the industrious, versatile, and overworked Gilbert Avery, were the brethren who persisted through the first decade. According to the scribe, Avery was the only one of the three brothers who met Shaker standards of diligence. Nothing but the sisters' exertions staved off the family's "annihilation" in those early years.[11]

One brother who was unable to stay at the Canaan gathering order was William Evans, an Englishman who arrived there in 1834. The diarist described him as "an aspiring would be gentleman who supposed he was called to be a leader. . . . He would not work, but was very willing to . . . give orders to those who would work. . . . He would take the manners book and bolt into the sisters' rooms and give instruction because he had discovered someone in the act of laughing and imagined he was the object of their mirth." Evans knew the sisters disliked him.[12]

When Evans criticized the sisters, they put up with him at first. They knew that communal life requires patience with individual foibles. But Evans eventually nettled them beyond their limits. The scribe wrote, "He wanted to go into the kitchen and teach the Sisters to cook and bake and would have succeeded had not the sisters rose en masse and threatened to leave the premises."[13] Evans's faux pas was serious. Because the kitchen was the center of the household, the women who worked there had to be treated with respect. In a society where food was the only sensual pleasure, community morale might depend on the cooks.

Up to this point, Shaker union had failed in three ways. Evans's arrogance was the most obvious failure. He had not internalized Shaker values and he was disinclined to learn. The second failure was that his behavior provoked the sisters to threaten a walkout—a gendered stand that pitted women against men. The conflict showed the divisive "party spirit" that could destroy Shaker union. The third failure belonged to other brethren, particularly Elders James Farnham and Thomas Estes. They should have counseled Evans, disciplined him, or sent him away, but they did not. By allowing such divisive behavior to continue, they condoned it.[14]

After two years of Evans's meddling, the sisters finally reached the end of their patience. "As the brethren had not the power or lacked the disposition to get rid of him the sisters undertook the job and succeeded admirably," the Canaan scribe explained. Hannah Bryant and Harriet Sellick solved the Evans problem with a fourth failure of Shaker union. They "took him by the collar and put him into the street and threw his clothes after him."[15]

Despite the drama of the Evans expulsion, it was not a rash act but a well-considered solution to ongoing vexation. The sisters had tolerated Evans for two years, ample time for him to mend his ways and adjust his attitude, but he did neither.[16] The expulsion tells us a lot about Shaker women's authority. Even at Shaker villages less egalitarian than New Lebanon, brethren had to respect the sisters or face the consequences. If the Elders did not eject an offender, the sisters could and did—an act that made the sisters the ultimate authority among Canaan Shakers.

The expulsion also shows that the official power structure was not necessarily the actual one. In theory, male Elders were responsible for disciplining rank and file brethren—but at Canaan, the first Elder, James Farnham, was a weak leader more inclined to making jokes than meting out discipline.[17] By casting out Evans, the sisters circumvented the Elders in ways not covered by the Millennial Laws—a reminder that lived experience could diverge from both the Shaker ideal and the norm.[18]

Another village's leader upheld the sisters' decision. Evans carried "his bitter tale of woe" to the Hancock Shaker village, fully expecting to be taken in there. He was disappointed. Elder Daniel Goodrich sent Evans away, saying, "A man that the sisters have turned out doors is not fit to be on consecrated ground."[19] Goodrich, like the Canaan Elders, respected women's authority to expel a troublemaker.

This expulsion raises the question, Who were the ultimate authorities in Shaker society, men or women? Some scholars believe that Shaker sisters were "powerless," relative to brethren, but that superficial impression ignores the Shakers' own perception of the sexes' equality.[20] On one hand, the Canaan sisters took the initiative because the Elders repeatedly failed to act. On the other hand, perhaps the sisters were, in fact, the final authorities on membership. If they were, that would explain the turnover of Canaan's brethren. Maybe sisters could shape a village, bolstering female membership while discouraging men and boys from joining. Even so, that authority did not give them complete power over brethren. However much the Canaan sisters might have wished to expel their good-natured but incompetent Elders, they did not. Most other brethren, though—those who did not become leaders—arrived and departed just as quickly. Some were run off in the same way that Ann Lee and her early followers had rejected unworthy potential proselytes. By 1841, the scribe wrote, "The lazy roughs that had graced the family had nearly all got scorched and cleared out."[21] If the sisters had the power to make fundamental decisions about membership, including expelling brethren, what else did they control?

If we are to credit the anthropologist Susan Rogers's views on female power and "the myth of male dominance" in agrarian societies, women effectively run some villages, gossiping and sharing information as they work or visit.[22] Power may have worked the same way among the Shakers, where men worked in scattered locations while women worked in groups within the village. Women gathered information, solicited opinions, drew conclusions, and made decisions—then informed the brethren. Occasionally they also carried out some of the brethren's duties.

Evidence of the sisters' influence among the Shakers persists in historical sources. Male apostates were a significant source of "petticoat government" complaints about the sisters, not only in Mother Lucy Wright's day but later, as well. Nicholas Briggs wrote that the sisters gradually acquired authority until they had the "deciding voice," which caused men to leave the Canterbury Shaker village in the late nineteenth century.[23]

According to the apostate Hervey Elkins, Shaker sisters carried out "female espionage," a sort of domestic surveillance to monitor behavior.[24] Elkins lived with New Hampshire Believers, far from New Lebanon, but this practice was institutionalized throughout the society. Their Millennial Laws required Believers to tell what they knew of their peers' sins.[25] David Lamson, who lived in a Shaker community for two years, explains how the system worked "to bring to light every hidden sin and every secret among the brethren and sisters."

> It is nothing against the character of a Shaker, but rather meritorious to be a listener and an informer. The Elders are very faithful not to expose an informer to those informed against. All heavy walking or loud talking in the halls of the house, is strictly forbidden. And it is alleged as a reason, that such things displease the invisible Spirits which are constantly present. This affords an excuse for listeners to be near in a sly and unexpected manner; suddenly appear in the rooms of others without any warning; and thus use all means of detection without seeming to design it.[26]

Though perhaps we should take into account that these are the words of an apostate, clearly, in such a setting, individuals with the lightest step would have the physical advantage in covert observation of their peers. Also, sisters were at an advantage because they cleaned everyone's room.

Even when men were in the village, sisters closely watched their behavior. At Enfield, New Hampshire, Robert Leavitt, a visitor, forgot the rule against touching and took the elderly Sister Margaret Appleton's elbow to steady her walking up the meetinghouse steps. She smiled at him and said, "Mr. Leavitt, the Sisters can't see us out of the window, but when they can see, you mustn't touch me."[27] Despite an innocent intent, the sisters would reprimand any transgressor.

Some incidents that seem relatively trivial take on larger significance when closely examined. In 1826, when Anne Royall visited the Shakers, she wrote of her arrival at New Lebanon, "One of the men, I think a shoemaker, accosted me very roughly, but he met with a sharp rebuke for it, from the females, and afterwards from the elders."[28] Shaker women did not hesitate to defend a female outsider even if it meant offending a Shaker brother. Furthermore, the incident shows that the sister who defended Royall also assumed authority over the brother she reprimanded; she did not call a deacon or Elder to intercede, even though brethren theoretically answered to other men, not women.

A later incident was also a telling one. In an 1892 "Home Notes" column for the *Shaker Manifesto,* the male author did not mention the sisters' work. It is not clear whether he was just thoughtless, or he had no idea of what work the sisters did, or he consciously valued men's work over women's. Nonetheless, when the sisters pointed out his error, he printed a correction. In his next column, he wrote, "Sisters of Center Family do not complain, only they are not quite satisfied with our last 'Home Notes,' though good as far as they went." He compensated for his earlier omission by describing the sisters' work on sale goods, including the unpleasant job of plucking raccoon fur for spinning into glove yarn. Shaker sisters demanded equal recognition for their labor and did not allow a brother to underrate their efforts. Even so, the male columnist had the last word on the subject, because he also noted that the sisters had brethren's help.[29]

One has to wonder whether this correction was just a small skirmish in an ongoing battle between Shaker men and women. In 1905, Leila Taylor wrote, "It is, so my observation goes, entirely possible to manage the masculine being, but it is not a good plan to put it too plainly beforehand that you're going to do it." The context of Taylor's comments was Laura Holloway-Langford's heavy-handed (and ultimately futile) contest with Brother Robert Valentine for use of a summer cottage.[30] Taylor's knowledge of managing "the masculine being," however, was probably hard won.

Other conflicts between men and women were more significant. Food was often the issue. Because of the large number of calories Shaker brethren needed to support their physical labor, meals were very important to them, and some brethren's journals make that clear. Isaac Newton Youngs often recorded seasonal treats such as strawberries, asparagus, and watermelon. In his history of the church, he wrote twenty pages on table fare, including breakfasts of fried ham and potatoes or broiled pork, beef, or mutton with biscuits and butter. Pie was on the table at every meal when the apple crop was good. Dinner included vegetables and meat. Supper was a lighter meal, with hash, bread, and milk, except on the Sabbath or holidays, when their richest meats, the best preserves, and cake were set on the table.[31] At one village, brethren discussed their meals so much that, as one seceder commented, they enjoyed the best dishes twice.[32]

Once in a while, though, provisions ran short. In 1833, Betsy Bates recorded a potentially divisive issue.

> Nicholas [Bennet] spoke some in our evening meeting, concerning our dairy, as he supposed we all well knew that it was coming short, especially the cheese. Wanted we should make use of it accordingly, & once in a while miss a meal, thought it would be better to miss one in a while than it would to get entirely out, spoke for our information, that we need not think strange, if it was not always on the table.[33]

After an evening spent paring pumpkins in 1834, Giles Avery explained an apple shortage with regret, "Weather was such last spring that we are deprived of Apples this season so pumpkins are a substitute for every thing even shortening." And in 1840, an Elder "spoke concerning being a little more sparing at table, particularly of apple pye, in this time of scarcity of apples."[34]

Food had been even less plentiful in 1816, "the Year Without a Summer," when even the best farmers had a skimpy harvest. Brethren must have complained about the quantity of food that year, because Mother Lucy Wright told them that they should be willing to "scant" a little and be thankful for what was put before them, rather than finding fault.[35]

In 1835, Grahamism arrived at New Lebanon, and food commentary spiked. Betsy Bates wrote, "A number of us go to eating according to the Graham manner of living for a trial."[36] Within two weeks, Isaac Newton Youngs noted that the new meatless diet of whole grains and vegetables had already provoked "party feeling."[37] The following summer he wrote some "Remarks" about food served during the haying season, the most labor-intensive time of the year: "As to our eating fare, I would observe that our food has been vegetable scarce any meat has been in the field. Milk for dinner, bread cracknels, potatoes, &c some butter, honey, apple pye, cake &c. and we also have bitting served round twice a day. Our drink is mostly water, sweetened with molasses, & some ginger or oatmeal in it, some beer, no cider, for 3 or 4 years."[38] Others also noted, with some dismay, the scarcity of meat in their new diet. Among them was Aaron Bill. After pickers brought home two bushels of "Whirtle Berries" during haying in 1837, he complained, "You must understand that berries is our main living having procured some thing near 20 bushels this season of all sorts & not much else to eat but rye bread & old potatoes of rather inferior quality."[39]

Dietary limitations continued to cause "party spirit" in a society that valued peace and union. Discontent flared up again in 1841, when "swine's flesh was entirely expunged from the table."[40] In 1850, Youngs wrote: "This is rather a questionable point in these days—some incline to be what is called Grahamites, & eat no meat, a part of those argue that it is wrong to take the life of any animals, that meat is not healthy, &c. These differences of opinion & practice make some trouble in furnishing our table. I think temperance & a medium are the chief requisites."[41] When he mentioned Grahamism again in 1856, he called it "a rigidly abstemious diet or regimen." "People have ran very wild on this subject," he said,

> and are of two parties, going to great extremes in opposite directions; the one discarding all indulgence of appetite, all rich or delicious, or high seasoned food, all flesh meat, all grease, butter &c. confining themselves to brown bread, or unbolted flour, and rejecting the whole train of variety and sorts of animal food; the others observing no particular restriction, but to eat what suits best, unless they know by experience that it injures their health, saying their own appetite is their best rule and judge of what is best for them.

Youngs wrote that the limited diet caused so much disagreement that the church had to back away from Grahamism and provide meals for both vegetarians and omnivores, even though the church was "in favor of the vegetable, or simple diet . . . in a general conviction that plain living is more conducive to health than luxurious."

> These differences of opinions have caused much affliction and additional labor, especially to the cooks as it has rendered it necessary for them to put upon the table both vegetable and animal food, at one meal, which instead of making less, has increased the number of sorts, so that those who do not adopt the simple diet have a wider range of variety.

Youngs clearly disapproved of Grahamism. He considered it an immoderate diet—but he did not complain about the food, only about the dissension the dietary change caused. He concluded, "It is also evidently a point of wisdom as well as necessity to endeavor to conform to each other, and come as near to a medium as possible in these things; & not to be so tenacious in our habits, but that we may harmonize."[42]

Among the New Lebanon Church Family sisters, leaders both spiritual and temporal agreed on the benefits of reducing meat consumption. Eldress Betsy Bates tried the Graham diet, and deaconess Betsy Crosman favored vegetarianism as a matter of principle. Crosman, who managed the family's food supplies, preferred to reduce the "blood shed." In 1852, after finishing her kitchen tour, she wrote, "Nothing has passed in the kitchen worthy of remark except our passing one week without cooking meat or fish."[43] Because the sisters controlled the brothers' diets, the brothers had to make do with less meat on the table, if only to reduce "party spirit."

The quantity of food brothers demanded inspired poems about the gripes and eating habits of gluttons. Those immortalized in Shaker poetry were men, whose overeating meant that the kitchen sisters had to make extra to accommodate them. One poem, titled "Hoggish Nature," observes: "When glutton goes in and sits down with the rest, / His hoggish old nature it grabs for the best / The cake and the custard, the crull and the pie / He cares not for others, but takes care of I." The glutton despised lighter fare such as soup, and made his feelings known. He searched the kitchen for choice tidbits, hoarded food, and ate more than his share.[44]

Shakers categorized overeating with drunkenness and other stupefying practices that fed natural lusts. Excess was to be avoided.[45] Though food was the Shakers' one acceptable sensual pleasure, the appetite was to be indulged in moderation—and the sisters were the arbiters in that line.

Furthermore, according to "Hoggish Nature," sisters could join forces to punish a gluttonous brother: "Now all that are wise they will never be dup'd; / They'll feed the old glutton on porridge and soup, / Until he is willing to eat like the rest, / And not hunt the kitchen to find out the best."[46] Like the women who ran their village's domestic affairs in Rogers's study, Shaker kitchen sisters conferred together, drew conclusions, and acted accordingly without consulting Elders, deacons, or other brethren. Sisters were a powerful force in Shaker society, and it did not pay to provoke them. The man who took their goodwill for granted might well have found himself on short rations.[47]

Gendered disagreements arose outside the kitchen, as well. One centered on the Potter children, who were indentured to the Shakers at New Lebanon. When their mother sought to retrieve the children in 1819, nearly all the brethren made it clear that they wanted to keep the children, but the sisters chose to give them up. The male scribe who recorded the incident wrote: "Mother [Lucy] spoke some concerning the children. Her mind in the matter was different from what the brethren were aware of but it appears that the sisters had found out more of Mother's feelings, which has occasioned a kind of strife between Br & sisters." Again, like the women in Rogers's agrarian village, the Shaker sisters discussed the matter and reached a conclusion. But they did not keep the brethren fully informed and as a result caused hard feelings among them. Their behavior is consistent with the finding of Beverly Chiñas, cited in the Introduction, that women have their own social universe because they share information that men do not circulate among themselves. As the Shaker scribe reveals, Lucy Wright had to repair the breach between sisters and brothers. He wrote: "Mother's gift I thought was calculated to heal."[48]

Other poems attacked gossips. One admonished, "Come, Sister, come, / Let all be one, / For you're as good as I am, / There is no cause / For picking flaws / For we're all going to Zion."[49] Another, more detailed poem is titled, "The Poison of the Tongue." The poet, Hannah Brownson, wrote of those who intentionally stirred up strife even though it was contrary to Shaker values. Describing the contagion of raging "malice & discord," she suggested that Believers curb their "vicious and idle" tongues and promised to curb her own, as well.[50] Despite the value of gossip in regulating behavior and building consensus in a Shaker village, as these poems show, it also had the potential to hamper union.

Other sisters' written criticism was much more public, and more clearly pitted sisters against brothers. In the late nineteenth century, two Shaker sisters were provoked enough to deride brothers in published poetry. One was Cecilia DeVere, whose poem, "Our Water Works," we saw earlier. The other, Lucy Bowers, wrote with revealing details about the relationship between Shaker sisters, brethren, and work in the poem "The Bird Legislator": "I thought of the men, the 'conference' men, / Who sat in converse from now till then; / How the women could toil in the self-same hall / Hanging new paper all over the wall." The able-bodied brother sat, talked, and "*conserved his strength*" while the women worked. Bowers concluded by wishing that "all the weak sex would rise in a mass," and set the men to doing hand labor.[51] She thought some brothers were lazy.

At Canaan, Gilbert Avery was the industrious exception, but that Shaker family had unusually indolent brethren.[52] At other Shaker villages, lazy brothers, like the subject of the song "The Slug" by "R. M." (probably Richard McNemar), were chastised.

> A lazy fellow it implies, Who in the morning hates to rise;
> When all the rest are up at four, He wants to sleep a little more.
> When others into meeting swarm, He keeps his nest so good and
> warm,
> That sometimes when sisters come To make the beds and sweep the
> room,
> Who do they find wrap'd up so snug? Ah! Who is it but Mr. Slug.[53]

A few outsiders suspected as much. Abigail May Alcott, wife of Bronson Alcott, for instance, upon visiting the Harvard Shakers, thought the brethren looked much too well-fed and sleek compared with the sisters. She inferred that men's exploitation of women might account for the difference. Perhaps she was right, but she may also have been drawing a parallel with her own situation as a hardworking woman married to a man who talked more than he worked.[54]

Anne Royall recorded additional evidence of men whose sense of entitlement may have allowed them to shirk their hand labor. When Royall visited New Lebanon in 1826, two Elders sat idle to talk with her, while "Miss Betsey," the Eldress in the room, kept busy with her needlework—a difference so conspicuous that Royall commented on it.[55] The Shaker Eldress worked every waking hour, while the Elders had the leisure to just sit and talk. That may be why New Lebanon Elder Rufus Bishop, ostensibly a tailor, sewed only one white vest and four pairs of drawers in six months of tailoring.[56] He was busy, primarily with travel, but did little else. Reciprocity meant that everyone was supposed to do his or her share of hand labor, but some did not. That difference was visible not only to Shaker sisters but also to outsiders who spent only a few hours with Believers.

One more gendered difference seems peculiar. Reading several thousand pages of Shaker journals, poetry, and visitor accounts, I found few brothers' criticisms of Shaker sisters—nothing comparable to the sisters' expulsion of William Evans or the poetry criticizing Shaker brothers. I have to wonder why. Is it possible that most brethren had no complaints about the sisters? Were brethren afraid to complain? Did women feel more free to criticize? Did the sisters' "female espionage" stifle criticism? Did some brethren encrypt journal entries because they did not want the sisters who cleaned their rooms to know what they were writing?[57] Such evidence may suggest how sisters shaped Shaker life or the documentary record or both. And considering that male apostates often sharply criticized Shaker sisters, we might infer that the men who were most resentful of sisters' authority were the men who left the society.

Sisters had another advantage in shaping Shaker life. The majority of Believers were women. Their numbers may have given the sisters authority that is not visible except in an occasional incident such as the expulsion of William Evans or in their publication of poems criticizing brethren. Among the Shakers, petticoat government lasted long after Lucy Wright's administration ended in 1821. If a brother did not like porridge for supper, he could always leave. If a brother did not respect women's authority, he had to go. Perhaps Shaker sisters always held the final word on membership. By policing the ranks, they promoted union among persisting Believers. Thus equality of the sexes—or the sisters' potential for hegemony in some villages—may have contributed to the dwindling of the society's male population.

9

Abuse by Spirit Messages during the Era of Manifestations

A hard time of it in this hurrycane of gifts,
to know what is revelation and what is not.

SPIRITUAL REVELATION IS THE FOUNDATION OF WESTERN religion. The Old Testament story of Moses, who alone heard the word of God and brought the Ten Commandments down from Mount Sinai, had something in common with the New Testament account of Mary, mother of Jesus, who related that an angel told her she would give birth while still a virgin. Both contributed to enduring religious traditions based on unseen beings' uncorroborated messages to chosen instruments. Though skeptics may challenge such revelations, the tradition persists.

Christianity's offshoot, Shakerism, is also based on spiritual messages. Mother Ann Lee's revelations were the foundation of Shaker belief. Her gifts exposed sin; Believers had to meet her standards of virtue.[1] A force for inclusion and exclusion, religion divides an in-group (members or the worthy) from an out-group (nonmembers or the unworthy). When Ann Lee assessed potential followers, she relegated some to the out-group. Perhaps it is axiomatic that a perfectionist society has to police itself for sinners, because religion derives power from its ability to influence human behavior.

Ann Lee also allowed her followers to expel the unworthy. When a young woman named Polly Swan came to see the Shakers, Abijah Worster recalled, "Elenor Pierce and Martha Prescot being full of zeal, and lacking both wisdom & charity, began to war at her for her lust and pride, and pushed her about, and Polly, when she got out of their hands, run." Questioned about the assault, Ann Lee said that Pierce and Prescot "have received the power of God, and are full of zeal; but lack wisdom to know how to improve their gifts; and if you strike at their zeal, they will be likely to lose their gifts, and go back to the world and be lost."[2] Lee was unwilling to restrain proselytes who had made a commitment to Shakerism. By allowing them to bully Swan, she set an unfortunate precedent. At the same time, however, Ann Lee gave women spiritual authority that they did not have in other religious groups.

After Ann Lee's death, Shakers regulated morality by more mundane means. Their domestic surveillance turned up misbehavior, which Believers were required to report to the Elders, who tried to persuade sinners to repent and confess.[3] The goal was to redeem those who truly repented their errors. During the Era of Manifestations, though, that system did not always work. Shakers tried to maintain a dynamic tension between gifts of inspiration and the society's need for order and union,[4] but from 1838 through 1841, inspiration prevailed. The Ministry and Elders gave visionists free rein, much as Ann Lee had done with Pierce and Prescot. As a result, instruments—most of them women—used spirit messages to threaten, intimidate, and expel their peers. Moreover, some of the New Lebanon visionists worked together to achieve their goals; what began as individual inspiration may have evolved into a team effort to oust Olive Gates and Sally Dean.

The story of Sally Dean began in 1821, when, at age twenty-one, she followed her brother John to the New Lebanon Church Family. Soon after her arrival, she wrote a searing testimony to her former church, stating her reasons for converting.[5] Having cut her former ties, she settled in and established herself as a capable, responsible Shaker sister.

In 1827, a revival brought spiritual gifts to "purge out the unfaithful, and sever dead branches,"[6] and thus, the Ann Lee tradition of expulsion continued. But that inspiration quickly faded. By late 1828, Elder Ebenezer Bishop was exhorting the Church Family to "wake up and be more zealous." However, enthusiasm continued to slump. In 1835, one brother complained that worship was so dull that he almost nodded off in meeting.[7] He did not foresee just how exciting worship would become.

Meanwhile, temporal life flowed along as usual. In 1832, Sally Dean roomed with Prudence Morrel, Joanna Kitchel, Zillah Potter, and Matilda Reed. Dean took her turn in the kitchen, the laundry, and the dairy, as needed, and joined in spring cleaning, painting, and apple picking. She worked in the palm-leaf bonnet business that the deaconesses started in 1835. For five years, she was the girls' caretaker. In September 1837, she was promoted to trustee (a deaconess who lived at the Trustees' Office to meet the public), working with Semantha Fairbanks.[8] Dean was evidently a good example of a Shaker sister, bright, personable, and reliable enough to interact with the world's people.

In 1834, twenty-three-year-old Olive Gates also joined the New Lebanon Shakers. Like Dean, Gates fit in. Her good voice put her at the top of the first class of singers, above Anna Dodgson and Miranda Barber. She, too, was a bonnet maker. In 1837, Gates assisted Zillah Potter, who had replaced Sally Dean as the girls' caretaker.[9] Occupational proximity to Zillah Potter (in child care) and Semantha Fairbanks (in bonnet making) was something both Gates and Dean had in common.

In late 1837, Shaker life was on the cusp of change. That fall, several girls at Watervliet, New York, experienced visions and received spirit messages. The Ministry counseled the visionists. "I warned them against letting their sense rise or taking the honor of those gifts to themselves," Rufus Bishop wrote. "To be honest about the matter," he added, "I think there was rather too much of the wind, fire & earthquake to satisfy Believers who have had a long and fruitful travel."[10] The Ministry investigated the phenomena and validated the manifestations,[11] which spread to other Shaker villages. Disturbing reports soon trickled back to New Lebanon; visionists were exposing other Believers' sins. In April 1838, Isaac Newton Youngs wrote that spirits revealed the errors of several Canaan Shakers "in a wonderful manner, rooting them up & bringing them to confession." One brother's sin "was such that he could not be suffered to remain, & was peaceably persuaded to go away."[12] Thus the Era's expulsions began. As Diane Sasson points out, spiritual manifestations offered the rank and file opportunities to shape community life. Unfortunately, spirit gifts were unpredictable and difficult to control.[13] And some visionists appear to have taken advantage of that opportunity.

The Ministry's village anxiously awaited the inspiration already prevalent elsewhere. In April 1838, Philemon Stewart brought a major spirit message to New Lebanon. By early May, he showed the strain of becoming an instrument. "Philemon is now almost constantly under the power of inspiration," Isaac Newton Youngs wrote. "He hardly seems like himself any of the time."[14]

By May 1838, the New Lebanon Church Family dwelling was "alive with new lights or such as are wro't upon," Youngs reported. "No comparison has ever been seen among us before. It is very different from the dark times of '35 & '36. I truly feel my soul filled with thankfulness; it is what I have long desired but never expected to see the like by a great deal."[15] New Lebanon's instruments began with physical manifestations—turning, shaking, and bowing—but soon began using spirit communications to manipulate their peers. One of Philemon Stewart's messages forced Calvin Green to make a public confession.[16] Sally Dean tried to smooth things over with a new communication.[17] Using one gift to combat another was an inspired response, whether spirits were involved or not—but it was also evidence of competing agendas.[18]

Shakers tried to police the phenomenon. Youngs noted that some gifts were "said to be real." He thought he could distinguish between genuine manifestations and fraudulent ones.[19] Much later, he had second thoughts, and wrote, "Much wisdom was needed, for the protection of the gifted ones, & to prevent those gifts from tending to wildness."[20] Because spirit messages could not be verified or corroborated (except by other, equally unverifiable, spirit messages), they were susceptible to misuse. The Ministry imposed a process to regulate matters. According to David Lamson, instruments were supposed to ask and receive the Elders' permission to manifest a gift before proceeding, but some did not. Barnabas Sprague, a Hancock Elder, admitted, "The elders have a hard time of it in this hurrycane of gifts, to know what is revelation and what is not."[21]

In June 1838, the girls' caretaker, Zillah Potter, told the Elders that ten-year-old Ann Eliza Goodwin had faked inspiration. Potter's report set off a cascade of problems. The child was expelled—not unusual for one who misbehaved—but repercussions followed.[22] Ann Eliza's older sister, Harriet Goodwin, remained a Shaker and assisted Potter with the girls in 1839 and 1840, but when Harriet left that job two years later, she reported a visionary dream that accused Potter of mistreating the girls and forcing someone out of the society by false accusations.[23] Spirit gifts could be used to settle old scores. Even so, Goodwin's exposure of Potter was a curious matter. Personal attacks were contrary to union, a fundamental Shaker virtue. If Goodwin had delivered that message in her own voice, it would have shown unreconciled feelings as well as the tale-bearing prohibited by their Millennial Laws.[24] Spirits, however, did not have to follow those rules, and some visionists took advantage of that gap in social control. These conflicts foreshadowed coming events.

In 1839, the spirits ousted Richard McNemar, a Shaker leader in the West.[25] McNemar sojourned at New Lebanon afterward, presumably seeking reinstatement, so his case was well known.[26] If a spirit could expel one of the founders of western Shakerism, no one was safe. Other villages suffered spirit-driven expulsions. At Harvard, Grove Blanchard noted that William Clapp had been "sentenced" to go to the world.[27] As manifestations proliferated during this period, the New Lebanon Ministry corresponded with Union Village about instruments being employed by evil spirits who were tools of the devil. As early as February 1839, the Ministry recognized the possibility of malice.[28]

At New Lebanon, Anna Dodgson began "fanning away the chaff" in mid-1840. She warned, "Woe, woe be unto you that shall now slight my manifestation saith Jehovah. . . . I will root you out from among my people; yea, I will cast you far from me, saith the Lord."[29] This message is a clue to New Lebanon Shakers' varying levels of belief in the manifestations. Some Believers' skepticism was so obvious that it irked the fully committed Dodgson.

In worship on October 4, 1840, Eleanor Potter announced a spiritual "writing of excommunication." In the persona of Mother Ann Lee, Potter warned that sinners would be purged out of the church. Olive Gates stepped forward to speak, but Potter rebuked her, "Go back, go back, depart, I know you not, depart, how dare you come forward." Turning and "warring in powerful exercise," Potter ranted while Gates retreated into the ranks. Potter harangued, "Evil doers could not be ownd, hypocrites, liars & deceitful workers nor whoremongers & adulterers, but would be exposed by the mighty powers of God."[30] Potter singled out Olive Gates when Gates stepped forward; if Gates had stayed put, she might have been safe. Potter seized authority, and the Elders let her.

Three days later, the Ministry left New Lebanon on a trip, and their absence boded ill.[31] That day, someone with the initials "S.F.," probably Semantha Fairbanks, delivered a spirit warning. She asked "if any one wished to speak, to seek for mercy . . . [erased here but still legible are the initials O.G., for Olive Gates] came forward & kneeled down . . . begged for mercy & forgiveness, saying she was willing to confess all her sins . . . rather than lose her soul's salvation." Gates acknowledged that she had doubted "the gifts of God." Potter's attack had made Gates conspicuous, and she broke under the pressure.[32]

Semantha Fairbanks had deaconess Betsy Crosman remove Gates from meeting, ostensibly so the Church Family could deliberate on the matter. After Gates left the room, however, they did not discuss her case; Fairbanks simply announced her expulsion. "By the mighty power of God is this woman exposed & that by her own means. She hath of herself shut the door of mercy against herself & her day of repentance has gone." Fairbanks concluded, "Sinners cannot abide in Zion. . . . Those who hide their sins, God will expose." Fairbanks asked whether all thought the expulsion was "perfect justice," an indication that she may have been uneasy about her peers' reaction. "If any did not feel satisfied [the spirit] desired they would speak or raise their right hand," the scribe noted. "None answered." On one hand, the rank and file may not have understood the situation's ramifications. On the other hand, they may have understood all too well, having just seen what happened to one who spoke up. Silent acquiescence was the safe response.

Dissatisfied with the lack of feedback, Fairbanks pressed for a reply. The spirit "wanted to know if we felt satisfied; some answered they did." Only a minority responded, so the answer was not unanimous. In a society that prized union, this lack of unity was significant. Finally Fairbanks tried to bolster her own credibility. She said the spirit wanted all to know that "the elders had never exposed this woman, nor had they said a word to this instrument to inform of her state or condition to expose her in any way, shape nor manner; what the instrument knew was by the mighty power of God."[33] Self-justification, however, resembled human agency more than divine.

Perhaps the Church Family did not realize that a visionist had the power to expel individuals. They may have expected the Elders to intervene. The Elders could have approved Potter's and Fairbanks's messages in advance to drive out miscreants but could not know who would admit transgression or how the visionists would react. After validating the manifestations, the Elders may not have known how to squelch a visionist without destroying faith in the phenomena or admitting their own error.

The following day, Zillah Potter, still the girls' caretaker, finished the ouster of her former assistant Olive Gates.[34] Potter spoke as Ann Lee's spirit, saying, "And now know ye concerning that woman, her day is past, & the time is come that she must be separated . . . before the going down of another sun that woman shall no longer be numbered among you; but must be removed to the Office & there remain till she peaceably withdraws." Potter told her peers, "Look ye well into your own hearts" and consider "a deceitful worker now cast out."[35]

In the normal course of events, confession and repentance were enough to allow a transgressor to remain in union. By one account, the New Lebanon Shakers had not expelled anyone for twenty years or more.[36] From 1838 to 1841, however, visionists expelled several Believers and terrified others. And neither the Ministry nor the family Elders reined them in.

Olive Gates, sequestered at the Trustees' Office, left "peaceably" before the Ministry returned to New Lebanon.[37] Her willing departure was taken as evidence of her guilt, but some of her peers were uneasy nonetheless. Joseph Babe, a Second Order brother, wrote that the week of Gates's expulsion was "the most extraordinary" that he ever witnessed—and cut short that journal entry.[38] Later Babe wrote that "l.t." delivered a spirit message saying she would "spew out" anyone who did not follow Ann Lee's precepts, then gagged and vomited. Another meeting "beggared description" with visionists "rolling and spewing" on the meeting room floor, Babe wrote, then added, "O—I must quit." He concluded, "Sufficient unto the day is the evil thereof, so rest, reader, in all the gospel peace you can obtain."[39] Joseph Babe was afraid to be candid, but he believed that evil had crept in among the Shakers.

Some Believers tried to ameliorate the situation. In November 1840, Calvin Green warned about spreading malice.[40] Several visionists, including Giles Avery and Jethro Turner, tried to smooth things over with benign spirit messages.[41] The Potter sisters and Semantha Fairbanks, in contrast, spoke for spirits who were not humble or kind—as did Miranda Barber, who soon came into her own as the voice of Holy Mother Wisdom.

Many Believers were dubious. The apostate David Lamson called the Era's spirit gifts "an outrage upon common sense." He believed that sisters pretended to be inspired and was amazed that no one else saw the absurdity of the situation.[42] Another apostate, Hervey Elkins, was careful not to "overstep the bounds of prudence" in showing skepticism.[43] At New Lebanon, several Believers also thought things had gone awry, as did Joseph Babe. Isaac Newton Youngs later concluded that "taking in the spirits" allowed evil to work through human instruments. Believers relied too much on spirit gifts, he thought, rather than relying on the Elders.[44] During the Era of Manifestations, however, prudent Believers did not show skepticism. Doubts were dangerous, and fear of retribution inhibited dissent.

Psychologists' studies of adult bullying show that it may begin as an individual's problem but quickly becomes an organizational issue that afflicts all members. Bullies isolate their victims, and potential allies fear being the next target. As a result, bystanders protect themselves however they can.[45] And so it was for Believers in 1840 and 1841, when several New Lebanon visionists intimidated their peers.[46]

Sally Dean's ordeal may have begun soon after Olive Gates was expelled. Dean left her job as second Office trustee under Semantha Fairbanks in December 1840. Eleanor Potter replaced Dean as deaconess.[47] Twice a Potter had replaced Dean in temporal employment, rising to a position of greater responsibility. In a Shaker family with about twenty women in the same age bracket, the selection of two Potter sisters seems more than a coincidence. In the light of subsequent events, one wonders whether "the spirits" were already at work. Deborah Burns says that family ties formed power blocs among natural kin in many Shaker villages.[48] New Lebanon was no different. The Ministry Elders' niece Betsy Crosman was a Church Family deaconess from 1837 to 1872, and her natural sister Abigail was a visionist. Moreover, unrelated individuals could form alliances. Though Betsy Crosman did not accuse anyone, Fairbanks had her remove Gates; she knew that Crosman would do as she asked.[49] Thus, deaconesses and visionists appear to have been allied.

Visionists demanded a great deal of time. On Sunday, April 11, the society spent ten hours in worship, laboring through mealtimes.[50] Threats continued. During another Ministry absence on May 22, 1841, spirits said God's judgment would "smite the hypocrite—none should be able to keep sin concealed." The warning foreshadowed worse accusations. At their next meeting, Isaac Newton Youngs wrote, "Indications of some soul's being shut out for hidden sins not fit to be spoken in this place—Solemn disclosure! I must be silent. Z.P."[51] Zillah Potter's spirit persona threatened, then tried to justify her actions. The visionist's self-justification was again indicative of human agency. By fending off challenge before it arose, Potter tried to bolster her own spirit persona's credibility with a pre-emptive defense. Youngs was intimidated, himself—never before had he felt he could not fully describe what he saw.

In meeting a few days later, he wrote, "Sally Dean stepped forward asked to speak—but said but little!—went back weeping. One of the inspired sisters instantly fell to the floor, in great distress [and] . . . after this there was a solemn & powerful communication from the holy angel of God, pronouncing wrath, indignation & final separation of sin & the sinner, for the hour was come & the soul of the sinner was rejected with an unalterable curse." The visionist denounced Sally Dean with curses shocking to hear.[52] That was only the start. Bullies isolate and exclude their targets, using intimidation, accusations, and public humiliation, and that is what visionists did to Sally Dean.[53]

Dean confessed nothing. Her weeping was unexplained. After months of intimidation, she may have wept in frustration because her society's leaders allowed visionists to operate through threats and fear, rather than union and love. At age forty-two, Dean had been a good Believer for more than twenty years but was cursed nonetheless. Isaac Newton Youngs wrote, "O what a solemn and distressing scene is this for us to pass thro'." His use of the plural "us" shows that the bullying afflicted the whole family, target and bystanders, as well.[54]

Later Youngs noted that the spirits said Dean could not stay, "tho nothing definite is alleged against her." Typically, when sinners were brought to judgment, they were charged with specific misdeeds.[55] But Sally Dean was not. Even so, she was so mortified that she wanted to die. Giles Avery wrote, she

> made her way for the M[ountain], where she was found . . . by J Dean & Benjamin Gates on a ledge N. east of the little pond. They brot her down and being asked her motive in this doing she confessed that she went with the intention of putting an end to her existence but fearing to do it she called upon the rocks & Mountains to fall upon her & hide her from the face of the Lord. Alas! O! Alas! how awful is such a situation.[56]

Dean was suicidal for good reason. She stood to lose all she held dear. Expulsion meant losing friends, home, livelihood, and support in old age, as well as her path to salvation. When a community member draws identity from the group, expulsion is a sort of dismemberment, and Dean felt that pain.[57] Giles Avery felt sympathy for her—not a typical Shaker response to someone accused of misbehavior, which usually provoked indignation. Nevertheless, the Ministry did not countermand the spirits. Dean was cursed, and she had to go. Her brother took her to live with kin in Rhode Island.[58]

Away from her attackers, Sally Dean quickly regained her emotional equilibrium. She kept her case before the Ministry. By October 22, 1841, Dean was back at New Lebanon, staying at the Trustees' Office as a visitor. On November 4, the Ministry decided to reinstate her. That decision showed their recognition that the expulsion had been an error. They also suspected that more trouble was brewing among the visionists, because the Elders "warned all to be wise and careful [and to] . . . let our words be few and not judge the matter: each one work in his own vineyard & keep the fear of God in all they do & say."[59] Sally Dean moved back into the dwelling.[60]

The visionists—or the spirits—were irate. Miranda Barber, who struggled to control her anger, spoke as the holy Angel of God and defied the Ministry. "I will not hold my peace," she thundered. "I will go forth in my fury, and will rend from before her face the vail of her covering, and she shall appear naked in the eyes of thy people. I will set upon her burning flames of fire, and she shall burn and burn in torment and vexation; —Heaven daring Mortal!" Barber vowed wrath against the "hypocrite, the liar, the vain pretender" and added, "Woe unto her."⁶¹ The Elders had lost control of the visionists.

The next three weeks were remarkably unpleasant. New Lebanon Shaker scribes recorded more than 150 pages of warnings. On November 11, Anna Dodgson joined the campaign to force Sally Dean out. On November 12, Dodgson derided the "Heaven daring mortal that doth yet continue to molest your habitation." She confirmed Dean's exile, saying, "Her spirit cannot blend with the spirits of the clean." Dodgson called everyone to the dwelling's center hall to be warned against doubt and unbelief.⁶²

On November 13, Youngs described "a great commotion among the sisters," which they attributed to "the presence of evil."⁶³ On November 15, Dodgson shared a spirit message about "that wicked woman who is among you." Dodgson said, "It is not meet that the visible Lead and the Elders in Zion should counsel that woman or advise her." The spirit had not come to accuse "that woman" but to reason with her. "But know ye it is not the decree of heaven, that that woman should ever utter with her tongue the abomination that hath cut her off from Zion. But if she still continued to remain in your dwellings to tempt the Lord, at the expiration of 10 days, the cries, lamentations, and wailing of the Holy Angels shall no more cease until her spirit is wearied, and her soul is vexed within her."⁶⁴ Dodgson did not name Dean's "abomination." This tactic may have made others think the worst and served to further isolate Dean. It also prevented the visionists from having to reveal her supposed sin, thus avoiding a rebuttal that might have weakened their position. By setting a deadline for Dean's expulsion, Dodgson effectively gave an ultimatum to the Ministry.

On November 17, Dodgson asked, "How long are ye willing the Holy Temple should be polluted by the steps of the unclean?"⁶⁵ The same day, the spirit of Mother Lucy Wright brought another message about Sally Dean, and the Ministry and Elders gave way. Youngs reported, "It was the revealed will, in union with the Lead, that she remain no longer in this house; but that she be as soon as convenient removed to another house." Accordingly, Dean moved to the Second Order.⁶⁶

That move did not satisfy the spirits. On November 18, Anna Dodgson brought a long message to "S.D." in the presence of the Ministry, Elders,

"J. D." (John Dean), and an unnamed visionist, as well as the scribe, who noted John Dean's and Sally Dean's responses in parentheses, as he recorded Sally Dean's ordeal. Speaking for Mother Lucy's spirit, Dodgson began:

> I have not come to admonish & chastise, neither to accuse, but merely to reason and talk with that Woman. For since she says she is following me, I am commanded by the powers of Heaven above, to speak my own word unto her; and if she has followed me, let her follow me still. Then Mother turning to J.D. said "Br. J.D. Have you come to help me your Mother to bear my heavy scene of tribulation? (Yea, Mother I have.) The Mother said, you need no more feel troubled because you drawed S.D. among Believers, you did but act the part of a brother in so doing. But unite your spirit said Mother, to your visible Lead. . . ."
>
> Mother then spake a few words to her witness, & then said she was ready for S.D. to enter. Then Mother said, "Is it in union with you & by your consent, Dear Ministry & Elders, that I speak a few words to this child, even to S.D. who is before me? (The Lead answered, Mother's will and the will of Heaven be done.)
>
> Mother proceeded, "S.D. child, do you really believe I am the Mother whom you have loved? (Answer, Yea Mother) Do you desire to hear the word which I . . . have to speak to you at this time? (Yea) Did you child follow me from Providence to Lebanon a few weeks ago? (I thot Mother told me to come home.) Will you follow me yet again? (Yea, I will go wherever Mother leads me.) Will you hear, receive, and withal obey the word of heaven. . . . (Yea I will always obey Mother's word to the laying down of my life.)"

Dodgson said that Mother Lucy Wright's spirit had come to advise Sally Dean on "the easiest and surest steps" she should take—and also to warn her of the wrath of God if she did not. Dean answered, "I do not care what comes upon me. I will bear it if I can only live here." Dodgson's response was to point out that Dean's union with Believers was already "separated and cut off," forever. If she walked in obedience, however, God would show her mercy. She continued:

> I accuse you of nothing; I do not say you are guilty of any crime under Heaven. But if you are innocent, pure & holy . . . you will have within your own soul that peace and consolation which men nor devils can ever take away nor hinder; let the dwelling place of your body be where it may, the peace of your spirit will never be disturbed. And if heaven

hath separated you from Zion, why child will you still continue to afflict those who yet are suffered to remain within Zion's walls?"

Dodgson then asked Dean to signify that she would obey the word of Heaven and said, "If you will, seal the same with seven bows in presence of the leaders of Israel & rap each time as you bow." The scribe added, "After some word passed between her and J.D. and the Ministry & Elders, she complied tho' reluctantly."

Dodgson continued her message: "Surely said Mother . . . the best counsel I can give you and the greatest mercy I can show you is that if you followed me from Providence to Lebanon, you should again follow me from Lebanon to Providence." Because God had already separated Dean from Believers, she could never again live within their walls. The Lead agreed, and John Dean united with them in asking Sally to obey. Sally Dean, however, "protested her innocence, & said she knew not for what she was cut off from Zion." No one else seemed to know why, either, but the spirits had spoken.

Dodgson pressed Sally Dean further: "But again said Mother, will you follow me, where I will lead you?" Dean replied, "Yea, Mother; but I cannot bear to go among the world, just suffer me to die in this street, it is all I ask." The answer nettled Dodgson, because she retorted, "I have not said anything to you about going to the world; and as for dying in the street, Heaven will not suffer it. But as for dwelling in Zion, you have no home here, & by returning back in disobedience, you have committed by far the greatest sin you ever committed in your life and have thereby cut yourself off from any union." If Dean would obey, Mother Lucy's spirit would accompany her to Providence and see her settled there—but would Sally obey? Dean reiterated, "Yea Mother but I can't bear to go to the world." Dodgson, increasingly exasperated at Dean's intransigence, answered:

> I have not said anything to you about going to the world. You may keep your faith; the laws and orders of Zion you know; you may walk the path and sound forth the songs of Zion. And if the world ask why you are there, you may tell them that you come in obedience to the command of Heaven to you and that is enough. And if you ever come to want, & circumstances deprive you of a home, then you may write to Zion; but one side of this, do not put your hand forth to write one word to come within her walls.

Dodgson continued to press Dean to signify her acceptance of exile: "Now if you will obey my word and follow me . . . you may bow yourself low and say, O Holy Anointed ye Leaders in Israel, will ye once more show mercy, charity and Loving kindness to me and safely conduct me to my destined abode?" "After considerable hesitation," the scribe added, "she said this by Mother's saying a few words at a time, and she repeated them after her." Dodgson tried to get Dean to repeat a second sentence, humbling herself to God's will, but she balked. Dodgson concluded the ordeal by telling Dean to make ready for her journey.[67] Significantly, though Ministry and Elders were present, they remained silent. Dodgson orchestrated Dean's humiliation.

Dean, however, remained stubbornly in place. She evidently did not accept a visionist's authority to expel her, and neither the Ministry nor Elders sent her away. Their failure to act immediately on Dodgson's message suggests that they were dubious.

The spirits went on a rampage. On November 23, Miranda Barber delivered a midnight message. Her spirit persona, she said, threatened to "sharpen my sword & send it among you [to] cut and slash you into atoms." She raged, "I will seek for your destruction. . . . I will curse your stock and herds; . . . your beautiful fields & pastures shall become as barren deserts; and your joy and mirth shall be gone. In all my devices I will contrive against you, and will be comforted in your afflictions."[68] Barber ordered the family to fall prostrate before her and kiss the dust—and they did. She mandated a day of fasting on bread and water, to cleanse away their sins. The Church Family spent the day in lamentation, with many wailing, prostrate in the dwelling's hallways. They roared out prayers of supplication until the instrument proclaimed, "I delight not in the distress of any souls—had ye taken warning when I called to you, this need not have been. Signified we must learn, & keep humble."[69] Miranda Barber, designated voice of Holy Mother Wisdom, also provided good recommendations for other instruments, which again suggests collaboration. Barber's recommendations, like Potter's and Fairbanks's self-justification, indicate human agency.[70]

Dodgson's deadline for expulsion passed, and the spirits remained agitated. One visionist warned of "a hidden abomination" and threatened to curse them.[71] On November 28, Semantha Fairbanks tried to reduce the conflict. Speaking as Mother Ann Lee, she told the female instruments to "confess every wicked and mean trick you ever did in your life."[72] She may have recognized just those sins among her peers, and perhaps she thought they had gone too far. On November 29, two visionists returned to the issue of Sally Dean. One delivered a message about "that certain object of God's displeasure," while another exhorted, "Behold what is past is forgiven you, if you will keep humble and low."[73] One threatened; another forgave.

Hannah Agnew prayed aloud for God to spare not the chastening rod; all deserved punishment.[74]

On November 29, a scribe wrote, "We hear some reading in relation to Sally Dean. The First Order singing a song of cursing around the 2d House."[75] The visionists had pursued Dean down the road. The situation was untenable, for Dean, as well as for the Second Order Believers who had given her sanctuary. Finally, Dean gave up. The visionists would not let her be. She returned to Rhode Island.[76]

The Church Family did not heave a sigh of relief when Dean departed. Holy Mother Wisdom stayed at New Lebanon through December, demanding "peculiar scenes" of humiliation, repentance, and cleansing, bread and water meals, and individual interviews with all adult Believers. Though Dean was gone, she was still very much on Believers' minds; Youngs wrote in his yearend review, "The singular case of Sally Dean has caused much labor & heavy tribulation this year, and we know not when it will end."[77] He suspected that it was not over yet, and he was right. Twice ejected, Dean should have been gone for good, but she continued to seek reinstatement, visiting several times in 1842 and 1843.[78] By maintaining contact, she probably discomfited the visionists who ousted her.

There the situation stood for more than a decade. By 1857, circumstances had changed, and Dean's exile ended. The Ministry was new, and so were the First Order's Elders. The other visionists remained in the New Lebanon Church Family, but the turnover in leadership broke the stalemate against Dean. The new Ministry decided she could return, a tacit admission of their predecessors' error. When the Elders announced the reinstatement, Polly Reed wrote:

> And alas, what a conflagration it kindled. We were positively told that there was not money enough in the Church to bear our expenses [to bring her back]; & then to have both of the Elder Sisters gone at once & the Ministry at Watervliet was considered very imprudent indeed. And another thing it had fallen to my lot to be gone considerable of the summer past, while it was the privilege of others more worthy than myself to stay at home & do the hard work.[79]

The financial objection was surely made by a deaconess.[80] The other objection implied that things had gotten out of hand earlier when the society's leaders were absent. The tirade degenerated into a personal attack on Polly Reed, Dean's advocate. Sixteen years after visionists ousted her, they (or their supporters) could not accept the Ministry's implied rebuke in allowing her return. Finally the Ministry compromised. Dean would not live at New Lebanon; she would start fresh at Watervliet.[81] And so she did.

In 1868, however, Sally Dean finally returned to New Lebanon "to finish her days in her former home."[82] Despite poor health, she outlived two of her younger tormenters.[83] And she evidently won over another. In 1874, Anna Dodgson wrote, "Watching with Mother Sarah D. discontinued. She appearing some better." The statement was significant: one of the visionists who had expelled Sally Dean in 1841 gave her the honorific title of "Mother." Dodgson must have enjoyed the older woman's company, because in another entry, she wrote, "Sarah D!! and writer go south Blackberrying!!! Lucky." She later called Dean "our beloved sister," a term of endearment she rarely used.[84] Sally Dean finally received a long-withheld portion of Shaker love.

Several conclusions can be drawn from these exiles' stories. Perhaps the most important is that by readmitting Sally Dean to the society, the new Ministry indicated that her expulsion might have been unjust. When the dynamic tension between gift and order lost its balance during the Era of Manifestations, unfettered instruments victimized some Believers, and frightened others—and not only at New Lebanon. Having validated spirit communications as gifts from God, and having accepted the exile of others farther away, how could the Ministry reject the spirits' expulsion of members from their home village? Perhaps they could not. The society had changed since the early days when some Shaker villages maintained an order just for backsliders. That historical forgiveness ended when Ministry Eldress Ruth Landon said, "A scabby sheep affects the whole flock."[85]

Moreover, the Ministry did not temper visionists' messages with common sense. Other religious traditions, such as Mormonism, have a vetting process for revelations, to apply the society's collective wisdom before instituting changes that revelation suggests.[86] In theory, the Shakers had such a process, but visionists outmaneuvered the 1840 Ministry (Ebenezer Bishop, Rufus Bishop, Ruth Landon, and Asenath Clark). The younger generation, including the 1857 Ministry (Amos Stewart, Daniel Boler, Betsy Bates and Eliza Ann Taylor), realized things had gone awry in 1841.[87] Elder Giles Avery wrote in 1880 that visionists were subject to the same negative aspects of human nature as everyone else. "If mediums are governed by prejudice, hatred, jealousy or any evil emotion, their gifts will be tinctured accordingly; and of course in a like degree be unreliable and false." Their reproofs therefore "bring great burden and trouble and injustice on the subjects of their manifestations."[88] He may have been thinking of Olive Gates and Sally Dean when he wrote those words.

Believers learned from their errors. In 1853, to their credit, Shakers published twelve tests for distinguishing between valid and spurious spirit messages. One of those tests is useful in Sally Dean's case. Frederick Evans wrote that warriors cannot be Christ's servants, regardless of what they profess, because Jesus repudiated war and bloodshed with "Blessed are the peacemakers, for they shall be called the children of God."[89] According to that standard, Miranda Barber's threats to set Dean on fire or slash her peers with a sword was not divinely inspired. The Ministry finally recognized that some visionists were suspect. Henry Blinn's later comments about the "unsubdued nature" of certain instruments showed their belated understanding.[90] Half a century after the Shakers developed their tests, psychologists and anthropologists began studying such manifestations of spirituality, but none of these scholars has yet devised a way to tell whether those who deliver spirit messages are possessed, or by whom or what.[91] In establishing their own tests of divine inspiration, the Shakers were ahead of the scholars in empirical understanding of inspired instruments, as well as in belief.

Ironically, Shakers recognized the problem of unsubstantiated allegations. Several of their poems, such as "The Tale Bearer," address the issue of Believers who would lie and, when caught, seek revenge.[92] Calvin Green, himself a target, wrote: "I've had many a serious tho't / Upon a slanderous tongue. / How many evils it hath bro't / Upon both old and young."[93] Anyone could slander, but women were the ones who expelled their peers. Frederick Evans commented years later, "Females need to be steadied, some."[94] As a male leader in a society with a female majority, he had keen insight into the ways some women operate in groups.

Even so, these expulsions raise more questions than they answer. Were they an exercise in power? Or a sort of religious performance art, where a few instruments tried to top their predecessors? Why did the visionists attack? Did they begin with a particular goal? Perhaps the most benign explanation is that visionists got carried away with their enthusiasm. Ruling other Believers, if only in meeting, was a heady experience, a temptation that some could not resist. When they realized that their excesses provoked doubt, perhaps they sought to consolidate their power by eliminating skeptics who might undermine their authority. After issuing warnings, they may have felt they had to expel someone and looked for an appropriate target. When Gates and Dean stepped out of the ranks in meeting, they became targets of opportunity. Perhaps anyone who moved forward at those times would have been expelled.

Scholars offer insights that can be used to set the Shaker experience into the larger context of spirit possession. According to Rodney Stark, spiritual revelations tend to occur in cultures with traditions of communication with the divine. Those who receive such revelations typically have a supportive role model who has already had revelations.[95] That certainly was true of the Shakers. Moreover, the spirits could be useful in practical ways. Judith T. Irvine addresses the societal functions of possession, especially as a means of protest.[96] Lawrence Foster points out that such phenomena can be used to challenge the status quo, and that, too, was true of the Shakers.[97]

Among the Shakers, spirit messages were often shared during family worship held at a predetermined time and place. The fact that many messages were scheduled, approved, and orchestrated suggests that they were voluntary and thus under the instruments' conscious control. Moreover, some visionists' messages reveal hidden motives that suggest they used spirit messages to promote specific changes. Philemon Stewart's first message, for instance, took the Elders to task for lax village maintenance.[98] And a Canaan sister's memoir said that by 1841, "the lazy roughs that had graced the family had nearly all got scorched and cleared out."[99] Canaan's spirit messages (probably delivered by sisters) proved effective in purging sluggards. In a society that generally eschewed open conflict, spirit gifts offered solutions to such problems.

Psychologists and anthropologists have a longstanding debate about whether spirit possession is evidence of mental illness. The problem is that when they viewed all possession as psychopathology, they overlooked some religions' normative possession practices and could not account for cultural variance.[100] The anthropologist Morton Klass compared what anthropologists call "spirit possession" with what psychologists call "dissociative identity disorder" and found psychopathology an unsatisfactory explanation. He credited community members with knowing who is mentally disturbed. He also wrote that spirit possession can be central to a religious culture. Within a particular belief system, members are aware of the difference between spirit possession and psychopathology. They seek help or treatment for those who are mentally ill, not for visionists.[101] The same was true of the Shakers; they knew the difference between derangement and inspiration. However, their leaders did not immediately recognize the possibility of malice or ambition.

The abuse of spirit messages reveals a fundamental weakness in Shakers' political structure: they had no approved way to satisfy ambition without being devious or manipulative.[102] Ambition is a worldly weakness, and self-promotion the antithesis of basic Shaker values such as humility and union. Nonetheless, according to Edward Alpers, people use spirit possession to manipulate their cosmology, force others to conform to their views, and evade the consequences.[103] Certainly that was true of New Lebanon visionists in 1840 and 1841. Anthropologists recognize spirit possession as a path to power.[104] The spirits undoubtedly gave the Potter sisters, Dodgson, and Barber authority that they otherwise lacked. Even a deaconess such as Fairbanks, already near the top of the village hierarchy, might use spirit gifts for her own purposes. She was eventually promoted to the Ministry. After such a promotion, Sally Promey points out, visionists "generally ceased to function as instruments."[105] That cessation of spirit gifts suggests that the former instrument's need for them had also ended—perhaps because a goal had been reached. Ambition can be powerful motivation, especially in a society lacking alternatives for self-promotion.

The requirement that they act with humility may have been more of a cross than some Shaker women could bear; perhaps a few of them gathered in cliques to satisfy frustrated ambition.[106] The five visionists, none having much family within their village, appear to have worked together in a shared enterprise, using criticism, ostracism, and public ridicule, just as bullies do. Their spirit messages eliminated two sisters who might have undermined their authority: Olive Gates, who confessed her doubt about the phenomena, and Sally Dean, who confessed no wrongdoing and adroitly resisted being maneuvered into doing so. She, however, had already used a spirit gift to combat an attack on Calvin Green. Other visionists may have wanted to neutralize her threat to their authority.

Another possibility is that a toxic clique exercised power just because they could. Bullying among women and girls is often expressed by exclusion from the group—and what is expulsion if not exclusion? Ostracism may be the most damaging psychological wound that female bullies inflict. The social aspect of spirit possession reveals that it is a group dynamic, just as bullying is. In this case study, the visionists depended on the acquiescence of the group, as bullies do. By that logic, we might expect that when the phenomena (or the visionists) became too frightening, group support would drop. Hints of dismay cropped up in Fairbanks's demand for visionists to confess their dirty tricks and Agnew's message about the chastening rod, just before Dean's second departure. They thought that some visionists had gone too far.

In Sally Dean's case, inspiration may have been misused by all-too-human instruments. With access to a source of power, someone will take advantage of it. The Shaker theologian Seth Youngs Wells might have agreed. In November 1842, he criticized the inconsistencies in spirit messages. Some messages clashed; others did not agree with Shaker doctrine. "We ought not to reject the wheat because of the chaff," he wrote, "but the chaff must be separated from the wheat." At Harvard, the effect of Wells's message was immediate; inspired communications "virtually ceased."[107]

When social support drops, spirit gifts should dwindle or be replaced with less threatening forms of expression—which seems to be what happened at New Lebanon. Isaac Newton Youngs described slackening inspiration from 1842 to 1856, with little to report after 1843. Some Believers recognized the difference between purging the faithless and harrowing the faithful and tried to counteract the latter. Polly Reed's heart-shaped spirit drawings, for instance, "beautifully written over with words of blessing," may have been her effort in 1844 to reassure persisting First Order Believers that the spirits loved them, despite other visionists' threats and curses.[108] She and Sarah Bates created many tokens of approbation for adult Believers from 1845 to 1854.[109] Perhaps the beautiful spirit drawings penned, painted, and drawn after 1842 were a positive response to the negative messages of 1840 and 1841, an effort for reconciliation. At the same time, spontaneous gifts of the spirit dwindled. By 1845, Isaac Newton Youngs wrote, "The gift and degree of devotion in meeting depended more upon our own voluntary exertions than upon the aid of the communications from the spirits."[110]

This critique should not be interpreted as an indictment of religious inspiration. The Harvard visionist Eunice Bathrick claimed that spirit messages that were not "true" in a literal or factual sense were nonetheless valid interpretations of the Shaker spirit world.[111] She did not witness the New Lebanon visionists' attacks but may well have understood that all believers, including Shakers, must separate spiritual wheat from chaff, just as the Israelites did. Moses' followers may have wondered whether he actually heard the voice of God, or whether the commandments came from his own imagination. Ann Lee was spiritually inspired, as well, and like Moses, was a brilliant manipulator. On one hand, Anna Dodgson may have followed that tradition in relaying messages from a spirit voice that no one else heard. On the other hand, she may have taken the initiative to resolve a conflict, reduce party spirit, and restore union when the village leaders failed to do so. In either case, hers was an inspired performance that showed the spiritual leadership of rank and file Shaker sisters—another benefit of equality of the sexes. We cannot know for sure what actually occurred, but we can judge the results. Revelation, whether it originates within the human imagination or is sent from the heavenly sphere, can be a source of faith, hope, and religious revitalization—as it was for many Shakers, though not for Olive Gates or Sally Dean.

10

The New Lebanon Deaconesses' Bonnet Business, 1835–1850

The females make fancy goods in a superior style of taste and elegance.

SOME SCHOLARS ASSERT THAT SHAKER DEACONESSES WERE "little concerned" with financial matters until late in the nineteenth century.[1] Shaker records, however, tell a different story. In a 1794 list of New Lebanon's first male and female Office Trustees, for instance, Rhoda Hammond was labeled the "Principal" trustee.[2] This is not to suggest that the sisters held financial power in every Shaker enclave. At the North Family, Antoinette Doolittle received the Ministry's permission for the sisters to retain control of their own earnings in 1850—and the sisters "acquired a competence" by thrift and careful management.[3] As we have already seen, the brethren's most lucrative businesses were founded on women's labor, but Shaker sisters had businesses of their own, as well. Living up to the ideal of Proverbs 31, the deaconesses sold goods, earned money, and managed their households. They did not fit the nineteenth-century stereotype of dependent, passive, and domestic middle-class women.[4] Instead, they were entrepreneurs, merchants, and innkeepers. Deaconesses met the public, marketed their products, and traded with merchants throughout the Northeast. Their diversion of sisters' domestic labor into the business of making bonnets for sale shows that they were vitally concerned about their society's finances and we can document their pursuit of profits beginning in the early nineteenth century. Shaker society produced shrewd businesswomen as well as businessmen.

Shakers recognized that women and men were equal partners in their communal society, and they structured their roles accordingly. Deaconesses' jobs resembled deacons' in managing temporal affairs. As Sister Aurelia Mace explained, "Where there is a Deacon, there is also a Deaconess, and they are considered equal in their powers of government."[5] Outsiders also recognized deaconesses' authority. In 1832, Carl David Arfwedsen, a visitor, reported, "The common fund is administered by a few select brethren and sisters, who account for every thing in a regular way."[6] Deaconesses' journals and account books show the extent of their management.[7]

Deaconesses met visitors at the Trustees' Office, sold goods from the store, and provided meals and overnight lodging.[8] Most deaconesses were outgoing, friendly, and helpful. And according to visitors' reports, some also were attractive. An 1860 visitor said of "Sister Rachel," perhaps Rachel Sampson, age fifty-seven, who worked at New Lebanon's Office, "The latter has been pretty."[9] Nathaniel S. Shaler, a visitor at the neighboring Shaker village in Hancock, Massachusetts, wrote: "At the communal store there was a buxom, pretty . . . happy woman, seemingly busy with a thousand things, and without one trace of care. She showed us the sleeping-rooms of the 'sisters,' which were miracles of neatness and taste . . . [and] sold us with skill all and more than we wanted from the store."[10] Another visitor, James Silk Buckingham, complimented a Watervliet deaconess's "cheerful and smiling countenance."[11] A disorderly Shaker brother also commented on the deaconesses' looks. When Semantha Fairbanks, Olive Brown, and Sarah Ann Lewis relocated from the Church Family dwelling to the Office, Aaron Bill lamented the absence of their "pretty faces."[12] In each of those villages, Shakers met the world with attractive, friendly women, who marketed their goods along with Shakerism.[13]

Deaconesses were good businesswomen who sold home manufactures as early as 1813.[14] By 1820, the New Lebanon sisters ran a store selling, among other things, "many articles in wicker-work, made very neatly by the women."[15] The village built the Trustees' Office and store in 1827.[16] Deaconesses staffed the Office and organized the sisters' production of merchandise for sale. By 1839, shop goods in the Hancock Shaker store were valued at more than two thousand dollars.[17]

Deaconesses' jobs were structured around temporal labor, but the women's duties were, as one Shaker brother put it, "easier understood than expressed."[18] Even the most astute brethren did not fully understand what deaconesses did. Family deaconesses managed the supply of food, textiles, and women's labor.[19] They scheduled sisters' work rotations in kitchen, laundry, and seasonal manufacturing jobs. They assigned sisters to work in the brethren's businesses, picking, processing, and packaging herbs and seeds for sale or weaving tape for chairs. In the New Lebanon First Order alone, feeding and clothing a family of more than a hundred and producing goods for sale meant organizing the workdays of sixty women, setting priorities, and assessing costs.

Like other shrewd Yankee farm women, deaconesses sometimes added new responsibilities to their jobs. For instance, they diversified their goods to include dozens of salable items that bolstered village profits. In 1830, a visitor listed the New Lebanon sisters' store goods: brushes, baskets, feather fans, brooms, reticules and bags, and domestic utensils. In 1835, another visitor, Andrew Bell, noted that most of the store's merchandise was sisters' handiwork. Harriet Martineau elaborated on their "simples": linen-drapery, knitwear, sieves, baskets, boxes, confectionery, palm and feather fans, and pin-cushions. "All of these may be had in some variety," she wrote, "and of the best quality."[20] That year, sisters made sixty fans, sixty brushes with feathers, fifteen pairs of thread gloves, thirty-four pairs of yarn footings, fifteen pairs of small mittens, and thirty pairs of small stockings. They sold silk-lined baskets and emery balls as early as 1832.[21] By 1842, they marketed many products in addition to fancy goods and palm leaf bonnets: "baskets, stockings, shirtings, gloves, shoes, butter, cheese, hams, garden and vegetable seeds of all kinds, cabinet ware, and worsted jackets, &c." A visitor was impressed by their display of goods, "all in exact order, and showing a neatness and arrangement that would shame a first-rate Bond Street milliner."[22]

Among the world's people, women's household manufactures were big business in the nineteenth century, but men rarely recognized the value of women's work. Because so much of women's artisanal production was done in the home, men dismissed it as unimportant. In the 1820s, for instance, a Massachusetts politician mentioned that straw products were made by young unmarried women "whose labor is not generally productive."[23] When Louis McLane surveyed U.S. manufacturers in 1832, male respondents described women's home manufactures as "trifling" or "inconsiderable." One respondent, a textile manufacturer, noted, "Comparatively nothing is done in the household manufactory; a female can now earn more cloth in a day than she could make in a household way in a week." He recognized women's traditional work of spinning and weaving but was oblivious to their other economic contributions. A few respondents, however, acknowledged that women made and sold more than cloth. In particular, they cited straw braid and straw bonnets made for the market.[24] Most men overlooked this "petti-coat economy" much the same way that they overlooked their wives' butter and egg money—until a fiscal crisis required it.

Bonnets, however, were a lucrative business because millinery was a fact of life for nineteenth-century women. A hat or bonnet protected a woman's skin when she went outdoors. The brim shaded her face and eyes and kept her head warm and her hair dry.[25] Head covering went beyond practicality; as we have seen, it was also an emblem of modesty, and Ann Lee taught her followers to uphold that standard.[26] In the nineteenth-century United States, bareheadedness at worship could provoke accusations of impiety.[27]

Ironically, worldly women adjusted the doctrine of modesty to show off; they made their Sabbath headgear into prideful display. The custom was so common that newspapers derided women for attending church just to show off their new bonnets. One editor wrote in 1872, "The fall styles having appeared, the gospel now reaches a larger number than usual."[28] Illustrations of Shaker Sabbath show worldly visitors in fancy bonnets.

Ann Lee's views on simplicity meant that sisters were not allowed to trim their bonnets. Echoing Isaiah 2:20, Mother Ann told her followers to "let all such things go to the moles and bats of the earth." Shakers enforced plainness, believing that "lust of the eye," a phrase drawn from 1 John 2:16, was worldly, not divine. "Articles which were forbidden, or thought not proper," included, "No frills on our bunnetts" and "No silk strings on every day bonnets."[29] The rules suggest that some sisters tried to embellish their bonnets, but a Shaker sister's plain bonnet promoted union in a society where everyone was supposed to have the same status.

The popularity of worldly women's expensive Italian Leghorn bonnets led to a new industry: palm leaf bonnets. It began with worldly women's fabrication of bonnets made from domestic straw in 1819 and grew into a home industry in Worcester County, Massachusetts, where women made hat braid in the 1820s.[30] Wholesalers imported palm leaves from the Caribbean for storekeepers to sell to local customers, who returned finished products for credit on their accounts. By 1837, about forty thousand rural New England women and children were braiding palm leaf for hats and bonnets.[31] This outwork gave them the opportunity to earn money or store credit.[32]

Because that cottage industry began near the Harvard and Shirley Shaker villages, those sisters may have been the first Believers to make palm leaf bonnets. By 1828, Sally Loomis had mastered the skill; she taught the Shirley sisters how to weave palm leaf for hats and may have passed the technique on to sisters farther west, as well.[33] At New Lebanon's Second Order, Rhoda

Blake was proficient enough by 1829 to teach Watervliet sisters how to braid palm leaf. Blake, a weaver, may have combined her areas of expertise to weave palm leaf for bonnets, as well.[34] At New Lebanon's First Order, "Betsy Crosman made a wove palm leaf hat for the first one," Semantha Fairbanks wrote in 1835.[35] When Shaker sisters wove palm leaf for the large parts of a bonnet (rather than braiding the strips of leaf, then coiling and sewing the braid into shape), they speeded up production and produced a more standardized and lighter-weight bonnet, as well.

In 1833, New Lebanon Eldress Betsy Bates mentioned that Hancock Eldress Rebecca Clark had given her a palm leaf bonnet.[36] Shaker women, however, did not yet wear palm leaf bonnets to meeting. Sisters had worn uniform bonnets since 1808; the first were made of pasteboard covered with black or gray silk.[37] In August 1835, the New Lebanon sisters continued to wear their older bonnets to meeting; Andrew Bell wrote, "Their head pieces were of a shape like that of our coal scoops, with retrenched handles, the material they were made of was apparently some cheap cotton fabric and its colour a slaty grey."[38] The New Lebanon sisters made more than two thousand palm leaf bonnets for sale that year, but either they did not wear such bonnets or they covered their palm leaf inside and out with gray fabric, an unlikely treatment for a summer bonnet. By 1837, however, the sisters had the new style; another visitor mentioned the New Lebanon sisters' plain straw bonnets. The "straw" was probably palm leaf.[39]

A Shaker bonnet was designed to promote chastity. It could be as much as thirteen inches long, front to back.[40] The bonnet directed attention straight ahead, in both the physical and the metaphorical sense; a sister would not be distracted from the straight and narrow path to salvation if she could not see out the sides of her bonnet. Nor could she cast flirtatious sidelong glances at men. Some Shaker bonnets were so deep that stealing a kiss would have been awkward, perhaps impossible.

Those bonnets were popular, however, with the New England farmers' daughters who became mill operatives. They came to town with country ways, including a shawl pinned under the chin for a head covering. A more citified operative wrote, "But after the first pay-day a 'shaker' (or 'scooter') sunbonnet usually replaced the primitive head-gear of their rural life."[41] The Shaker-style bonnet was fashionable among working-class mill girls with money to spend, and the rise of New England's textile industry increased the demand. Despite its restrictiveness, the Shaker bonnet became an object of worldly women's desire. Thus the feminine public's lust for fashionable bonnets created a business opportunity for Shaker sisters.

Shakers' earliest production of bonnets resembled the pattern of other rural women who did outwork, working in their "spare" time to earn money without neglecting other responsibilities. When the Shakers' bonnet business expanded, however, it absorbed massive amounts of sisters' labor. The journal of a Watervliet sister, perhaps Polly Vedder, records how the bonnet trade grew from a part-time, occasional occupation into a full-time job. In the fall of 1830, the Watervliet sister braided 2 palm leaf hats. In 1832, she produced 11 more. In 1833, she assisted in weaving 33 palm leaf bonnets, an indication that construction was evolving from braiding to weaving. Then the numbers spiked; in 1834, she made 283 bonnets: 17 for home use, the rest for sale. Four sisters together made 424. By June 1835, the Watervliet woman was teaching sisters at other families how to make bonnets. By March 1836, the job had expanded so much that it interfered with her duties as junior Eldress. On July 18, 1836, she noted that the senior Eldress "thinks it is best for me to give up the burden of the bonnets to Lucy Fairchild & Elizabeth Sealey, & even so I will do." She cut back but continued to work on bonnets. She and the other women made 1,606 bonnets to sell that year.[42]

New Lebanon's First Order also had a thriving bonnet business in 1835. Deaconess Semantha Fairbanks noted more than 160 bonnets finished in May and July, when worldly women needed summer bonnets. Their manufacturing cycles ranged from two weeks to two months and the number of bonnets per delivery varied from 7 to 87. The First Order sisters made 500 palm leaf bonnets for sale that year.[43] The even number suggests that they set a production goal and met it by working when hands were available.

Their "manufactory" ran through the winter. In mid-December 1835. Fairbanks wrote, "Mercury 8 degrees below cypher. The sisters stay in as before mentioned, excepting the bonnet makers." Eldress Annie Williams made a similar notation about the Second Order.[44] They must have felt pressure to work every daylight minute because they braved the cold and built additional fires to heat another workplace in subzero weather. Perhaps they had advance orders for the spring trade. Sisters may have appreciated the distraction in midwinter. Making goods for sale alleviated cabin fever and promoted union in the coldest, darkest months.

The Second Order's production cycle went unrecorded, but at the end of 1835, Eldress Annie Williams estimated that they had made 1,811 bonnets—almost four times the First Order's production, even though the Second Order had fewer than half as many sisters.[45] The Second Order's huge production suggests high levels of competence and efficiency—and perhaps competition with the First Order. The New Lebanon bonnet business may have begun there under Rhoda Blake's tutelage.[46]

Bonnets were a valuable addition to Shaker industries, so much so that the New Lebanon Church Family reallocated resources to expand their bonnet business. On March 1, 1836, deaconess Semantha Fairbanks wrote, "The Ministry, Elders, Deaconesses both at the office and family together with Zipporah [Cory] & Betsy C[rosman] meet together in Deaconesses room, and have some conversation on making bonnets & buying our cloth for frocks and trowsers, gowns, aprons &c &c. We all agree not to have any clothes made this year only for present necessity." Zipporah Cory was the senior deaconess in the Second Order, an indication that the two orders were collaborating. Rhoda Blake and Betsy Crosman were probably their resident experts. The deaconesses' room must have been thick with discussion as fourteen Believers worked toward consensus. Their reason for investing in a new trade at that time was "so that we can make bonnets while they are readily mar[ketable]."[47] The deaconesses recognized that worldly styles were short-lived. Years earlier, Lucy Wright had pointed out that the "vain fashions of the world" ran from one extreme to another and suggested that interest in such things was a loss to the people of God.[48] The Shakers, however, had increased their dealings with the world's people, and the deaconesses seized the opportunity to turn worldly fashion to Believers' profit.

To have enough hands, however, they had to divert needleworkers and weavers to bonnet making, which meant that the sisters had to forgo unnecessary new garments and purchase cloth rather than weaving their own. The issue of sacrificing clothing, however, was ticklish one that required a careful approach. Junior deaconess Semantha Fairbanks accompanied senior deaconess Lydia Matthewson in visiting all the sisters' rooms, one at a time, to lobby for support for the new plan.[49] By approaching sisters in small groups, they reduced the possibility that opposition would derail their plan before they gained support. Evidently they convinced the sisters that sacrificing new clothing for a bonnet business was worthwhile.

The First Order bonnet makers forged ahead. In March 1836, twelve days after deciding to expand their millinery trade, Fairbanks reported, "75 bonnets made this week." The increase in personnel immediately upped the numbers of bonnets made. As soon as the boys' winter school ended, the basket and bonnet makers converted the schoolhouse into a shop. Bonnets proliferated through March. The sisters rolled through the palm leaf. Hannah Reed wove 14 bonnets in one day. In one week, the First Order sisters made 142 bonnets. By the end of the month, they had carried 250 bonnets to the office for sale, then in April they finished 300 more and in May, 330.[50]

In June, Betsy Bates gave each of the Ministry sisters a palm leaf bonnet, a politic move. In December 1836, Fairbanks noted that they had intended to make 2,000 bonnets but they surpassed their goal with 2,174 bonnets sold.[51] New Lebanon deaconesses paid $463 for supplies, including palm leaves, gingham, cambric, silk, ribbon, bonnet wire, velvet and emery (which suggests that their bonnet accounts included materials for other sale items, as well).[52] From April through November 1836, their total income from bonnets was $1,742.14.[53] The New Lebanon bonnet business was a going concern.

In addition to the deaconesses' astute business sense, their new enterprise required many competent hands. Each bonnet maker had qualities of the worldly milliner. She was an accomplished needlewoman, with all the skills and attributes required. She could sew quickly, neatly, and invisibly, hiding knots and stitches so they would not show on the outside of the finished product. She could not just "nail the material on," with the novice's heavy hand and large stitches; she had to have a light touch. She had to be patient and persistent to get the design right if it went awry. The women who made silk capes or linings had to have dry hands; sweaty palms could ruin fine silk. The bonnet maker also had to be neat, clean, and well-organized so her materials were not so "tumbled and crushed" that they were ruined; she had to be thrifty.[54] Shaker bonnet makers followed the same tradition of perfectionism and were probably as competent and meticulous as the cap maker Thankful Goodrich, who had once been chided by Mother Lucy Wright for her unseemly pride in her work.[55]

The bonnet business also required a good organization. Bonnet makers had to work well together because workdays were long and the manufacturing pace was brisk. Deaconesses must have recruited sisters with essential skills, but the division of labor could have caused dissension. Rhoda Blake later recalled that her years as a deaconess included "unusual afflictions." On occasion, for instance, the deaconesses had to divert the best needle-workers from other jobs into bonnet making. In May 1836, Semantha Fairbanks wrote, "Polly Reed and Mary Wicks comes out of the kitchen for this purpose. Jane Smith & Mariah Lapsley work in the kitchen in their stead."[56] Reed, a tailoress, was a highly skilled needlewoman whose meticulous attention to detail was an asset to the bonnet business. Smith and Lapsley, who took Reed's and Wicks's places in the kitchen, probably did not have bonnet-making skills, but that does not mean that they relished an extra tour of kitchen work. The bonnet business tended to separate sisters into two classes, a possible source of tension in a society that valued equality and union. Profits, however, took precedence, and Believers had to humble themselves to the needs of their communal society.

Until they reached their production goals, Shaker bonnet makers were as busy as worldly milliners. "All hands are engaged making bonnets," Fairbanks wrote, "even myself." Their urgency about the spring trade resulted in a prodigious effort. In only twelve days, the First Order sisters finished 250 bonnets—half the number they had made in 1835.[57] The Second Order also accelerated their work. In early May, Eldress Annie Williams wrote, "We sisters start a bonnet bee." In eight days, they made 210 bonnets.[58] On December 31, 1836, Williams reported, "The bonnets made at this house amounted to 2000 and 60 and the number made at the S H 1200." During bees, they averaged 43 bonnets a day.[59]

As in a worldly millinery workroom, every woman had her assigned place. The business had a clear hierarchy. The deaconess who acted as forewoman directed the work, provided instruction, and monitored the quality of the bonnets. Before apprentices learned the trade, she may have been the only one with all the skills to make a bonnet from start to finish. Beginners in the bonnet shop started with simple tasks and, gradually, as they learned more advanced skills, progressed from helper to apprentice to journeywoman or bonnet maker. In March 1836, Isaac Newton Youngs listed the many tasks.

> The sisters have this week performed, as I may say, wonders at making Bonnets. They have wove 120, and did the sewing to 142! Betsy Crosman made 28, Jane Blanchard 28, & Tabitha Lapsley 14 to the binding. Dolly Chauncey 18, Rachel Sampson 27, & Mary Wicks 27 to the Cape. Betsy Bates & Sarah Fairchild put the capes to 92, Hannah Ann Treadway 41, & Lucy Clark, 9. Molly Smith wove 17, [Olive] Brown 4, Maryann [Mantle] 17, Hannah [Reed] 40, Elizaette [Bates] 40 & Hortency [Lockwood] 3 = 121 in all. Olive Gates wove binding all the week & Rhoda [Wilson] all but one day. Abigail [Hathaway] braided all the week. Five hands worked at sorting. Hannah [Treadway?] made capes &c. Sally Dean worked more or less at some parts—& various, too numerous to mention. A good many hands have worked at bonnets & baskets in the school room, since the school closed.[60]

By Youngs's account, at least twenty-one First Order sisters worked on bonnets. Betsy Crosman and Jane Blanchard made bonnets from start to finish with little assistance. They must have been the forewomen who kept the bonnet brigade going. Chauncey, Sampson, and Wicks may have been just as capable, but they made bonnets only to the cape to provide work for sisters who did nothing but sew capes. Other sisters did smaller jobs.

Most of the bonnet makers were young: two in their teens, five in their twenties, and four in their thirties. Only Molly Smith, age fifty-nine, represented the older 50 percent of New Lebanon sisters.[61] Good eyesight and steady hands were essential to the millinery trade, and those attributes are often the province of youth. Children helped, as well. "The girls do abundance of braiding, for binding of palm leaf work," Youngs wrote.[62]

A few New Lebanon brethren helped with the bonnet business. Henry DeWitt and Benjamin Gates cut and ironed palm leaf. Philemon Stewart split leaves. Brothers also made some of the tools; David Rowley built a small loom for weaving palm leaf in 1845.[63] One brother constructed a bonnet. In late January 1836, Eldress Annie Williams wrote, "Jethro [Turner] goes to Hancock S family to carry them a bonnet he has been making."[64] That was Williams's only reference to a brother's participation in the Second Order's bonnet making, so we may assume that most of the work was done by sisters.

Bonnet construction worked like an assembly line, each sister doing what she did best. Each bonnet required dozens of steps. Once the palm leaves were in hand, they had to be processed for use. In the spring of 1836, deaconess Semantha Fairbanks and Eldress Betsy Bates washed, whitened, and cut palm leaves for bonnets.[65] Palm leaves may have been cut with the same hand-held cutters used earlier to split straw and later for poplar.[66]

After the strips were cut to a uniform one-eighth-inch width, they were tied to threads through the harness and reed of a hand loom. Shorter strips were threaded through a wooden needle, then woven on the loom.[67] The palm leaf fabric (a "chip" or sheet roughly ten inches by thirty inches for each bonnet) was singed to remove loose fibers, and a thin cloth pasted on the other side to stabilize the fabric. Next, a sister cut out the bonnet pieces, using a wooden or metal pattern as a template. Bonnets came in different sizes, and all parts had to match.[68]

Meanwhile, another sister hand-braided trim or wove it on a smaller loom, either with palm leaf on a thread warp or using leaf for both warp and weft. The crown braid, one-half inch wide, was used to cover the seam between brim and crown. The fore braid, one inch wide, was for edging. Such braid could cover a multitude of construction errors such as visible stitches or a frayed edge, but it had to be well made and tightly woven.

Next came assembly. The assembler handled the pieces carefully to avoid loosening the edges of the chip. First, she sewed bonnet wire around the crown and the front edge of the fore piece. Her stitches had to be tight, strong, and invisible from the outside of the bonnet. She sewed the back edge of the fore piece to the crown, then sewed a length of crown braid over the seam to give the bonnet a finished look. If the bonnet was to be lined, the sister added the lining before the braid. (Some extant Shaker palm leaf bonnets have a lightweight silk lining tacked over a thin wool batting with stitches invisible on the outside of the bonnet.) Then the bonnet maker used one-inch fore braid, folded over to hide the wire, to finish the front edge.[69] If the bonnet was for home use or to be sold finished, other sisters would attach cape and strings. For bonnets sold wholesale, cape and lining may have been omitted.[70] The New Lebanon First Order bonnet makers finished more than twenty bonnets a day in their six-day week.

The sisters wore bonnets they made. By 1840, each sister owned as many as three palm leaf bonnets, the best for Sunday, a common one for everyday, and an old one for dirty work.[71] Most Shaker bonnets, however, were wholesaled to city milliners. Watervliet's bonnet prices varied from $.60 to $1.44 apiece in 1836, depending on size and accouterments, such as cape, lining, and strings. By 1869, New Lebanon bonnet prices ranged from $.75 to $5.00.[72] In an era when a decorated bonnet ranged from $20 to $200, a Shaker bonnet was a bargain.[73]

The deaconesses' bonnet business contributed to the Shakers' economic health at a time when the U.S. economy was increasingly cyclical. The Panic of 1837 caused bank failures, factory closings, layoffs, high unemployment, and inflation. "The greater part of the banks have stopped paying specie," Isaac Newton Youngs wrote, "and it is extremely difficult to get any hard money." The Shaker bonnet business weathered 1837; Watervliet sold 1,000 that year, and sales rebounded to almost 2,000 in 1838.[74] As long as worldly demand remained high, the bonnet makers met it. From April 1836 to June 1837, the New Lebanon deaconesses sold 1,866 bonnets for $1,963.71. In October 1838, they shipped $528.95 worth of bonnets to New York and Philadelphia. Martha Osbourne Barrett, a Danvers factory operative who left mill work to become a millinery apprentice, wrote that millinery work was "as lucrative as any I could have," and so it was for the Shakers.[75]

Shaker bonnet makers had several advantages over worldly milliners. Sisters expected to be busy every waking hour, and they worked hard because diligence was a virtue in their communal society. Shaker products were known for their high quality, and the sisters tried to maintain that reputation of perfectionism. Moreover, the deaconesses did not risk much capital in their bonnet business. Overhead was low because they used existing workplaces, paid no rent, and had no labor costs.

Shaker bonnets brought much-needed revenue into the society. In 1839, the New Lebanon First Order made $1,993.68 on expenditures of $662. The brethren's three most lucrative enterprises, the seed, herb, and extract businesses (all dependent on sisters' labor) were expected to return less than $10,000 that year. Thus, the deaconesses' $1,331 bonnet profit was not a paltry sum.[76] Watervliet netted $4,096 on their bonnets from 1836 to 1839.[77] That income could have been the margin between profit and loss, and a cash-poor, depressed economy added weight to the sisters' contribution.

New Lebanon's bonnet business employed a significant number of sisters through 1840, when thirteen sisters in the First Order (22 percent of the females over age thirteen) were in the business. Former deaconess Molly Smith and Amy Reed wove bonnet fabric. Sarah Smith, Mariah Buck, Mary Hazzard, Olive Gates, Elizaette Bates, and Lucy Gates made bonnets. Anna Dodgson, Abigail Hathaway, and Elizabeth Sidle wove bonnet binding. Olive Wheeler and Sarah Ann Standish also worked on bonnets.[78]

Unfortunately, the popularity of palm leaf bonnets soon waned. By the 1850s, the Shaker bonnet was no longer fashionable. Younger women were wearing hats rather than bonnets, and a worldly woman in a Shaker bonnet was considered a comic sight, notable for her outdated apparel. One fictional penny-pincher wore "an immense Shaker bonnet of antediluvian make, projecting a quarter of a yard over her weather-beaten face, to protect it from the summer sun and wintry blast."[79] Her ancient Shaker bonnet symbolized her old-fashioned views as well as her thrift. She valued it for its durability. Shakers made their goods to last. In 1871, a worldly visitor wrote, "Shaker bonnets are out of fashion as common sunbonnets in the world outside—so these are only made for the Shakeresses themselves."[80]

From 1840 to 1863, the New Lebanon First Order's sales ranged from zero to over six hundred bonnets a year, but the trade never regained the volume of 1836 through 1838.[81] As the demand for Shaker bonnets declined, deaconesses reassigned sisters to other work. In 1845, only three sisters in the First Order were bonnet makers, and all had additional jobs.[82] By 1850, only Jane Blanchard was listed as a bonnet maker, but several others occasionally made bonnets for sale. In the Second Order, Jane Rea, Hannah Ann Agnew, and Loiza Sears were palm leaf workers.[83] In January 1855, deaconess Betsy Crosman wrote, "EJ & BC finished our 6 doz Order of bonnets, cut & pressed 2 doz. more to be sold in the Office. [Molly] Bennet &

EP [Eleanor Potter] are to cape them."[84] A journal entry from August 1856 noting that Mary Hazard taught Maine sisters to weave palm leaf on cotton warp shows that the sisters were still adjusting their methods.[85]

When the Shaker bonnet lost favor with fashionable women of the world's people, the sisters did not let their millinery skills or their business acumen atrophy. Crosman's successors sold millinery and fancy goods into the twentieth century. Like other good businesswomen, deaconesses simply shifted production to different wares. In 1839, they made palm leaf boxes with drawers. In 1846, they wove more than three thousand palm leaf fans. In 1847, they added palm leaf "reticles" (reticules) for sale. Through the 1840s, their diversification was impressive. Moreover, their work in palm leaf may have led to their later "popple" fancy goods made of split poplar.[86]

In 1854, the New Lebanon deaconesses' sale goods included only 36 palm leaf bonnets, but they made hundreds of other articles for sale: 2,000 splint baskets, 250 drawer boxes, 10 dozen emery balls, 23 dozen floor mops, 100 dozen cup mops, 29 feather dusters, 40 needle books, 11 yards of shagging, 4,400 yards of palm leaf notched braid, 560 pin cushions, 100 feather fans, 28 pairs of wings, and dozens of cushions, door mats, and table mats. Each order's sisters had their own specialties. Including food, the First and Second Order sisters sold $3,168 worth of goods after expenses of $1,660. By 1870, the Shaker bonnet may have been only a special-order item, but their business thrived.[87]

The deaconesses' palm leaf bonnet trade was a success as long as that style remained fashionable. The sisters were astute about manufacturing bonnets and marketing goods. They did not work by men's orders or under men's supervision. Deaconesses set goals, secured the support of their labor force, ran the business, and recorded their profits. By enlarging women's work to include entrepreneurship, the deaconesses exercised individual initiative and political savvy, and in doing so they demonstrated their society's flexibility in gender roles. As Suzanne Thurman points out, the Shakers integrated the public and private spheres, recognizing women's authority to participate in the economic realm as men did.[88] This, then, was one more manifestation of equality of the sexes among the Shakers.

Conclusions on Shaker
Equality of the Sexes

The female must have her equal rights in a
corresponding order with the male.

WHEN I BEGAN RESEARCHING SHAKER SISTERS' LIVES, I
was dubious about the Shaker tenet of equality of the sexes. Judging
from other scholars' assessments, I was not alone in being unable to imagine
how it might have worked. After several years of research, however, I found
enough evidence to see how the Shakers constructed and maintained equality of the sexes within their communal society.

Scholars assess equality in several ways: authority (in managing members,
dealing with the outside world, or controlling money), religion or spirituality (whose voice predominates), and social relations (who defers to whom).
Unlike academics, however, Believers did not parse equality into its compo-
nent parts. They structured their society to express their ideals and pursued
those ideals in daily life. Equality of the sexes appeared in the leadership of
each village, in Shakers' pursuit of union, and in their consensus decision-
making. If everyone upheld Shaker values, their village might approach
the ideal. Because of differences in personalities, however, the practice of
equality could vary. And consensus does not mean unanimity.

Scholars have written extensively about Shaker equality. Some suggest
that it was only theoretical. Those who draw this conclusion base it on
limited evidence. Moreover, researchers often apply late-twentieth-century
standards to nineteenth-century Shaker life in an ahistorical effort to make

the evidence fit their theories.[1] A review of the evidence, however, validates the Shakers' claim that they practiced equality of the sexes.

Having more interest in evidence than theory, I would suggest that Shaker sisters were equal to Shaker brothers because they said they were equal. It would be a mistake to shortchange Shakers' own beliefs about equality. By their standards, the sexes were equal within their society. They recognized, however, that men and women had different duties, and that each sex had to be in charge of their own responsibilities and had to respect the other sex's authority in theirs.[2] As D'Ann Campbell points out, for the Shakers, equality for women did not mean doing the same work men did.[3]

Shaker equality of the sexes began with Mother Ann Lee, the founder of Shakerism in the United States. Ann Lee was one of only ten women preachers that Catherine Brekus identified in the eighteenth century.[4] Ann Lee provided Shaker women with an assertive role model. For a woman to preach to the public was radical, and a woman's leadership of a communal society was even more so. Moreover, a later Believer, Sister Aurelia Mace, wrote, "Our Mother gave unto her daughters equal rights with their brothers in all the offices established for the government of the Shaker Order."[5] Some men rebelled at her leadership. In 1783 Benjamin West complained that Shaker men were "in entire subjection to the woman."[6] Neither he nor the Shakers who left testimonies of the early church left any doubt about who was their leading light.[7]

Ann Lee's charismatic gifts so far outstripped those of her male associates that she is remembered as their leader. She was the one who healed the sick and the lame, knew newcomers' secret sins, and had "the power of God" in her touch. The fact that Ann Lee was a woman set a precedent for women's leadership and established the authority of women among her followers, who believed she was the second incarnation of the Christ spirit.

Mother Ann explained her spiritual leadership by using a "deputy husband" metaphor.[8] When Jesus of Nazareth walked the earth, he was the embodiment of Christ. But in his absence, Ann Lee, his female counterpart or spiritual wife, became the leader. That comparison was culturally relevant, because farmers and farmwives recognized the resemblance to their own partnerships. At the same time, Ann Lee promoted the radical view that a woman could serve as well as a man could, at the highest level of religion.[9] Equal partners could share leadership, each one respecting the other's authority.

For Shaker sisters, equality began with celibacy, which was another radical aspect of Shakerism. Control of sexuality is a source of women's power.

For Shakers, celibacy ameliorated the inequality of patriarchal tradition, which is based on the gendered hierarchy of marriage, as well as socialization in male domination and female submission.[10] Because marriage gave men legal authority over women, eliminating marriage flattened the hierarchy. Among Shakers, where the marital relationship ended upon joining the church, men lacked their traditional source of authority over women. Shaker sisters were not under any man's thumb.

After Ann Lee's death, patriarchy persisted in some respects among the Shakers; her immediate successors were men. But when Joseph Meacham became the head of the society in 1787, he took another radical step toward equality of the sexes: he elevated Lucy Wright to be his partner in leadership. Together they restructured Shaker social relations to provide women with opportunities that, if not exactly equal, were equivalent to those of men.

According to Isaac Newton Youngs, who wrote the official history of the New Lebanon Shaker village between 1856 and 1860, the Ministry was committed to the concept that "the female must have her equal rights in a corresponding order with the male" as early as 1788, when Shakers began "gathering in" to live together in their own separatist communities.[11] In 1794, when the Shakers listed their society's officials, Eldresses' and deaconesses' names appeared alongside those of Elders and deacons; the men's names were written first, by a male scribe, at the left-hand side of the page, and the women's on the right. Women, however, were not necessarily secondary or subordinate in those partnerships; Sister Rhoda Hammond was the "Principal" trustee, rather than the two men whose names were in the other column.[12] The Shakers recognized that a woman could be the best candidate for the job—but both sexes had to be represented.

Furthermore, when new Elders and Eldresses were appointed to lead Shaker societies, the Ministry did not assume that the men would dominate the women. A newly appointed Elder and Eldress in 1814 had to figure out "which shall be the Elder to bear rule—have the lead."[13] The Ministry did not assume male dominance or female submission. After joining the Shakers, converts had to learn a new form of social relations.

When Joseph Meacham died in 1796, the movement toward Shaker equality might well have ended, but Lucy Wright remained in place as the society's leader for twenty-five years more. She was a strong leader, and some men contested her authority. Angell Matthewson complained that not only was the church led by a woman but they were "entirely ruled by women." Unwilling to live under petticoat government, Matthewson left. It was significant that he resented the authority of other Shaker sisters in addition to Lucy Wright's power. The society lost Believers who could not adjust to equality of the sexes, which meant that persisters were free to pursue that ideal. Moreover, it is significant that *those who objected to women's equality with men did not succeed in dismantling it.*

Over the next few decades, Shaker society's demographics shifted until women outnumbered men. This change suggests that Shakerism, including equality of the sexes, had more to offer women than it did to men accustomed to the traditional perquisites of masculinity. Persisting Shakers, male and female, had to acquiesce, avoid, or gracefully resist the pressures that the female majority brought to bear on individual members and on the society as a whole. Evidently women were more comfortable living within that system than men were, because the demographics grew more lopsided as time passed. Allison Newby suggests that the demographic imbalance shows women's dissatisfaction with mainstream social realities, as well as Shakerism's more satisfying alternative.[14]

Shakers consolidated their view of equality in publishing their theology. Around 1805, they began to systematize their use of music, and by 1807 the various societies were sharing songs. Their hymnal printed in 1813 includes lyrics that document their view of God as both female and male. The first song, "The Testimony of Eternal Truth," written about 1811 by Richard McNemar, includes the words, "The Father's high eternal throne / Was never fill'd by one alone: / There Wisdom holds the Mother's seat, / And is the Father's helper-meet. / This vast creation was not made / Without the fruitful Mother's aid." Another McNemar hymn, "The Everlasting Parents," begins, "The everlasting Father, / And Spirit two in one, / Liv'd in eternal union, / Before the world begun."[15] Thus Shakers documented their view of a deity who was both Holy Mother Wisdom and Father God. Their theology did not elevate one sex over the other. Having men and women on an even theological footing strengthened the foundation of Shaker equality of the sexes.

In 1808, the Shakers began to publish books that promoted their view that a woman could be equal to a man within a Christian worldview. *The Testimony of Christ's Second Appearing* explains their belief in God as both male and female and cites scripture to support their views, including, "God created man in his own image—male and female created he them." The work of the redemption of humankind, begun by a male Christ, would be completed by a female.[16] In 1816, the Shakers published *Testimonies of the Life, Character, Revelations and Doctrines of Our Ever Blessed Mother Ann Lee*, which documents Ann Lee's spiritual gifts and paranormal abilities resembling those of Jesus of Nazareth. In 1823, they printed *A Summary*

View of the Millennial Church or United Society of Believers, which reiterates their theology.[17] Those early publishing ventures documented more than the Shaker belief in Ann Lee as the embodiment of the Christ spirit; they also showed that their society incorporated the equality of male and female into their belief system.

After Lucy Wright died in 1821, someone evidently questioned women's equality; some must have thought that Wright alone had maintained equality of the sexes. Nonetheless, her successors made sure that equality did not end with her death. A New Lebanon Elder said, "Mother Lucy's work was to establish and support an equ[ality] in the Church between brethren and sisters," and he expected Believers to support it. He wanted the sisters "to consider that they have the same right as ever they had when Mother was with us, the[y] must not be deprived of their lo[t] & equality in the gospel: they really have influence in matters as ever. It is in the perfect union between the two that we shall find our relation in the kingdom."[18] If one sex felt elevated over (or subordinate to) the other, that situation would create a dangerous division within their communal society. Equality promoted union, one of their society's most basic ideals.

The first outsider who explicitly described Shakers' gender relations was Anne Royall in 1826. She wrote that a New Lebanon Eldress told her that Shaker sisters were "held in no subordination whatever." Royall questioned the Eldress closely enough to be convinced.[19] At New Lebanon, at least, equality of the sexes was in effect.

Shaker manuscripts show how equality of the sexes worked in daily life. Some journals show that sisters negotiated with brothers, in groups, under the auspices of Elders, Eldresses, deacons, and deaconesses. For instance, when the New Lebanon brethren wanted to use the sisters' shop for hat-making in 1835, the sisters postponed their use of that shop so the brothers could make hats—but demanded another shop of their own. They negotiated as a group, and an Eldress recorded their agreement. The brothers fulfilled their part of the agreement and built a new shop the following year.[20]

The evidence on Shakers' practice of equality of the sexes, however, does not show that all things were exactly equal. Visitor accounts reveal that at public worship, for instance, brethren gave most of the Sabbath addresses. But sisters also spoke when the spirit moved them—a privilege rarely indulged among the world's people in Christian meetinghouses other than Quakers'. Moreover, visitors' illustrations of the Shakers' choreographed Sabbath performances show the balance between men and women in Shaker society. They were at the same task, in the same fashion, neither sex exalted over the other. Sisters and brothers alike policed outsiders' behavior during Shakers' public services, and sisters were forceful in ridiculing or expelling those who misbehaved.

Neither were Shaker women's and men's work responsibilities exactly the same. They maintained a traditional division of labor, as did other farm families. Sisters cooked, sewed, knitted, did housework and laundry, and were responsible for a multitude of chores that might be collectively termed "women's work." Nevertheless, the sisters expected to have equal rights in ways that reached beyond housework. In a manner of speaking, Shaker sisters earned their equality. The brethren's herb, extract, and seed businesses depended on the sisters' labor in picking, drying, sorting, and packaging. Thus the brethren's most lucrative businesses were built on a foundation of women's labor. But the brothers did not command the sisters' time; they had to request the sisters' help through the deaconesses, who assigned the sisters' work. If the sisters had other priorities, the brethren's work had to wait.

Sisters expanded their textile skills into basket, bonnet, and fancy goods businesses that helped support their village. The sisters traveled to sell their wares, leaving behind the "domestic sphere" as they sold its products elsewhere. Brethren supported the sisters' businesses by buying, transporting, and preparing the raw materials and finding markets for the goods. Thus men and women were partners in Shaker businesses.

Sisters challenged traditional gender relations in other ways. At New Lebanon, tailoresses resisted making the brethren's heavy outerwear when there was a shortage of male tailors to do the work—and made the brothers' garments only after they finished their own sewing. Brethren eased the sisters' work by buying sewing machines and later on, by buying ready-made clothing. Though New Lebanon sisters sometimes felt oppressed by their work, they seem not to have felt subjugated to the brethren.

The efforts of New Lebanon brothers to lighten the sisters' work by building sisters' shops, purchasing sewing machines, and installing the most up-to-date conveniences in kitchen, dairy, and laundry as early as 1818 are outlined in Chapter 7. Watervliet's historian noted in 1877 many improvements there that benefited the sisters. He mentioned washing, boiling, wringing, and ironing laundry by steam, as well as new "ranges for cooking, soapstone ovens for baking, coal stoves for heating, and refined oils for giving light." "As we strive for equality of feeling and action," he wrote, "we endeavor to give them the right hand of fellowship in most things."[21] Visitors who toured the New Lebanon village on weekdays often commented on the Shakers' exceptionally well-appointed kitchen. Hester Poole concluded in 1888: "The Brethren have devised unheard-of comforts for the indoor workers, and the visitor leaves with the feeling of pity for the housewife who does her cooking in the ordinary way. Here every step tells, every movement counts."[22]

It may seem odd to consider the kitchen as evidence of women's equality, but it is important to recognize that Shaker equality can be measured both by comparing sisters' status to that of women among the world's people and by comparing sisters' status to that of brethren. The kitchen provides material evidence of both. Shaker kitchen sisters had the best equipment available. This is remarkable because most worldly farmers did not care how much work women had to do. Farmers among the world's people privileged men over women, so they improved the outdoor equipment men used but rarely eased women's work. Because marriage meant that a woman was subordinate, many wives received only the assistance their husbands deigned to give them. Shakers, in contrast, had to build a partnership based on the equality that many marriages lacked. Brethren were obliged to devote time and money to easing the sisters' work with mechanical conveniences just as they eased their own labor with the latest farm equipment.

Among non-Shakers, some couples develop a "myth of equality," based on their gender ideology and their concept of what seems fair. The underlying premise is that equality is a good thing to be consciously pursued, even though the actual thing may remain elusive. They identify inequalities in their relationships, and negotiate a compromise on points of contention. For partners dedicated to the pursuit of equality, having the goal is important, whether or not it is perfectly attainable.[23]

Nineteenth-century Shaker families did much the same thing in their partnerships between groups of sisters and groups of brethren. They publicly affirmed their goal of equality, supported women's activities, monitored their roles and addressed inequalities through negotiation and compromise. They had to be flexible. Probably no one was completely satisfied all of the time, but that is the nature of compromise. When displeased, Shaker women challenged men—and often succeeded. They had the advantage of working collectively within a system that recognized women's authority as well as men's. Among the Shakers, those who remained unreconciled to a negotiated arrangement could always leave. Those who stayed, however, shared a commitment to maintaining union, which meant supporting equality of the sexes.

Some aspects of the relations between Shaker brethren and sisters were thoroughly traditional. Recall, for instance, Anne Royall's observation that

Eldress Betsey sewed as she talked to a visitor, while two Elders sat idle in the same conversation, and another sister's poetic description of struggling to hang wallpaper while a brother sat nearby talking. In both instances, the unspoken subtext is that a woman's work is never done, but a man's talk alone merits designation as labor. Those brethren performed what sociologist Patricia Yancey Martin calls "a masculinity" by sitting idle; their sense of entitlement let them feel that conversation was their work. The sisters practiced "a femininity" by not challenging the brethren. Perhaps they felt little would be gained by raising the issue, and union would have suffered. Despite their collective and publicly avowed commitment to equality, both sexes practiced some aspects of their socially constructed gender roles in traditional ways.[24] Shaker sisters, however, were pragmatists who chose their battles wisely and fought only the ones they could win, or that were worth the effort.

Nevertheless, sisters challenged gender norms in other ways. They acted collectively to achieve their goals. During the Era of Manifestations, they shaped their society's membership, using spirit edicts to expel other Believers; they wielded the power of the spirits over their Elders and Eldresses, as well as their peers. At other times, they enforced moral standards through domestic espionage.[25] Sisters sometimes assumed authority over brothers. In one instance they corrected a brother by rebuking him for rudeness to a visitor. In another case, the Canaan sisters threatened a walkout when harassed by a brother; his obnoxious behavior finally provoked two sisters to physically eject him. Moreover, another village's Elder upheld their right to do so—a significant validation of sisters' authority. Sisters also had the right to control or withhold their own labor, which would not have been possible if they had been subordinate to brethren. At New Lebanon and Watervliet, sisters refused to do the milking when they felt they were working harder than the brethren.[26] Before the end of the nineteenth century, sisters challenged and changed their dress code, finally giving up the Shaker cap, an itchy symbol of Christian patriarchy. The outnumbered brothers were unable to keep groups of determined sisters from getting what they wanted—and probably realized it was in their own best interest to keep the women content. Some might suggest that the sisters' power went beyond equality and approached hegemony.

The Shakers proved that change is possible despite patriarchal tradition. They owned their belief in equality, structured their society to reflect that belief, wrote about it in their publications, and tried to practice it in their daily life. In 1853, William Leonard wrote that Shakerism brought an end to the "degradation and oppression of WOMAN" and suggested that the public discussion of woman's rights, as well as other reforms, originated with Shakers and was due to their recognition of God as both male and female.[27] In 1859, Elder Frederick Evans stated their beliefs forcefully, writing that Shakers were "the first to disenthrall woman from the condition of vassalage to which all other religious systems (more or less) consign her, and to secure to her those just and equal rights with man that, by her similarity to him in organization and faculties, both God and nature would seem to demand."[28] In the 1870s, other Shakers published their views of women's rights. Chauncey Sears blamed "the history of woman's unnatural slavery" to man on the Judeo-Christian concept of a male God. Sister Asenath C. Stickney asserted that Shaker women were the only women "in the civilized world who have equal rights with their brothers in the daily struggles of an earthly career." She added that unselfish Shaker brothers, "impressed with singular views of their moral obligations toward God and their earthly companions," were "among the best advocates of woman's rights." Sister Rosie Morse criticized the concept of "woman's sphere" and promoted women's suffrage.[29] As historian Wendy Benningfield suggests, the Shakers were more than a radical religious sect on the fringes of American society; they spent the nineteenth century putting equality of the sexes into practice. They showed that equality could be achieved and how to do it.[30]

By the late nineteenth century, a few outsiders recognized that Shakers were a living example of equality and suggested that the world's people should emulate them. A visitor wrote in 1875, "Each sex works in its own appropriate sphere of action, there being a proper subordination, deference and respect of the female to the male in his order, and of the male to the female in her order, so that in any of these communities the zealous advocates of 'women's rights' may here find a practical realization of their ideal."[31] That mutual respect was the basis of their reciprocity, and the foundation of their equality.

Some outsiders were dubious about Shaker equality of the sexes. William Hinds, who visited several communal societies, wrote in 1876, "The women of the Shaker Societies claim to be fully emancipated—to have equal rights with the men in all respects." Despite his use of the word "claim," he included this affirmation:

> The Shaker government is dual in all its departments and offices. The women appear to have as much influence and voice as the men; a woman founded the organization, and a woman held its first office for

twenty-five years during its greatest period of prosperity; women are as free as men to speak in their meetings; women are as free as men to write for their paper; women manage their own departments of industry independently of the men.[32]

Hinds may have been unwilling to believe what he saw—but the notion of equality of the sexes was so radical that it made many men uneasy. In 1888, however, a visiting Mormon missionary noted without quibbling that Eldresses were "equal in authority" with Elders.[33] These two descriptions shows that men's power and authority were the standard against which women's power and authority were judged—and indeed, that remains the standard applied to issues of equality for women today.

The problem with judging women against a male standard is that both the standard and the judgment are androcentric; they value men over women. Men are seldom judged by a feminine standard; indeed, the idea seems ludicrous because it is so unlikely. This disparity shows that the standard itself is male-centered or androcentric.

Furthermore, applying the masculine standard devalues women because it ignores issues of responsibility that, between the two sexes, usually devolve on women. Childbearing and nurturing, for instance, are duties traditionally gendered female because of women's biological role in reproduction. Those roles make women responsible for the survival of the next generation. In biological or Darwinian terms, however, successful rearing of offspring is the standard by which all species are measured.

The Shakers did not judge brothers' and sisters' roles by a masculine standard. They did not expect women to fill exactly the same roles men held, though either sex could be called on to assume the other sex's duties when necessary. By eliminating marriage and childbearing, Shakers reduced women's biological role; brethren and sisters shared the responsibility of nurturing children. The fact that more girls remained Shakers into adulthood suggests that the sisters did a better job of rearing the next generation of girls than brethren did with the boys. In a Darwinian organizational sense, the sisters were more successful in ensuring the perpetuation of Shakerism into the next generation. Girls' persistence as Shaker adults may reflect the fact that among the world's people, women had less protection and fewer economic opportunities than men, but the fact remains that Shaker sisters ensured their society's survival by recruiting and maintaining the majority of the next generation of Believers.

Shaker sisters' equality went beyond equal rights and responsibilities. Shaker women working together expanded their power throughout the nineteenth century. Because sisters were the majority in a society that made decisions by consensus, they could bring pressure to bear on the male minority. In 1878, a visiting Frenchman recognized that Shaker society had become a "woman-ocracy ('gynécratie'), or a government by women."[34] He may have been the first outsider to suggest that Shaker society was actually run by the sisters. The brethren's complaints about petticoat government in the 1790s revealed that the New Lebanon sisters' power had been apparent nearly a century earlier, as well. In 1881, a woman visitor, with a keen interest in the Shakers' practical application of the principles of women's rights, recognized that women were the "real strength" of Shakerism, while men assumed "no air of superiority" in either religious or temporal matters—though some brethren did complain.[35]

A woman familiar with the Canterbury, New Hampshire, Shakers, had strong opinions about Shakers and wrote this of the brethren in 1899: "Men among these people are of two types, . . . the vigorous, spiritualized, self-controlled; and those weak, to the point of servile obedience to any stronger will. Average men are not found among Shakers. It is a matter of leading or being led." She had quite a different view of Shaker sisters: "Women there impress you as intellectually stronger than women of the world. Their equality with men recognized in all daily life, it has the effect of centering their energies and expanding their self-esteem."[36] Both of her views were correct, as far as they went. A member of a communal society, male or female, had to be comfortable with being led. Moreover, sisters were well aware of their equality, but most visitors did not fully appreciate its ramifications.

According to Lida Kimball, who visited New Lebanon in 1897, Shakers had "perfect equality of the sexes."[37] Because the sisters' equality at that Shaker village was evident even to outsiders, there can be little question about women's status there. Without assessments of other Shaker villages, however, it would be hard to say whether the same was true in every community. In 1899, a former resident of the Hancock Shakers wrote, "Theoretically the sisters enjoy perfect equality with the brethren," but added that the "lead" were men.[38] That may have been true when and where the seceder lived—but the lead did not *have* to be male. Equality means that either sex could be the lead. Isaac Newton Youngs noted that only Watervliet and New Lebanon maintained the standard of equality in 1816.[39] Nevertheless, the sisters ostensibly remained equal throughout the society, and Eldresses had the "leading gifts" in other bishoprics, as well. The Shakers' desire to achieve perfection meant that they were well aware of which communities fell short of the ideal, perhaps including Canterbury, New Hampshire.[40] Nevertheless, they did not abandon their effort to promote equality of the sexes, nor could a noncompliant community restructure its administration to eliminate women entirely, as was the norm for government among the world's people.

Perhaps other researchers will want to assess more villages' practice of equality of the sexes. Close reading of journals, visitor accounts, and poetry, to see who complained about whom and why and how (or if) their complaints were resolved will reveal discrepancies where they exist. Recognizing masculinities and femininities may be useful in determining which traditional gendered social behaviors were used and whether they were challenged and how those practices supported equality or hampered it. Reports of meetings held to secure consensus can be revealing, as are indications of sisters working to support each other — or not. In some instances, the telling detail might be a note about party spirit or open conflict; in others, a comment on what was not done. There are hundreds of manuscripts for some Shaker villages; more evidence is waiting to be found. This research is important because Shakers had an impact on national politics.

In the nineteenth century, thousands of non-Shakers visited Shaker villages, and a significant number of them had heard or read about Shaker equality of the sexes. In published accounts of their visits, some of those outsiders discussed Shaker equality in political terms, referring to "women's rights" and "women's emancipation," terms that functioned within a national political context beyond Shaker ideas of social and spiritual equality. We cannot know exactly how much influence the Shakers had, but the fact remains that some non-Shakers thought the society's practice of equality had an impact outside the boundaries of Shaker villages.[41] Shakers established equality of the sexes as the ideal between 1788 and 1796, and that was accepted doctrine before 1821. In 1856, when Isaac Newton Youngs was writing his history of the New Lebanon Shaker society, the Shakers used the term "equal rights" in referring to the distribution of authority. Youngs read his history aloud to the Ministry, making corrections when needed, but the manuscript shows no revision in his use of the term "equal rights."[42] That was, therefore, the understood relationship between the sexes at the time Youngs wrote (and the Ministry approved) the text.

By 1869, Shakers advocated women's equality, including the right to vote, in the worldly press. New York editors ridiculed the idea — but the Shaker ideal was being discussed on the national level.[43] Several worldly contemporaries were satisfied that Shaker sisters were equal to Shaker brothers and noted their example in equality of the sexes. In 1879, a female visitor observed that Shakers had swayed public opinion regarding women's rights. She wrote that the "best writers on political economy" were approaching Shaker views of the advancement of women. She felt Shaker beliefs had influenced the United States' political culture—and she may have been correct. Many prominent nineteenth-century authors and editors had visited the Shakers, and through them, Shakers funneled their ideas into national politics. Historians who believe that the United States' women's movement began at Seneca Falls, New York, in 1848 might more accurately date it to the arrival of Ann Lee in America on August 6, 1774, as the theologian J. R. Hyland has suggested.[44] Equality of the sexes was Shakerism's gift to the world.

This is not to suggest that Shaker equality of the sexes was a *fait accompli* at any point. It cannot have been easy to push against mainstream traditions in which many Believers had grown up. Shaker sisters had to muster their forces over and over again to maintain their equality, to hold their own without damaging the union that they valued—and sometimes they failed. Nevertheless, Shakerism can serve as a model. The Shakers show that it is possible to establish a more androgynous personal ideal, and judge women and men by the same measures: cooperation, diligence, fairness, competence, humility, and spirituality. Their example shows that relics of patriarchy can crumble under pressure, and that cooperation is a source of women's power. Working together, women gain ground.

NOTES

ABBREVIATIONS

In citations, the numbers immediately following the repository refer to the microfilm reel number and the document designation.

BA   Berkshire Athenaeum, Pittsfield, Massachusetts
FM   Library, Fruitlands Museums, Harvard, Massachusetts, manuscripts.
HCDC   Hamilton College, Clinton, New York, Digital Collection of Shaker imprints online, http://library.hamilton.edu/collections
HSV   Hancock Shaker Village, Pittsfield, Massachusetts
LC   Library of Congress, Washington, D.C.
NYPL   New York Public Library, New York, New York
NYSL   New York State Library, Albany, New York
SM   Emma B. King Library, Shaker Museum, Old Chatham, New York
WCA   Williams College Archives, Williamstown, Massachusetts
WM   Edward Deming Andrews Memorial Shaker Collection, Winterthur Library, Winterthur, Delaware
WRHS   Western Reserve Historical Society, Cleveland, Ohio

INTRODUCTION

1. Glendyne R. Wergland, "Women, Men, Property, and Inheritance: Gendered Testamentary Customs in Western Massachusetts, 1800–1860" (Ph.D. diss., University of Massachusetts, 2001).
2. "Grass widow" Mercy Brazie and "California widow" Caroline Austin are listed thus in the 1860 U.S. Census, Great Barrington, Mass., families 296 and 507.
3. Lee Virginia Chambers-Schiller, *Liberty, a Better Husband: Single Women in America; the Generations of 1780–1840* (New Haven: Yale University Press, 1984), chap. 1.
4. Virginia Penny, *The Employments of Women* (Boston: Walker, Wise and Company, 1863), xv.
5. Anna White and Leila S. Taylor, *Shakerism: Its Meaning and Message* (Columbus, Ohio: for the Shakers, 1905), 72–76; Isaac N. Youngs, A Concise View of the Church of God and of Christ on Earth, 25–27, WM 861.

6. White and Taylor, *Shakerism*, 74, 108–9.

7. Stephen J. Paterwic, *Historical Dictionary of the Shakers* (Lanham, Md.: Scarecrow Press, 2008), 154. The decline continued until the New Lebanon village disbanded in 1932, selling the property to a group who established a boys' prep school in the historic buildings. "Darrow School: A Unique Sense of Place," available at Darrow School website, "History," http://www.darrowschool.com/, accessed April 12, 2007.

8. Metin M. Coşgel, "The Commitment Process in a Religious Commune: The Shakers," *Journal for the Scientific Study of Religion* 40.1 (2001): 36.

9. [Unattributed note], WRHS 1, I:A-2. Language and spelling resemble Joseph Meacham's, though the handwriting does not. See Meacham's letter to Lucy Wright "a short time before his decease [August 16, 1796]," WRHS 19, IV:A-30.

10. Isaac N. Youngs, Family and Meeting Journal (1815–23), August 17, 1816, LC 3:42.

11. In Chapter 7 we meet Betsy Bates negotiating both sexes' use of the same work space and in Chapter 10, Semantha Fairbanks and Lydia Matthewson practicing consensus-building before establishing a bonnet business.

12. Edward D. Andrews, *The People Called Shakers* (New York: Dover, 1963), 56, 60.

13. James R. Gregory, "The Myth of the Male Ethnographer and the Woman's World," *American Anthropologist*, n.s., 86.2 (1984): 323.

14. D'Ann Campbell, "Women's Life in Utopia: The Shaker Experiment in Sexual Equality Reappraised—1810 to 1860," *New England Quarterly* 51.1 (1978): 27.

15. Susan Carol Rogers, "Female Forms of Power and the Myth of Male Dominance: A Model of Female/Male Interaction in Peasant Society," *American Ethnologist* 2.4 (1975): 753.

16. Michelle Z. Rosaldo, "The Use and Abuse of Anthropology: Reflections on Feminism and Cross-Cultural Understanding," *Signs* 5.3 (1980): 397, 407–9, 416.

17. Mary Farrell Bednarowski, "Outside the Mainstream: Women's Religion and Women Religious Leaders in Nineteenth-Century America," *Journal of the American Academy of Religion* 48 (1980): 207, 211, 213, 224.

18. Louis J. Kern, *An Ordered Love* (Chapel Hill: University of North Carolina Press, 1981), 132–33.

19. Jean M. Humez, "'Weary of Petticoat Government': The Specter of Female Rule in Early Nineteenth-Century Shaker Politics," *Communal Societies* 11 (1991): 1–17; Jean Humez, *Mother's First-Born Daughters: Early Shaker Writings on Women and Religion* (Bloomington: Indiana University Press, 1993), 66–67.

20. Priscilla J. Brewer, "'Tho' of the Weaker Sex': A Reassessment of Gender Equality among the Shakers," *Signs* 17.3 (1992): 611, 635.

21. Sally Kitch, *Chaste Liberation: Celibacy and Female Cultural Status* (Urbana: University of Illinois Press, 1989), 6–7.

22. Lawrence Foster, *Women, Family, and Utopia: Communal Experiments of the Shakers, the Oneida Community, and the Mormons* (Syracuse, N.Y.: Syracuse University Press, 1991), 18.

23. Elizabeth A. De Wolfe, *Shaking the Faith: Women, Family, and Mary Marshall Dyer's Anti-Shaker Campaign, 1815–1867* (New York: Palgrave, 2002), shows how hard it was to challenge that system.

24. Stephen J. Stein, *The Shaker Experience in America: A History of the United Society of Believers* (New Haven: Yale University Press, 1992), 132–33.

25. Suzanne Thurman, *"O Sisters Ain't You Happy?" Gender, Family, and Community*

among the Harvard and Shirley Shakers, 1781–1918 (Syracuse, N.Y.: Syracuse University Press, 2002), 56–59.

26. Ernestine Friedl, "The Position of Women: Appearance and Reality," *Anthropology Quarterly* 40 (1967): 97, 108.

27. Rogers, "Female Forms of Power," 727–56.

28. Beverly Chiñas, *The Isthmus Zapotecs: Women's Roles in Cultural Context* (New York: Holt, Rinehart and Winston, 1973), 108–9.

29. Andrei Simic, "Machismo and Cryptomatriarchy: Power, Affect, and Authority in the Contemporary Yugoslav Family," *Ethos* 11 (1983): 66.

30. Hervey Elkins, *Fifteen Years in the Senior Order of Shakers* (Hanover, N.H., 1853), 26. If Shakers witnessed a sin, they had to report it. Theodore E. Johnson, ed., "The Millennial Laws of 1821," *Shaker Quarterly* 7.2 (1967): 46–47.

31. Rogers, "Female Forms of Power," 748.

32. Susan Carol Rogers, "Gender in Southwestern France: The Myth of Male Dominance Revisited," *Anthropology* 9 (1985): 67–69, 84.

33. Gregory, Myth of the Male Ethnographer," 318.

34. See Simic, "Machismo and Cryptomatriarchy," 66–86; David D. Gilmore, "Men and Women in Southern Spain: 'Domestic Power' Revisited," *American Anthropologist*, n.s., 92.4 (1990): 953–70. When women are excluded from political roles, they can still be "political actors" through gossip or spirit possession: Sharon W. Tiffany, "Models and the Social Anthropology of Women," *Man*, n.s., 13.1 (1978): 45. Women's visiting creates a "solidarity network": Augusta Molnar, "Women and Politics: Case of the Kham Magar of Western Nepal," *American Ethnologist* 9.3. (1982): 485–502. Women use gossip for social control: Yael Katzir, "Yemenite Jewish Women in Israeli Rural Development: Female Power versus Male Authority," *Economic Development and Cultural Change* 32.1 (1983): 46. Gossip empowers women: Joann Martin, "Motherhood and Power: The Production of a Women's Culture of Politics in a Mexican Community," *American Ethnologist* 17.3 (1990): 470–90.

35. Susan Carol Rogers, review of Peggy Reeves Sanday, *Female Power and Male Dominance: On the Origins of Sexual Inequality,* in *American Anthropologist*, n.s., 86.2 (1984): 436.

36. Christopher Boehm, "Egalitarian Behavior and Reverse Dominance Hierarchy," *Current Anthropology* 34.3 (1993): 228, 230, 239.

37. Susan Starr Sered, "Ideology, Autonomy, and Sisterhood: An Analysis of the Secular Consequences of Women's Religions," *Gender and Society* 8.4 (1994): 488, 492, 500–1, 503.

Chapter 1. Ann Lee

The first version of this chapter was presented at Hancock Shaker Village in January 2005.

1. In addition to Ann Lee, only nine women preachers have been identified before 1800. Catherine A. Brekus, *Strangers and Pilgrims: Female Preaching in America, 1740–1845* (Chapel Hill: University of North Carolina Press, 1998), 343–46.

2. Sketch of Life & Experiences of Rhoda Blake, written 1864–92, Alonzo Hollister transcription, 49–50, WRHS 51, VI:B-33. Vedder: Edward D. Andrews, *The People Called Shakers* (New York: Dover, 1963), 17; Anna White and Leila Taylor, *Shakerism: Its Meaning and Message* (Columbus, Ohio: Fred J. Heer for the Shakers, 1905), 100.

3. Nardi Reeder Campion, *Mother Ann Lee: Morning Star of the Shakers* (Hanover, N.H.: University Press of New England, 1990), 69–70; Richard Francis, *Ann the Word: The Story of Ann Lee, Female Messiah, Mother of the Shakers, the Woman Clothed with the Sun* (New York: Arcade, 2000), 105–6.

4. David J. Goodall, "New Light on the Border: New England Squatter Settlements in New York during the American Revolution" (Ph.D. diss., New York State University–Albany, 1984), 315–16, 323.

5. J. E. A. Smith, *History of Pittsfield,* vol. 1 (Boston: Lee and Shepard, 1869), 261, 390–92.

6. Metin M. Coşgel points out that theories of commitment are not mutually exclusive; all are part of securing and maintaining commitment. He summarizes deprivation theory in "The Commitment Process in a Religious Commune: The Shakers," *Journal for the Scientific Study of Religion* 40.1 (2001): 28.

7. Stephen Marini blames the New Light Stir on the war, exacerbated by westward migration and Congregationalists' waning authority. Stephen A. Marini, *Radical Sects of Revolutionary New England* (Cambridge, Mass.: Harvard University Press, 1982), 5–6, 52; Smith, *History of Pittsfield,* 453.

8. White and Taylor, *Shakerism,* 35–36.

9. "A Short Account of the People known by the Name of Shakers, or Shaking Quakers," *Theological Magazine* 1 (September–October 1795), quoted in Glendyne Wergland, *Visiting the Shakers, 1778–1849* (Clinton, N.Y.: Richard W. Couper Press, 2007), 20.

10. Seth Youngs Wells, comp., *Testimonies Concerning the Character and Ministry of Mother Ann Lee* (Albany: Packard and Van Benthuysen, 1827), 87–88. The 1827 testimonies appear less heavily edited than those from 1816: [Rufus Bishop and Seth Youngs Wells, comps.], *Testimonies of the Life, Character, Revelations and Doctrines of Our Ever Blessed Mother Ann Lee* (Hancock, Mass.: J. Talcott and J. Deming Junrs., 1816).

11. "Short Account," 22.

12. Marini, *Radical Sects,* 52.

13. Goodall, "New Light on the Border," 330; Wells, 1827 *Testimonies,* 157, reported in Francis, *Ann the Word,* 111.

14. Seth Youngs Wells, comp., Unpublisht Testimonies of Mother's First Born Children in America, Forming a Cloud of Witnesses, vol. 1, recopied by Alonzo Hollister, 58, 84, WRHS 52, VI:B-42.

15. *Diary of Matthew Patten of Bedford, N.H., 1754–1788* (Concord, N.H.: Rumford, 1903), 414; Sarah A. (Smith) Emery, *Reminiscences of a Nonagenarian* (Newburyport, Mass.: W. H. Huse, 1879), 176; Francis, *Ann the Word,* 130–31; *Diary of Rev. Ebenezer Parkman of Westborough, Massachusetts,* ed. Harriette M. Forbes (Westborough Historical Society, 1899), 235–36.

16. Ross W. Beales, Jr., "The Ecstasy of Sarah Prentice," Death, Re-Birth, and the Great Awakening in Grafton, Massachusetts," *Historical Journal of Massachusetts* 26.2 (1997), 120; White and Taylor, *Shakerism,* 100; Francis, *Ann the Word,* 132–33; Isaac Newton Youngs, Memorandum, WRHS 29, V:A-3.

17. "Short Account," 22. Rathbun headed the Baptist Church in Richmond, Massachusetts. He first visited the Shakers at Watervliet on May 26, 1780.

18. Wells, 1827 *Testimonies,* 108–9, 125.

19. Daniel Goodrich, Narrative History of the Shakers (1803), HSV ms. 6140a, 3b.

20. Lucy Wight, wife of Reuben, should not be confused with Lucy Wright. Wells, 1827 *Testimonies,* 67, 125, 127; Records Kept by Order of the Church (1780–1929), 159, NYPL 2.7.

21. Goodrich, Narrative History, 3b–4. The Goodrich property became what is now Hancock Shaker Village, west of Pittsfield, Massachusetts.

22. Wells, 1827 *Testimonies,* 24–25.

23. "Short Account," 21.

24. Campion, *Mother Ann Lee,* 122; "Short Account," 22–23. An apostate who sold anti-Shaker pamphlets corroborated the warm greeting and foreknowledge of the visit. See Valentine Rathbun, *An Account of the Matter, Form and Manner of a New and Strange Religion* (Providence, R.I.: Bennett Wheeler, 1781), 4.

25. In one study, library patrons who were briefly touched on the hand (while checking books out) rated library services significantly higher than those not touched. J. D. Fisher, M. Rytting, and R. Heslin, "Hands Touching Hands: Affective and Evaluative Effects of an Interpersonal Touch," *Sociometry* 39 (1976): 416–21, reported in Jacob Hornik, "Tactile Stimulation and Consumer Response," *Journal of Consumer Research* 19.3 (1992): 449–58.

26. Coşgel, "Commitment Process," 28–29.

27. Michael R. Solomon, Carol Surprenant, John A. Czepiel, and Evelyn G. Gutman describe the importance of face-to-face marketing, in "A Role Theory Perspective on Dyadic Interactions: The Service Encounter," *Journal of Marketing* 49.1 (1985): 99–111.

28. Wells, Unpublisht Testimonies, 1:82, WRHS 52, VI:B-42.

29. Wells, 1827 *Testimonies,* 93,122; [Bishop and Wells], 1816 *Testimonies,* 261.

30. According to folklore, a few women are born with "healing hands," which some nurses have credited with spontaneous remissions or cures. One version says that the patient has to believe that such healing is possible for it to work. "Healing Hands," http://www.humanhand.com/healinghands.html;.Phylameana Desy, "Hands-on Healing," http://healing.about.com/od/empathic/a/empath_foltyn.htm, accessed March 10, 2009; Joseph Bernard Hutton, *Healing Hands* (New York: D. McKay, 1967). Note, however, that folklore is not hard science. See Sara Wuthnow, "Healing Touch Controversies," *Journal of Religion and Health* 36 (September 1997): 221–29. Social scientists believe that psychosocial support or placebo effect are responsible for such cures. See James McClenon, "Shamanic Healing, Human Evolution, and the Origin of Religion," *Journal for the Scientific Study of Religion* 36 (September 1997): 345–54; Jaap J. Beutler, Johannes T. M. Attevelt, Sybo A. Schouten, Joop A. J. Faber, Evert J. Dorhout Mees, Gijsbert G. Geijskes, "Paranormal Healing And Hypertension," *British Medical Journal,* Vol. 296, No. 6635 (May 28, 1988: 1491–94.

31. [Bishop and Wells], 1816 *Testimonies,* 257–59; Wells, Unpublisht Testimonies, 1:22, 78, WRHS 52, VI:B-42; Wells, 1827 *Testimonies,* 52.

32. In Matthew 8 and 9, Jesus heals cases of leprosy, demon-possession, paralysis, hemorrhage, and blindness.

33. Rosabeth Moss Kanter, *Commitment and Community: Communes and Utopias in Sociological Perspective* (Cambridge, Mass.: Harvard University Press, 1972), 113.

34. Ezra Stiles, 1786, quoted in Wergland, *Visiting the Shakers, 1778–1849,* 134.

35. Rathbun, *Account of the Matter,* 7–8.

36. Ibid., 7, 17–18.

37. Wells, 1827 *Testimonies,* 19, 68, 159, 175.

38. "Short Account," 22.

39. Ibid., 23.

40. Rathbun, *Account of the Matter,* 10.

41. Kanter, *Commitment and Community,* 82–91, cited in Suzanne Thurman, "*O Sisters*

Ain't You Happy?" Gender, Family, and Community among the Harvard and Shirley Shakers, 1781–1918 (Syracuse, N.Y.: Syracuse University Press, 2002), 48.

42. Angell Matthewson, Reminiscences, letter 1 (1780), NYPL 9.119; Wells, 1827 *Testimonies,* 17, 51, 169; Elizabeth Wood testimony, WRHS 49, VI:B-1.

43. [Bishop and Wells], 1816 *Testimonies,* 38. See also Seth Youngs Wells and Calvin Green, *A Summary View of the Millennial Church or United Society of Believers (commonly called Shakers)* (Albany, N.Y.: Packard and Van Benthuysen, 1823), 18.

44. John P. Demos, *Entertaining Satan* (New York: Oxford University Press, 1982), 57–94.

45. Wells, Unpublisht Testimonies, 1:171–75, WRHS 52, VI:B-42.

46. Wells, 1827 *Testimonies,* 108–9, 125; "Short Account," 22.

47. [Bishop and Wells], 1816 *Testimonies,* 21–22, quoted in Jean M. Humez, "Weary of Petticoat Government": The Specter of Female Rule in Early Nineteenth-Century Shaker Politics," *Communal Societies* 11 (1991): 1.

48. Marini, *Radical Sects,* 89.

49. Rathbun, *Account of the Matter,* 5, 10.

50. Matthewson, Reminiscences, letter 4 (1783), NYPL 9.119; Testimony of Sixty, a Cloud of Witnesses, Alonzo Hollister, comp., 30–31, WRHS 52, VI:B-40.

51. [Bishop and Wells], 1816 *Testimonies,* 226.

52. Abijah Worster, Sayings of Mother Ann, comp. Thomas Hammond, 1–2, WRHS 54, VII:B-22.

53. Albert Matthews, 1790, in Wergland, *Visiting the Shakers, 1778–1849,* 139; François Marquis de Barbé-Marbois, in ibid., 15. He visited on September 26, 1784, just after Ann Lee died.

54. Wells, 1827 *Testimonies,* 77.

55. Kanter, *Commitment and Community,* 76–80, cited in Thurman, "O Sisters," 48.

56. Testimony of Sixty, 30–33, 135, WRHS 52, VI:B-40.

57. Marini, *Radical Sects,* 90.

58. Rathbun, *Account of the Matter,* 5–6.

59. Kanter, *Commitment and Community,* 103–11, cited in Thurman, "O Sisters," 48.

60. "Short Account," 23.

61. Wells, 1827 *Testimonies,* 127.

62. "Short Account," 23. Public confessions: Thankful Rice (drunkenness, 1744), in *The Diary of Ebenezer Parkman, 1703–1782,* ed. Francis G. Walett (Worcester, Mass.: American Antiquarian Society, 1974), 91–93; church records, Westborough Public Library; Deacon Andrew Everett (debt, 1809), Dalton, Mass., Congregational Church Records, Cooke Collection, BA, 24.

63. Wells, 1827 *Testimonies,* 12.

64. Wells, Unpublisht Testimonies, 1:101–2, WRHS 52, VI:B-42.

65. Wells, 1827 *Testimonies,* 12, 67–68, 90, 109.

66. David R. Lamson, *Two Years' Experience among the Shakers* (West Boylston, Mass.: for the author, 1848), 165.

67. "Short Account," 23. Shakers considered long hair to be the mark of the beast. Rathbun, *Account of the Matter,* 4.

68. Kanter, *Commitment and Community,* 80–82, cited in Thurman, "O Sisters," 48.

69. Rathbun, *Account of the Matter,* 9.

70. Ibid., 12–13.

71. Elizabeth Youngs to Benjamin Seth Youngs, February 16, 1830, WRHS 29, IV:B-35.

72. Bibliography of apostate accounts: Elizabeth A. De Wolfe, *Shaking the Faith: Women, Family, and Mary Marshall Dyer's Anti-Shaker Campaign, 1815–1867* (New York: Palgrave, 2002), 221–24.
73. Watson and Smith, 1790, in Wergland, *Visiting the Shakers, 1778–1849*, 137, 139.
74. Dr. Benjamin Waterhouse, 1794, in Wergland, *Visiting the Shakers, 1778–1849*, 142.

CHAPTER 2. THE SHORT MARRIAGE OF MOTHER LUCY WRIGHT

1. Early New Lebanon Believers included sixty-six couples, one widower, thirteen bachelors, and fourteen single women and widows. Thus, most members were already married when they became celibate. Records Kept by Order of the Church (1780–1929), 159, NYPL 2.7.
2. The Shakers exploited the legal tradition that made it a father's right to decide where his family (or children) lived. When the father was a Shaker, and the mother was not, the Shakers supported the father in retaining custody of the children. See Elizabeth A. De Wolfe, *Shaking the Faith: Women, Family, and Mary Marshall Dyer's Anti-Shaker Campaign, 1815–1867* (New York: Palgrave, 2002), and Ilyon Woo's book on Eunice Chapman, *The Great Divorce: A Nineteenth-Century Mother's Fight to Save Her Children from the Shakers* (New York: Atlantic Monthly Press, 2010).
3. J. E. A. Smith, *History of Pittsfield to 1800* (Boston: Lee and Shepard, 1869), 475.
4. Frederick W. Evans, *Shakers. Compendium of the Origin, History, Principles, Rules and Regulations, Government, and Doctrines of the United Society of Believers in Christ's Second Appearing* (n.p.: for the Shakers, 1859), 184; Calvin Green, Memoir of Lucy Wright, 75, Sayings of Mother Lucy, WRHS 56, VII: B-60.1. Green calls Lucy Wright's mother Molly; Alonzo Hollister's copy refers to her as Martha, and Evans calls her Mary. According to Stephen Paterwic, Lucy's mother was Mary (Robbins) Wright, nicknamed Molly. Paterwic e-mail message to author, October 20, 2008. John Wright was slightly above the mid-point of property owners. Pittsfield tax records, reel 1, 1785 worksheet, west side, BA.
5. Smith, *History of Pittsfield*, 86, 97–107, 116, 120–21; Josiah Wright, Journal at Pontoosuck, April 29, 1756–February 21, 1757, in Col. Israel Williams papers, vol. 2, p. 8: May 10, June 4, 5, 10, August 14, October 8, 1756, January 8, 10, 1757, Massachusetts Historical Society, Boston, Blanche Stockwell typescript, Wright family file, BA.
6. Bettye Hobbs Pruitt, ed., *Massachusetts Tax Valuation List of 1771* (Camden, Maine: Picton Press, 1978), 478–82. Trading work: Laurel Thatcher Ulrich, *Age of Homespun: Objects and Stories in the Creation of an American Myth* (New York: Knopf, 2001), chap. 6.
7. Smith, *History of Pittsfield*, 102–4, 107, 115, 120, 122; Josiah Wright, Journal at Pontoosuck, May 4, July 4, 1756.
8. David Hackett Fischer, *Albion's Seed: Four British Folkways in America* (New York: Oxford University Press, 1989), 132–33; Smith, *History of Pittsfield*, 137; Green, Memoir, 76, 111.
9. Isaac N. Youngs, Family and Meeting Journal (1815–23), March 27, 1818, LC 3:42.
10. Philip Greven, *The Protestant Temperament: Patterns of Child-Rearing, Religious Experience, and the Self in Early America* (Chicago: University of Chicago Press, 1988), 45.
11. Calvin Green quoted in Anna White and Leila S. Taylor, *Shakerism: Its Meaning and Message* (Columbus, Ohio: Fred J. Heer for the Shakers, 1905), 150, 106; Green,

Memoir, 89–90. Eunice Chapman, *No. 2, Being an Additional Account of the Conduct of the Shakers* (Albany, N.Y.: I. W. Clark, 1818), 58, corroborates Wright's beauty. My thanks to Ilyon Woo for this reference.

12. Lafayette W. Case, *The Goodrich Family in America* (Chicago: Fergus Printing Co., 1889), 48; Smith, *History of Pittsfield,* 230, 235–40, 486, 492–93.

13. Smith, *History of Pittsfield.,* 295–99.

14. Case, *Goodrich Family in America,* 48, 78.

15. William Gouge, *Of Domesticall Duties* (London: Haviland, 1622; facsimile of the first edition, Amsterdam: Theatrum Orbis Terrarum, 1976), 301.

16. Green, Memoir, 78.

17. Theodore E. Johnson, ed., "The Millennial Laws of 1821," *Shaker Quarterly* 7.2 (1967): 46.

18. Smith, *History of Pittsfield,* 88–89.

19. Greven, *Protestant Temperament,* 50; Seth Youngs Wells, comp., *Testimonies Concerning the Character and Ministry of Mother Ann Lee* (Albany: Packard and Van Benthuysen, 1827), 125–27.

20. Greven, *Protestant Temperament,* 127–31.

21. White and Taylor, *Shakerism,* 107.

22. Thomas Brown, *Account of the People Called Shakers* (Troy, N.Y.: Parker and Bliss, 1812), 339; Chapman, *No. 2,* 58. This is not to suggest that Wright and Goodrich did not consummate their marriage. They may even have had a child. The Goodrich family historian wrote of them, "No record has been found of any children." Genealogists generally just leave the space blank or note "no issue." In 1798 a Shaker journal said, "Young Elizur Goodrich about the Church with a pistol, threatening." Joseph Bennet, Dayly Journal (1795–1802), February 5, 1798, WRHS 32, V:B-65. Wright's husband, then an Elder, was in his forties and therefore no longer young by the standards of their day. If Wright had gotten pregnant during their brief union in 1779–80, their child would have been seventeen or eighteen in 1798. Supporting this possibility was Joseph Bennet's earlier mention of "Elizur Goodrich Junr.," on June 24, 1796. "Junior" generally refers to the son of a "Senior" by the same name. It is possible, though, that Bennet misidentified "young Elizur," who could have been Elder Elizur's nephew, the son of Ezekiel and Eunice (Rathbun) Goodrich. That boy, born in 1765, left the Shakers at twenty-one, moved to Vermont, and married. Case, *Goodrich Family,* 80.

23. White and Taylor, *Shakerism,* 107.

24. Economy: Smith, *History of Pittsfield,* 390–92; Christopher Clark, *Roots of Rural Capitalism: Western Massachusetts, 1780–1860* (Ithaca, N.Y.: Cornell University Press, 1990), 44–47. Inflation: *Connecticut Courant and the Weekly Intelligencer,* October 12, 1779, 3. Merchant: Case, *Goodrich Family,* 80. Son's portion: Edmund S. Morgan, *The Puritan Family: Religion and Domestic Relations in Seventh-Century New England,* new ed. (New York: Harper and Row, 1966), 81–82. Land: Berkshire Registry of Deeds, Middle District, Pittsfield, Massachusetts, grantor and grantee indices, 1761–1830. Elizur had an undivided right in Lot 49, perhaps his father's land in Richmond, but signed a quitclaim for £20 in 1791. Berkshire Registry of Deeds, Middle District, 31:155–56.

25. Elizur's first case as a defendant began in 1777 with a £580 debt that was still unpaid in 1783. Berkshire County Court of Common Pleas, vol. 5 (1782–83), 284, 363, BA.

26. Stephen A. Marini, *Radical Sects of Revolutionary New England* (Cambridge, Mass.: Harvard University Press, 1982), 52–53; White and Taylor, *Shakerism,* 36, 40, 107; Smith, *History of Pittsfield,* 453.

27. White and Taylor, *Shakerism,* 107; Case, *Goodrich Family,* 48, 78–80; Ezra Stiles, 1786, in Glendyne R. Wergland, *Visiting the Shakers, 1778–1849* (Clinton, N.Y.: Richard W. Couper Press, 2007), 134; Smith, *History of Pittsfield,* 453.

28. [Rufus Bishop and Seth Youngs Wells, comps.], *Testimonies of the Life, Character, Revelation and Doctrines of Our Ever Blessed Mother Ann Lee* (Hancock, Mass.: J. Tallcott and J. Deming, Junrs., 1816) (hereafter 1816 *Testimonies*), 31–32, 46–47.

29. Ibid., 259–60.

30. [Bishop and Wells], 1816 *Testimonies,* 306. Ann Lee separated other newlyweds, including Eliphalet Slosson (son of Elijah of West Stockbridge) and his wife, who lived in the New Lebanon and West Pittsfield/Hancock Shaker villages. [Berkshire Hills Conference and Federal Writers' Project of the WPA], *Berkshire Hills* (New York: Duell, Sloan and Pearce), 99–100.

31. Testimony of Sixty, a Cloud of Witnesses, Alonzo Hollister, comp., 8, WRHS 52, VI:B-40.

32. Ibid., 5.

33. "A Short Account of the People known by the Name of Shakers, or Shaking Quakers," *Theological Magazine* 1 (September–October 1795), quoted in Wergland, *Visiting the Shakers,* 23; Testimony of Sixty, 9.

34. [Bishop and Wells], 1816 *Testimonies,* 222–23.

35. Jan Kurth, "Wayward Wenches and Wives: Runaway Women in the Hudson Valley, N.Y., 1785–1830," *NWSA Journal* 1.2 (1988–89): 199–220.

36. Green, Memoir, 93.

37. [Bishop and Wells], 1816 *Testimonies,* 76.

38. Green, Memoir, 79–80; White and Taylor, *Shakerism,* 107.

39. Stiles, 1786; "Short Account," 21, 133.

40. Green, Memoir, 82. Other converts remained in their own homes because they were not yet gathered into villages. Throughout his book *Account of the People Called Shakers,* Brown describes Elders traveling to keep an eye on scattered Believers.

41. Massachusetts passed laws in the late 1700s to allow abandoned wives to divorce, freeing them to remarry and thus keeping them off the public dole. Richard Chused, "Married Women's Property and Inheritance by Widows in Massachusetts: A Study of Wills Probated between 1800 and 1850," *Berkeley Women's Law Journal* 2 (1986): 49.

42. Nancy F. Cott, "Divorce and the Changing Status of Women in Eighteenth-Century Massachusetts," *William and Mary Quarterly,* 3d. ser., 33.4 (1976): 597.

43. De Wolfe, *Shaking the Faith,* 130–34.

44. Occasionally, Lucy Wright's family ties surface in Shaker records: "Woodbridge Wright, of the 2nd Family Hancock Deceased aged 76—He was half Brother to Lucy Wright & half Uncle to Elder Grove Wright." Thomas Damon, Memoranda (1845–60), November 5, 1853, Dirk Langeveld transcription, HSV. See also Wealthy Storer [and Anna Erving?] journal (1846–52), May 10, 1849, June 19, 1850, and October 29, 1850 (out of sequence) WM 851, HSV copy.

45. Women's occupations in Boston: milliner, seamstress, mantua-maker, boarding-house keeper, innholder, taverner or liquor retailer, shopkeeper, starcher and dyer, schoolmistress, victualler, baker, and smallpox nurse. *Boston Directory* (Boston: John Norman, 1789); *Report of the Record Commissioners of the City of Boston, containing the Selectmen's Minutes from 1769 through April, 1775,* vol. 23 (Boston: Rockwell and Churchill, 1893). In Albany, many grocers were women; two advertised as washerwoman and one as a leather dresser. *Albany Directory* (Albany: Webster and Skinner, 1813).

46. Mary Beth Norton, *Liberty's Daughters: The Revolutionary Experience of American*

Women, 1750–1800 (New York: HarperCollins, 1980), 41–42. Lee Virginia Chambers-Schiller, *Liberty, a Better Husband: Single Women in America . . . 1780–1840* (New Haven: Yale University Press, 1984), chap. 1, covers the cult of single blessedness. Terri Premo, *Winter Friends: Women Growing Old in the New Republic, 1785–1835* (Chicago: University of Illinois Press, 1990), addresses the issues of singleness in old age.

47. Green, Memoir, 81.

48. Youngs, Family and Meeting Journal, March 23, 1818, LC 3:42.

49. Green, Memoir, 82–83. In 1782, Elizur was working at Watervliet for Ann Lee. Elizabeth Wood testimony: Jean Humez, *Mother's First-Born Daughters: Early Shaker Writings on Women and Religion* (Bloomington: Indiana University Press, 1993), 61.

50. [Bishop and Wells], 1816 *Testimonies*, 281.

51. Brown, *Account of the People Called Shakers*, 339; Chapman, *No. 2*, 58. Apostate views may be a biased source, but these two corroborate Elizur's continued affection.

52. Elizur did not dispose of his mercantile interests in Pittsfield until 1787. Case, *Goodrich Family*, 80; White and Taylor, *Shakerism*, 108. Scarlet coat: Rufus Bishop correspondence, WRHS 29, IV:B-37, 159–60, cited in Priscilla Brewer, *Shaker Communities, Shaker Lives* (Hanover, N.H.: University Press of New England, 1986), 11.

53. White and Taylor, *Shakerism*, 108.

54. Angell Matthewson, Reminiscences, letter 11 (1788), NYPL 9:119; Isaac N. Youngs, A Concise View of the Millennial Church, 443, WM 861; Priscilla Brewer, "The Demographic Features of the Shaker Decline, 1787–1900," *Journal of Interdisciplinary History* 15.1 (1984): 36–37; [Freegift Wells], Records of the Church at Watervliet, vol. 1 (1788–1851), WRHS 44, V:B-279. James Whittaker started gathering in 1786. Matthewson, Reminiscences, letter 9 (1786).

55. Elkanah Watson, in Wergland, *Visiting the Shakers*, 137.

56. Dr. Benjamin Waterhouse, in ibid., 142.

57. Joseph Meacham to Lucy Wright "a short time before his decease" [August 16, 1796], WRHS 19, IV:A-30.

58. Joseph Bennet, Domestic Journal (1789–94), WRHS 32, V:B-64, esp. 1790–91.

59. Matthewson, letter 23 (1798). My thanks to Christian Goodwillie for pointing out this source.

60. Seth Youngs Wells to David Darrow, April 25, 1822, WRHS 25, IV:A-78, cited in Humez, *Mother's First-Born Daughters*, 10n10. Goodrich died in New Lebanon's Second Order. Records Kept by Order of the Church, February 2, 1812, NYPL 2:7, 35.

61. White and Taylor, *Shakerism*, 108.

62. Stephen J. Stein, *The Shaker Experience in America: A History of the United Society of Believers* (New Haven: Yale University Press, 1992), 117.

63. Daniel Goodrich, Narrative History of the Church (1803), 9, HSV 6140a. My thanks to Christian Goodwillie for sharing this source.

64. Memorandum Kept by Jethro [Turner] (1784–1836), February 1821, LC 5:83.

65. Green, Memoir, 116.

CHAPTER 3. WHY WOMEN JOINED THE SHAKERS, 1780–1840

1. D'Ann Campbell, "Women's Life in Utopia: The Shaker Experiment in Sexual Equality Reappraised, 1810–1860," *New England Quarterly* 51.1 (1978): 32–36.

2. The women I surveyed were born between 1733 and 1825 and left testimonies dating from 1816 into the 1890s, describing their experiences from childhood to about 1840.

3. Seth Youngs Wells, comp., *Testimonies Concerning the Character and Ministry of Mother Ann Lee* (Albany: Packard and Van Benthuysen, 1827) (hereafter 1827 Testimonies), 26, 30, 93.

4. Ibid., 90–91, 92–93. Pentecostals say "baptism of the Holy Spirit" has a sensation like an electrical shock. Michael J. McClymond, "Issues and Explanations in the Study of North American Revivalism," in *Embodying the Spirit: New Perspectives on North American Revivalism,* ed. Michael J. McClymond (Baltimore: Johns Hopkins University Press, 2004), 8–9.

5. William Plumer, "Original Shaker Communities in New England," ed. F. B. Sanborn, *New England Magazine,* May 1900, 309.

6. Merlin Stone, *When God Was a Woman* (New York: Harcourt, 1976), 54–61, 216–23.

7. Christian Goodwillie and Jane Crosthwaite, eds., *Millennial Praises: A Shaker Hymnal* (Amherst: University of Massachusetts Press, 2009), 49.

8. Wells, 1827 Testimonies, 50.

9. McClymond, "Issues and Explanations," 9, 13.

10. Seth Youngs Wells, comp., Unpublisht Testimonies of Mother's First Born Children in America, Forming a Cloud of Witnesses, vol. 2, recopied by Alonzo Hollister, 89–91, WRHS 52, VI:B-43.

11. Diane Sasson, *Shaker Spiritual Narrative* (Knoxville: University of Tennessee Press, 1983), 193.

12. Wells, Unpublisht Testimonies, 1:59, 61, 84, WRHS 52, VI:B-42.

13. Ibid., 1:160–61.

14. Ibid., Unpublisht Testimonies, 2:107–8, WRHS 52, VI:B-43.

15. Ibid., 2:124–25, 130, 135–36.

16. Wells, 1827 Testimonies, 32–33, 60–61.

17. Wells, 1827 Testimonies, 90–92.

18. "Shaker Sister's Funeral," *Pittsfield Sun,* July 1, 1897, 5.

19. Book of Immortality, 63, WRHS 52, VI:B-37.

20. Wells, 1827 Testimonies, 66–68, 92–93.

21. Sasson, *Shaker Spiritual Narrative,* 171.

22. Wells, Unpublisht Testimonies, 2:129, WRHS 52, VI:B-43.

23. Book of Immortality, 324–25, WRHS 52, VI:B-37.

24. Wells, Unpublisht Testimonies, 1:100–106.

25. Eliza Rayson testimony (1842?), WRHS 49, VI:A-6.

26. Selah Youngs, Jr., *Youngs Family: A History and Genealogy* (New York: for author, 1907), 87–88, 115–18; Lafayette Wallace Case, *Goodrich Family in America* (Chicago: Fergus Printing Co., 1889), 48, 78–80.

27. Chet Raymo, "Genetics of Belief," *Notre Dame Magazine,* Spring 2005, http://magazine .nd.edu/news/10465-the-genetics-of-belief/; James Sage, review of *The God Gene: How Faith Is Hardwired into Our Genes,* by Dean H. Hamer (New York: Anchor, 2004), *Metapsychology Online Reviews* 11.28 (July 2007), http://metapsychology.mentalhelp .net/poc/view_doc.php?type=book&id=3723&cn=403.

28. Wells, Unpublisht Testimonies, 1:77–78, WRHS 52, VI:B-42; Archibald Montgomery Maxwell, *A Run through the United States,* vol. 1 (London: H. Colburn, 1841), 130–31; Wells, 1827 Testimonies, 87–89.

29. Stephen Paterwic, "From Individual to Community: Becoming a Shaker at New Lebanon, 1780–1947," *Communal Societies* 11 (1991): 26–27.
30. Win Arn, "Is TV Appropriate for Mass Evangelism?" *Christianity Today* 16 (1987): 50, quoted in McClymond, *Embodying the Spirit,* 287n81.
31. Metin M. Coşgel, "Family in Utopia: Celibacy, Communal Child Rearing, and Continuity in a Religious Commune," *Journal of Family History* 25.4 (2000): 499; Coşgel, "The Commitment Process in a Religious Commune: The Shakers," *Journal for the Scientific Study of Religion* 40.1 (2001): 36.
32. Before the 1830s, male property owners were more likely to bequeath assets to other men than to women. Glendyne Wergland, "Women, Men, Property, and Inheritance: Gendered Testamentary Customs in Western Massachusetts, 1800–1860" (Ph.D. diss., University of Massachusetts, 2001).
33. "The Shakers," *The Ariel* (Philadelphia), December 28, 1827. Elizabeth Baker, Esq., kindly shared this account of Harvard Shaker village.
34. Youngs, *Youngs Family,* 117.
35. Isaac N. Youngs to Nancy Farrell, January 30, 1830, WRHS 20, IV:A-36. Also see Elizabeth A. De Wolfe, *Shaking the Faith: Women, Family, and Mary Marshall Dyer's Anti-Shaker Campaign, 1815–1867* (New York: Palgrave, 2002).
36. William Dean Howells, "A Shaker Village," *Atlantic Monthly,* June 1876, 700, 707, Cornell University Making of America collection of nineteenth-century publications, http://cdl.library.cornell.edu/moa.
37. Book of Immortality, 320, WRHS 52, VI:B-37; [Rufus Bishop and Seth Youngs Wells, comps.], *Testimonies of the Life, Character, Revelations and Doctrines of Our Ever Blessed Mother Ann Lee* (Hancock, Mass.: J. Talcott and J. Deming, Junrs., 1816), 36.
38. Garret Lawrence obituary, *Hampshire Republican,* n.d., in Isaac N. Youngs, Domestic Journal (1834–46), February 8, 1837, NYSL 10.
39. Nicholas Bennett, Domestic Journal, WRHS 32, V:B-68, May–September 1816; [Bishop], Ministry Day Book, May 12–16, June 1, 1816, WRHS 33, V:B-85; Samuel Griswold Goodrich, *Recollections of a Lifetime,* vol. 2 (New York: Auburn, Miller, Orton and Mulligan, 1857), 78–80; Diaries of William Partridge of Pittsfield [Mass.], August 21, 28, 1816, Russell C. Taylor transcription, 2004, BA; Calvin Green, Sayings of Mother Lucy Wright, 14, WRHS 56, VII:B-70.
40. Priscilla Brewer, *Shaker Communities, Shaker Lives* (Hanover, N.H.: University Press of New England, 1986), 215.
41. Fredrika Bremer, *Homes of the New World: Impressions of America,* trans. Mary Howitt (New York: Harper and Brothers, 1853), 1:562.
42. Wells, 1827 Testimonies, 59.
43. [Rhoda Blake], Sketch of the Life, Experience and Recollections of Rhoda Blake, written 1864–92, Alonzo Hollister transcription, 3–5, 7–8, 9–12, 15–16, WRHS 51, VI:B-33.
44. Ibid., 35.
45. Betsy Crosman to Sister Harriet, n.d. [after September 29, 1840], WRHS 19, IV:A-30.
46. Wells, 1827 Testimonies, 60.
47. Wells, Unpublisht Testimonies, 1:24–252, WRHS 52, VI:B-4.
48. Ibid., 2:138–41.
49. Wells, 1827 Testimonies, 52.
50. Cory's parents returned to Connecticut. Wells, 1827 Testimonies, 54–59. Boys also suf-

fered domestic violence and neglect. See James Wilson's 1843 testimony. Sasson, *Shaker Spiritual Narrative,* 70.

51. Wells, Unpublisht Testimonies, 1:82, WRHS 52, VI:B-42.

52. Ibid., 171–75.

53. Book of Immortality, 292–96, 303, WRHS VI:B-37.

54. Early Shakers' reasons for joining the sect combine the "cognitive minority," "revivalist-centered," "economic deprivation," and "functionalist" models—four of the six reasons McClymond postulates in "Issues and Explanations," 32–41.

55. Wells, Unpublisht Testimonies, 1:88, WRHS 52, VI:B-42.

56. Suzanne Thurman, "Shaker Women and Sexual Power: Heresy and Orthodoxy in the Shaker Village of Harvard, Massachusetts," *Journal of Women's History* 10.1 (1998): 82.

57. Beirne Stedman, "Right of Husband to Chastise Wife," *Virginia Law Register,* n.s., 3.4 (August 1917): 241–48; Reva B. Siegel, "'The Rule of Love': Wife Beating as Prerogative and Privacy," *Yale Law Journal* 105.8 (June 1996): 2117–207. On obedience, see also Nancy Cott, *Bonds of Womanhood: "Woman's Sphere" in New England, 1780–1835* (New Haven: Yale University Press, 1977), 76–80.

58. Testimony of Sixty, a Cloud of Witnesses, Alonzo Hollister, comp., 98, WRHS 52, VI:B-40.

59. Marianne Finch, *An Englishwoman's Experience in America* (1853; reprint, New York: Negro Universities Press, 1969), 152–53.

60. Lee Virginia Chambers-Schiller, *Liberty, a Better Husband: Single Women in America . . . 1780–1840* (New Haven: Yale University Press, 1984), chap. 1.

61. Pattie Cowell, "'Womankind Call Reason to Their Aid': Susanna Wright's Verse Epistle on the Status of Women in Eighteenth-Century America," *Signs* 6.4 (1981): 800.

62. Susan Starr Sered, "Ideology, Autonomy, and Sisterhood: An Analysis of the Secular Consequences of Women's Religions," *Gender and Society* 8.4 (1994): 487–88.

63. Isaac N. Youngs, Family and Meeting Journal (1815–23), August 17, 1816, LC 3:42.

64. Chambers-Schiller, *Liberty,* chap. 1; Terri Premo, *Winter Friends: Women Growing Old in the New Republic, 1785–1835* (Chicago: University of Illinois Press, 1990), 38–47.

65. [Seth Youngs Wells], Remarks on the necessity of reforming the morals . . . of our youth and children, 1830, WRHS 56, VII:B-66, 4–5; Brewer, *Shaker Communities,* 213–14; Louis J. Kern, *An Ordered Love* (Chapel Hill: University of North Carolina Press, 1981), 133.

CHAPTER 4. SHAKER GIRLHOOD

1. Memorandum Kept by Jethro [Turner], April 1811, LC 5:83; Shaker names index, WRHS 123. See also Elizabeth A. De Wolfe, *Shaking the Faith: Women, Family, and Mary Marshall Dyer's Anti-Shaker Campaign, 1815–1867* (New York: Palgrave, 2002), 19–53, 89.

2. Rufus Bishop, Daily Journal of Passing Events (1830–39), August 17, 1833, NYPL 1.1.

3. Wealthy Storer [and Anna Erving?] journal (1846–52), May 18, 1849, WM 851, HSV copy.

4. Hancock Ministry Journal (1849–56), September 13, 1850, Crete collection, HSV; Storer [and Erving?] journal, September 13, 1850, WM 851, HSV copy.

5. Anita Gurian, "Gifted Girls—Many Gifted Girls, Few Eminent Women: Why?" NYU Child Study Center, available at http://www.aboutourkids.org/; Susan Jones and Debra

Myhill, "'Troublesome Boys' and 'Compliant Girls': Gender Identity and Perceptions of Achievement and Underachievement," *British Journal of Sociology of Education* 25.5 (2004): 547–61.

6. Carol Lynn Martin and Richard A. Fabes, "Stability and Consequences of Young Children's Same-Sex Peer Interactions," *Developmental Psychology* 37.3 (May 2001): 431–46.

7. Hervey Elkins, *Fifteen Years in the Senior Order of Shakers* (Hanover, N.H., 1853), 26.

8. Edward Deming Andrews and Faith Andrews, "The Shaker Children's Order," *Winterthur Portfolio* 8 (1973): 202.

9. Harriet Hanson Robinson was a bobbin doffer in a textile mill at age ten. She discusses her experiences in her book *Loom and Spindle; or, Life among the Early Mill Girls* (New York: Thomas Y. Crowell, 1898).

10. Watervliet indentures, NYSL 5:367.

11. [Aaron Bill, Sr.], Canaan journal (1813–43), June 1838, LC 3:40.

12. [Abigail Crosman et al.], Journal of Domestic Events & transactions . . . Kept by the Deaconesses, Chh 2nd Order (1843–64), February 15, 1854, HSV 9758. Weather: Isaac N. Youngs, Domestic Journal (1847–55), February 1854, WRHS 32, V:B-70.

13. Garret K. Lawrence obituary, Isaac N. Youngs, Domestic Journal, end, NYSL 10.

14. Calvin Reed, Sarah Bates, Polly Reed, et al., [New Lebanon School Journal] (1852–87), 200, HSV 9758.

15. [Rhoda Blake], Sketch of the Life, Experience and Recollections of Rhoda Blake, written 1864–92, Alonzo Hollister transcription, 7, 35, WRHS 51, VI:B-33.

16. Storer [and Erving?] journal, December 1848–1849, WM 851; Youngs, Domestic Journal, January 25, 1848; Isaac N. Youngs, Personal Journal (1839–54), December 13, 1848, WRHS 35, V:B-134.

17. Storer [and Erving?] journal, January 24, March 20, 1849, October 18, 1851.

18. Rev. David Macrae, "A Day with the Shakers," *Americans at Home: Pen-and-Ink Sketches of American Men, Manners, and Institutions,* vol. 2 (Glasgow: John Smith and Son, Ltd., 1908), 339. This was not an isolated occurrence for the Shakers near Pittsfield. See also "Accident," Berkshire County Eagle, October 24, 1861, 2; "The Foundling at the Shakers," Berkshire County Eagle, February 13, 1862, 2; and "T.," "The Shaker Baby," *Pittsfield Sun,* September 3, 1873.

19. Andrews and Andrews, "Shaker Children's Order," 213–14.

20. Storer [and Erving?] journal, March 20, 1849.

21. Andrews and Andrews, "Shaker Children's Order," 202–3. Winterthur Museum owns 142 Shaker indentures.

22. [Bill], Canaan journal, April 22, October 15, 1834.

23. [Abigail Crosman et al.], Journal, January 31, 1855, November 12, 1857, June 18–19, 1858, September 15, October 3, 1860, HSV 9758.

24. [Catherine Ann Slater], "Fifteen Years a Shakeress," *Galaxy* 13 (March 1872): 31.

25. Shaker censuses: Names of the Brethren and the Sisters in the First and Second Order April 1835 [New Lebanon], LC 5:92; Youngs, Domestic Journal, January 1, 1840, January 1, 1845, NYSL 10; Youngs, Domestic Journal, January 1, 1850, January 1, 1855, WRHS 32, V:B-70; Isaac N. Youngs and John Brown, Domestic Journal (1856–69), January 1, 1860, WRHS 32, V:B-71.

26. My thanks to Jane Crosthwaite for sharing "Polly Reed: Shaker Minister and Shaker Artist," her talk to American Society of Church History, April 1993, 7–8.

27. Youngs, Domestic Journal, April 28, 1856, WRHS 32, V:B-71.

28. Glendyne Wergland, "Shaker Discipline and Bad Boys 'more fit for the company of pirates than here'" (paper presented at the Dublin Seminar for New England Folklife, Deerfield, Mass., June 15, 2002).

29. As early as preschool, girls' compliance contrasts with boys' noncompliance. Jane Brown, "Time, Space and Gender: Understanding 'Problem' Behaviour in Young Children," *Children & Society* 21.2 (2007): 98–110. Another study discusses boys' diverging from expectations, while girls conform. Tony Eaude, "Should Teachers Adopt Differential Strategies for Young Boys and Girls in Relation to Spiritual Development?" *International Handbook of the Religious, Moral, and Spiritual Dimensions in Education*, vol. 1, ed. Marian de Souza, Gloria Durka, Kathleen Engebretson, Robert Jackson, and Andrew McGrady (London: Springer, 2006).

30. Reed et al., [New Lebanon School Journal], 21; Isaac N. Youngs, Idle Company: A Treatise on Disorderly Communication, particularly for boys and youth (1851–54), WRHS 57, VII:B-103; Sister Frances A. Carr, *Growing Up Shaker* (Sabbathday Lake, Me.: United Society of Shakers, 1995), 14.

31. Seth Youngs Wells, Remarks on the necessity of reforming the morals . . . of our youth and children (1830), 5, WRHS 56, VII: B-66.

32. Lizzie Horton to Emma B. King, *Shaker Manifesto* 15.5 (1885): 113, HCDC; Lizzie Horton, "My Choice," *Shaker Manifesto* 23.9 (1893): 206, HCDC.

33. Isaac N. Youngs and Derobigne Bennett, Journal of Inspirational Meetings (1840–41), December 6, 1840, WRHS 77, VIII:B-138.

34. See Shaker censuses cited above. Names of the Brethren and the Sisters . . . April 1835, LC 5:92; Youngs, Domestic Journal, January 1, 1840, January 1, 1845, NYSL 10; Youngs, Domestic Journal, January 1, 1850, January 1, 1855, WRHS 32, V:B-70; Isaac N. Youngs and John Brown, Domestic Journal (1856–69), January 1, 1860 and January 1, 1865, WRHS 32, V:B-71.

35. Amy Reed journal (1832–56), January 1, 1841, SM 10,465.

36. Glendyne R. Wergland, *One Shaker Life: Isaac Newton Youngs, 1793–1865* (Amherst: University of Massachusetts Press, 2006), chap. 3.

37. Youngs, Domestic Journal, January 1, 1840, January 1, 1845, NYSL 10; Youngs, Domestic Journal, January 1, 1850, WRHS 32, V:B-70; Youngs, Domestic Journal, January 1, 1860, WRHS 32, V:B-71.

38. Generally speaking, men notice women's work only when it is not done, or not done correctly. I am reminded of an anecdote I heard years ago. An anthropologist was interviewing an older man in an African village, videotaping their conversation. She asked what the women in his village did, and he seemed stumped by the question, finally making a general comment about child care. Behind him, clearly visible on the video, a group of women were building a house.

39. Eloise Myers, *Tyringham: A Hinterland Settlement* (Tyringham, Mass.: Hinterland Press, 1989), 85–86. At Sabbathday Lake, kitchen work was done by a head cook, baker, vegetable girl, and sink girl. Carr, *Growing Up Shaker*, 68–69.

40. "S. P.," "From the Little Children," *Shaker Manifesto* 16.5 (1886): 119, HCDC.

41. "Sister Marcia," "Recollections of My Childhood," *Good Housekeeping*, August 1906, 127.

42. Carr, *Growing Up Shaker*, 20; Trudy Reno Sherburne, *As I Remember It* (Holland, Mich.: World of Shaker, 1987), 22.

43. "Sister Marcia," "Recollections of My Childhood," 127.
44. Anna P. Carll, "Reminiscences of My Shaker Childhood: Autumn," *Shaker Manifesto* 16.10 (1886): 235, HCDC.
45. Youngs, Domestic Journal, January 1, 1860, WRHS 32, V:B-71.
46. Nathaniel Hawthorne, *American Notebooks,* ed. Claude M. Simpson (Columbus: Ohio State University Press, 1972), 465.
47. Myers, *Tyringham,* 86; Judith A. Graham, "The New Lebanon Shaker Children's Order," *Winterthur Portfolio* 26.4 (1991): 220; Carr, *Growing Up Shaker,* 10, 57.
48. Hattie to Elder Henry, February 1886, *Shaker Manifesto* 16.4 (1886): 96; L. Horton to Sister Caroline, May 1883, *Shaker Manifesto* 13.5 (1883): 111, HCDC.
49. Betsy Crosman, Small Record Book (1848–72), December 31, 1859, December 31, 1860, WRHS 36, V:B-143.
50. Ibid., December 31, 1865, 1867, 1868, 1869.
51. Anne L. MacDonald, *No Idle Hands: The Social History of American Knitting* (New York: Ballantine Books, 1988), 88.
52. Lorraine Lauzon, "Pittsfield Woman Had a Shaker Upbringing," *Catholic Observer,* January 13, 1978, 10. At Sabbathday Lake, girls had to weave six inches of poplar each weekday. Carr, *Growing Up Shaker,* 71.
53. Myers, *Tyringham,* 86; "Sister Marcia," "Recollections of My Childhood," 127; Martha A. Hulings, *Shaker Days Remembered* (Albany, N.Y.: Shaker Heritage Society, 1983), 28.
54. Anna P. Carll, "Reminiscences of My Shaker Childhood: Winter," *Shaker Manifesto* 17.2 (1887): 45–46, HCDC.
55. Hulings, *Shaker Days Remembered,* 27–29, 36–37.
56. Carr, *Growing Up Shaker,* 19; [Rufus Bishop], Ministry Day Book, August 19, September 4, 1815, WRHS 33, V:B-85.
57. D. A. Buckingham, Records of the Church at Watervliet (1788–1851), 193, August 23, 1841, WRHS 44, V:B-279; Shaker Names index, WRHS 123.
58. Hattie to Elder Henry, February 1886, *Shaker Manifesto* 16.4 (1886): 96.
59. "Sister Marcia," "Recollections of My Childhood," 127; Sherburne, *As I Remember It,* 26.
60. Seth Youngs Wells, A plain statement of the custom and manner of receiving, managing, teaching, governing and disciplining children (1815), 10–11, WRHS 56, VII:B-62; "Child Life in Shakerdom," *New York Times,* September 21, 1874, 3.
61. "Striking Children," reprinted from *Congregationalist* in *Shaker Manifesto* 18.4 (1888): 95, HCDC; Hulings, *Shaker Days Remembered,* 59–63. Sister Frances Carr says, "Shakers never have believed in corporal punishment." To her, staying home from a day at the beach or a Thursday night movie was punishment enough. Carr, *Growing Up Shaker,* 57–58.
62. Carr, *Growing Up Shaker,* 24, 53–54.
63. Youngs, Domestic Journal, April 30, 1856, WRHS 32, V:B-71; "Shaker Sister's Funeral, *Pittsfield Sun,* July 1, 1897, 5. On a mentor as a surrogate parent, see Wergland, *One Shaker Life,* chap. 7.
64. Herrick Kenyon, "The Shakers of Mount Lebanon," *Sunday Magazine* 15 (1886): 95.
65. Fairs quoted in Lauzon, "Pittsfield Woman," 10; Sherburne, *As I Remember It,* 9; [Slater], "Fifteen Years a Shakeress," 32.
66. Carr, *Growing Up Shaker,* 3, 10, 31–33, 40, 53–56.
67. [Slater], "Fifteen Years a Shakeress," 35; Hulings, *Shaker Days Remembered,* 81–84.

68. Isaac N. Youngs, A Concise View of the Church of God (1856), 363–67, 374, WM 861; Isaac N. Youngs et al., Memorandum of the Proceedings and Expenses of the School, 11, March 9, 1820, SM 21:10,469 (vol. 181).

69. Youngs, Domestic Journal, May 6, 1851, WRHS 32, V:B-70; Youngs, Domestic Journal, April 30, 1856, WRHS 32, V:B-71; Youngs, Concise View 373.

70. Youngs et al., Memorandum, 23, 29, 35–39, 46, SM 21:10,469.

71. "The Scholar's Soliloquy," n. p., WRHS 116, X:A-2.

72. Jeremiah Hacker, "Traveler's Cabin," *Portland Pleasure Boat* 3 (August 28, 1847): 1. Jerry Grant kindly shared this source.

73. [Lewis Gaylord Clark], "Editor's Table: A Visit to the Shakers at New-Lebanon and Hancock," *Knickerbocker* 32 (July 1848): 77.

74. John W. Barber, *Historical Collections of the State of New York* (New York: Clark, Austin & Co., 1851), 79, Cornell University Making of America collection of nineteenth-century publications, http://cdl.library.cornell.edu/moa (hereafter Cornell MOA).

75. Editor's Drawer, *Harper's*, June 1852, 135, Cornell MOA. Polly Reed was the previous teacher. Youngs, Domestic Journal, May 6, 1851, WRHS 32, V:B-70. Anna Dodgson may have been the next teacher. Youngs, Domestic Journal, April 30, 1856, WRHS 32, V:B-71.

76. Kenyon, "Shakers of Mount Lebanon," 96. North Family teachers were Mary A. Bowers or Brown [semi-legible], 27, and Lucy Bowers, 21. The Church Family teacher was Sarah Cutler, 32. 1880 U.S. Census, New Lebanon, N.Y., 451, 457.

77. [Charles Dudley Warner], "Out of the World," *Scribner's Monthly* 18.4 (August 1879): 552, Cornell MOA. Teacher Mary Nelson: 1880 U.S. Census, Watervliet, N.Y., 430.

78. Youngs, Domestic Journal, July 2, 1857, WRHS 32, V:B-71; Reed et al., [New Lebanon School Journal], 203–4.

79. Amelia Calver, Some Verses, in Specimens of Composition . . . written by the girls in school, New Lebanon (1856–68), comp. Anna Dodgson, 25, SM 12,064.

80. [Rufus Bishop and Seth Youngs Wells, comps.], *Testimonies of the Life, Character, Revelations and Doctrines of Our Ever Blessed Mother Ann Lee* (Hancock, Mass.: J. Talcott and J. Deming, Junrs., 1816), 279.

81. "Sister Marcia," "Recollections of My Childhood," 127; [Slater], "Fifteen Years a Shakeress," 31–32, 36, 338.

82. Hulings, *Shaker Days Remembered,* 78–84; Carll, "Reminiscences of My Shaker Childhood: Winter," 46.

83. Sherburne, *As I Remember It,* 16, 28–29, 35–36. At Canterbury, girls took a steamboat to a resort. Anna P. Carll, "Reminiscences of My Shaker Childhood: Summer," *Shaker Manifesto* 16.8 (1886): 186, HCDC.

84. Youngs, Domestic Journal, April 1–2, 1857, WRHS 32, V:B-71.

85. Anna P. Carll, "Reminiscences of My Shaker Childhood: Spring," *Shaker Manifesto* 17.5 (1887): 116–17, HCDC.

86. "Sister Marcia," "Recollections of My Childhood," 129.

87. Crosman, Small Record Book, April 2–4, 1857; 2nd Order Deaconesses' journal, April 10, 1857, HSV 1086a; Youngs, Domestic Journal, April 17, 1868, WRHS 32, V:B-71.

88. Youngs, Domestic Journal, August 28, 1838, NYSL 10.

89. Carll, "Reminiscences of My Shaker Childhood: Summer," 186; "Sister Marcia," "Recollections of My Childhood," 129.

90. Betsy Bates, Journal of Events (1833–35), July 7, 1835, WRHS 35, V:B-128.

91. A Trip to the Berkshires: The 1860 Summer Diary of Lucius Manlius Sargent, Jr., HSV photocopy and transcription, gift of Alex and Nancy Burgess (1995), 69.

92. "Sister Marcia," "Recollections of My Childhood," 128–29.

93. "Innominato," "An Old Time Shaker Meeting: Observances of Thirty Years Ago," *Pittsfield Sun,* February 2, 1899, 2.

94. Isaac N. Youngs, Family and Meeting Journal, February 27, 1820, 48, LC 3:42.

95. Youngs, Domestic Journal, August 20, 1857, July 7, 1862, WRHS 32, V:B-71.

96. Sisters over age sixty lived elsewhere. Ministry Sisters' Journal, September 1832, WRHS 32, V:B-60; Youngs, Domestic Journal, January 1, 1840, NYSL 10.

97. [Slater], "Fifteen Years a Shakeress," 468; Elizabeth Baker, "Everything You Always Wanted to Know about the Shaker Covenant" (Shaker Seminar talk, Hancock Shaker Village, Pittsfield, Massachusetts, July 27, 2006). Slater's statement could be the thesis of a study of seceders' economic problems. Another seceder failed at several businesses. See DeRobigne Bennet, *The World's Sages, Thinkers, and Reformers* (New York: Liberal and Scientific Publishing House, 1876), 1061–64.

98. [Julia H. Johnson], "Reminiscences of Shaker Life," *Credit Foncier of Sinaloa* [Mexico], 4.24 (September 1, 1889), clipping in Wallace H. Cathcart Shaker scrapbook (1811–1912), WRHS 120, XIII: 47.

99. Kenyon, "Shakers of Mount Lebanon," 93; Seth Youngs Wells, Remarks on the necessity of reforming the morals, 4–5, WRHS 56, VII: B-66. Shakers compensated for boys' relative immaturity by keeping them in the children's order until age sixteen, whereas girls were moved into adult quarters at fourteen (or so). 1845 Millennial Laws: Edward D. Andrews, The *People Called Shakers* (New York: Dover, 1963), 277.

100. John E. Murray, "Human Capital in Religious Communes: Literacy and Selection of Nineteenth-Century Shakers," *Explorations in Economic History* 32 (1995): 217–35. One of the University of Massachusetts Press's anonymous readers also points out that girls had fewer economic opportunities in the world than boys did.

101. Priscilla Brewer, *Shaker Communities, Shaker Lives* (Hanover, N.H.: University Press of New England, 1986), 213–14.

CHAPTER 5. CHASTITY AND THE SHAKER CAP

1. Wealthy Storer [and Anna Erving] journal (1846–52), April 6, 1851, WM 851, copy at HSV; Deborah E. Burns, *Shaker Cities of Peace, Love, and Union: A History of the Hancock Bishopric* (Hanover, N.H.: University Press of New England, 1993), 146; Edward Deming Andrews and Faith Andrews, "The Shaker Children's Order," *Winterthur Portfolio* 8 (1973): 204. In 1847, the Irvings joined the Shakers, but the parents left before August 1850. 1850 U.S. Census, Hancock, Mass., p. 139/277; Hancock Record database, HSV.

2. Headgear is often used to declare beliefs or status. Marguerite de Angeli discusses the symbolism of the Quaker bonnet in the children's classic *Thee, Hannah* (Scottdale, Pa.: Herald Press, 2000). My thanks to Elizabeth Hansen for this reference.

3. Irving's violence gave his daughters a good reason to stay with the Shakers. One scholar believes that Shaker-raised children lacked the love and security of biological kin, but Justina might have disagreed. Judith A. Graham, "The New Lebanon Shaker Children's Order," *Winterthur Portfolio* 26.4 (1991): 224. My thanks to University of Massachusetts Press's anonymous reader for pointing out the economic value of a daughter's work.

4. Laura H. Weaver ponders acculturation in "Plain Clothes Revisited: Empathy for Muslim Women," *Mennonite Life* 57.2 (June 2002), available online at http://www.bethelks.edu/mennonitelife/2002june/weaver.php.

5. Mary M. Crain review of *Religion, Dress and the Body*, ed. Linda Arthur, *American Ethnologist* 27.3 (2000): 790.

6. Linda B. Arthur, Introduction to *Religion, Dress, and the Body*, ed. Gabriella Lazaridis and Linda B. Arthur (New York: Berg, 1999), 3–4; Margaret C. Reynolds, *Plain Women: Gender and Ritual in the Old Order River Brethren* (University Park: Pennsylvania State University Press, 2001), 76–77.

7. Reynolds, *Plain Women*, 2.

8. [Emily Smith], "Lines on a Shaker Dress," in [book of transcribed writings] (1775–1857), 112, WRHS 26, IV:B-3.

9. Nina Baym, *Woman's Fiction: A Guide to Novels by and about Women in America, 1820–1870*, 2d ed. (Urbana: University of Illinois Press, 1993), 158; Glendyne R. Wergland, "Designing Women: Massachusetts Milliners in the Nineteenth Century," *Dublin Seminar for New England Folklife Annual Proceedings*, 1997, 203–11.

10. Elie Reclus, "A Visit to Mount Lebanon in 1878," trans. and ed. Marius B. Péladeau, *Shaker Quarterly* 11 (Spring 1971): 37.

11. Frances Trollope, *Domestic Manners of the Americans* (1832; reprint, New York: Dodd, Mead, 1894), 74, 300; Mrs. L. G. Abell, *Woman in Her Various Relations* (New York: William Holdredge, 1851), 137–38.

12. Shakers (their mode of worship), Kellogg and Comstock lithograph, 1850–51, HSV.

13. Joanne B. Eicher and Mary Ellen Roach-Higgins, "Definition and Classification of Dress: Implications for Analysis of Gender Roles," *Dress and Gender: Making and Meaning*, ed. Ruth Barnes and Joanne B. Eicher (Providence, R.I.: Berg, 1992), 12–13; Reynolds, *Plain Women*, 14, 55, 69.

14. Eunice Chapman, *Account of the Conduct of the People Called Shakers* (Albany: author, 1817), 23. My thanks to Ilyon Woo for this quotation.

15. Reynolds, *Plain Women*, 85.

16. Arthur, introduction, 1–3.

17. Paul Erb, *We Believe* (Scottdale, Pa.: Herald Press, 1969), 60–63, explains the Christian doctrine that women must cover their heads while praying. Joseph W. Yoder, *The Prayer Veil Analyzed* (Huntington, Pa.: Yoder, 1954) says that the practice of women wearing a veil or cap of subordination is based on a misinterpretation of Paul.

18. Giles Avery to Eldress Polly Lee, Groveland, April 19, 1869, WRHS 21, IV:A-43.

19. Eicher and Roach-Higgins, "Definition and Classification of Dress," 15, 19.

20. Sherry B. Ortner, "On Key Symbols," *American Anthropologist*, n.s. 75.5 (1973): 1338–39.

21. [Rufus Bishop and Seth Youngs Wells, comps.], *Testimonies of the Life, Character, Revelations and Doctrines of Our Ever Blessed Mother Ann Lee* (Hancock, Mass.: J. Talcott and J. Deming, Junrs., 1816), 278.

22. Crain review, 790.

23. Jean Humez, *Mother's First-Born Daughters: Early Shaker Writings on Women and Religion* (Bloomington: Indiana University Press, 1993), 70.

24. Giles Avery to Polly Lee, April 19, 1869, WRHS 21, IV:A-43.

25. Isaac N. Youngs, A Concise View of the Church of God and of Christ on Earth, 327, WM 861; "Shakers in Niskayuna," *Frank Leslie's Popular Monthly*, December 1885, 666.

26. Nineteenth-century Quaker girls received their caps before they were "fairly grown up." Amelia Mott Gummere, *The Quaker: A Study in Costume* (Philadelphia: Ferris and Leach, 1901), 181–82. My thanks to Isabel Jane Penraeth for this source. Old Order River Brethren girls "take the covering" by age twelve or thirteen. Reynolds, *Plain Women,* 73.

27. Rules for Dressing Little Girls' Heads, LC 22.305.

28. In other communal groups, adulthood was a function of age. A Hutterite rite of passage was on a girl's fifteenth birthday, the end of childhood. Ruth Baer Lambach, "Colony Girl: A Hutterite Childhood," *Women in Spiritual and Communitarian Societies in the United States,* ed. Wendy E. Chmielewski, Louis J. Kern, and Marlyn Klee-Hartzel (Syracuse, N.Y.: Syracuse University Press, 1993), 249.

29. A visitor noticed one "demure little maid with her hair in a single braid instead of hidden under a cap." O. A. Bierstadt, "The Shakers," clipping in Wallace H. Cathcart Shaker scrapbook, 97–98, WRHS 120, XIII-47.

30. Isaac N. Youngs, Domestic Journal (1856–77), August 20, 1857, July 7, 1862, WRHS 32, V:B-71; Shaker Names index, WRHS 123; [Semantha Fairbanks] journal (1835–36) following John DeWitt Memorandum, November 21, 1836, WRHS 33, V:B-92; Names of the Brethren and the Sisters in the First and Second Order April 1835, LC 5:92.

31. [Shirley journal] (1816–29), December 2, 1827, WRHS 38, V:B-197.

32. Betsy Bates, Journal of Events (1833–35), August 13, 1833, WRHS 35, V:B-128.

33. In the United States, menarche has declined from age 17 in the early 1800s to 14 in the 1920s and 12.8 in the 1980s. Museum of Menstruation and Women's Health, "Average Age at Menarche," http://www.mum.org/menarage.htm.

34. Beverly Gordon, *Shaker Textile Arts* (Hanover, N.H.: University Press of New England, 1980), 149; Reynolds, *Plain Women,* 83.

35. Stereopticon of Canaan Upper Family schoolgirls, HSV 1991-5298.

36. David R. Lamson, *Two Years' Experience among the Shakers* (West Boylston [Mass.]: for the author, 1848), 39; Brother Arnold Hadd, Sabbathday Lake Shaker Village, New Gloucester, Maine, e-mail message to author, May 12, 2008.

37. [Catherine Ann Slater], "Fifteen Years a Shakeress," *Galaxy* 13 (1872): 337–38.

38. [Slater], "Fifteen Years a Shakeress," 467.

39. Eloise Myers, *Tyringham: A Hinterland Settlement* (Tyringham, Mass.: Hinterland Press, 1989), 81.

40. Asenath Clark, Ministerial Journal, New Lebanon and Watervliet, N.Y. (1834–36), June 1, 1835, HSV 1480, copy of SM original; Kimberly D. Praria, "Visions of Others: Changes in Shaker Doctrine as Viewed through the Acceptance or Denial of Popular Worldly Fashion" (master's thesis, State University of New York–Oneonta, 2003), 8.

41. Charles Giles B. Daubeny, 1837, in Glendyne R. Wergland, *Visiting the Shakers, 1778–1849* (Clinton, N.Y.: Richard W. Couper Press, 2007), 264.

42. Thankful Goodrich, A Brief Sketch of Experience & Testimony, copied into Book of Immortality, comp. Alonzo Hollister, WRHS 52, VI:B-37.

43. Eliza Babbit, Office Sister's Journal (1855–57), February 16, 1856, FM 31.3.

44. Eldress Annie Williams journal (1832–55), February 21, 1842, August 3, 1836, WRHS 35, V:B-127; Canaan, N.Y., Lower Family Sister's journal (1850–53), November 20, 1850, LC 3:39.

45. Olive Chandler Journal, November 11, 25, 1870, FM 32.7.

46. A List of what is thought proper for the Sisters wearing apparel, 1840, LC 22:305, 306; Instructions for clothing young females according to Mother Lucy, NYPL 8.113i.

47. Eunice Chapman, *No. 2, Being an Additional Account of the Conduct of the Shakers,* (Albany: I. W. Clark, 1818), 25. My thanks to Ilyon Woo for this reference.

48. Canaan Lower Family Sister's journal, May 28, 1852, LC 3:39.

49. Bates, Journal of Events, August 19, 1835, WRHS 35, V:B-128.

50. Olive Hatch, Ministry Journal, (1851–54), December 1851, March 2, September 29, 1853, WRHS 39, V:B-218, FM transcription.

51. Elkanah Watson and William Loughton Smith, in Wergland, *Visiting the Shakers, 1778–1849,* 136, 138.

52. Rebecca Clark, A little memorial showing how we lived in the time of the first gathering of the church, Writings of Daniel Goodrich, 105–6, WM 821.

53. "Joshua Evans" [diary, September 1795], in *The Friend* (n.p., July 28, 1890), 378.

54. Henry Blinn, Historical Record of the Society of Believers, 1:92, HSV 9768.C3 B648, 6437a.

55. Youngs, Concise View, 311–12, WM 861.

56. Ibid., 326, WM 861.

57. Citizen of Kentucky, "The Shakers," *Farmer's Repository,* January 13, 1814, 1 (reprinted from *Gospel Herald*).

58. Molly Goodrich to Ruth Landon, May 10, 1817, in Humez, *Mother's First-Born Daughters,* 167–68.

59. Youngs, Concise View, 329–30, WM 861.

60. Anne Newport Royall, in Wergland, *Visiting the Shakers, 1778–1849,* 207.

61. Bates, Journal of Events April 7, 1835, WRHS 35, V:B-128.

62. Daubeny, in Wergland, *Visiting the Shakers, 1778–1849,* 261.

63. James Silk Buckingham, in ibid., 70.

64. Isaac N. Youngs, Personal Journal (1839–58), August 18, 1856, WRHS 35, V:B-134; [Benson Lossing], "The Shakers," *Harper's New Monthly Magazine,* July 1857, 165–77.

65. Polly Reed, Journal of Miscellaneous Items, Kept by the Elder Sisters (1855–64), April 28, 1863, SM 10,452.

66. "On the Improved Muslin Caps," Wisdom Valley [sisters] to the Ministry, 1863, In Memory of Elder Rufus Bishop (1848–63), [101–4], WRHS 117, X:B-33.

67. Robert Fowle, Ephraim Dennett, Marcia Hastings, and Mira Bean, "Plain Dealing with Square Work," 25, WRHS 116, X:B-1.

68. Crain review, 791.

69. Giles Avery to Eldress Polly Lee at Groveland, April 19, 1869, WRHS 21, IV:A-43. Polly Lee description: Shaker names index, WRHS 123.

70. 1845 Millennial Laws in Edward D. Andrews, *The People Called Shakers* (New York: Dover, 1963), 282.

71. Chandler Journal, May 10, 1870, FM 32.7.

72. Betsy Crosman, Small Record Book (1848–72), December 8, 1871, May 27, June 6, 1872, WRHS 36, V:B-143; Blinn, Historical Record, 93.

73. Jane Crosthwaite, "Polly Reed, Shaker Minister and Shaker Artist" (paper presented at American Society of Church History meeting, April 1993), 5; quantifying information from Polly Reed, Daily Pocket Diaries, WRHS 37, V:B-165–66.

74. *New York Tribune* quoted in J. M. Brown, Domestic Journal (1856–77), June 11, 1869, WRHS 32, V:B-71.

75. Reclus, "Visit to Mount Lebanon," 29; Lady Correspondent, "Canterbury Shakers," *San Francisco Bulletin,* July 9, 1880.

76. "Shakers in Niskayuna," 666.

77. Reynolds, *Plain Women,* 70, 79.
78. Priscilla Brewer, *Shaker Communities, Shaker Lives* (Hanover, N.H.: University Press of New England, 1986), 211, 217.
79. It is possible, also, to be strict about the wrong things. Laurence R. Iannaccone, "Why Strict Churches Are Strong," *American Journal of Sociology* 99.5 (March 1994): 1181–82, 1204.
80. Henry Blinn, "Notes from our Diary," Shaker *Manifesto* 28.10 (1898): 152, HCDC.
81. Records Book No. 2 (1825–1929), 353, NYPL 2.6. My thanks to Stephen Paterwic for this citation. Brother Arnold Hadd, e-mail messages to author, May 12, 15, 2008.
82. Gordon, *Shaker Textile Arts,* 177.

CHAPTER 6. THE WORLD'S VIEWS OF SHAKER SISTERS, 1782–1865

This chapter began as "Shakers and the Public Roads: Burdens and Blessings, 1780–1875" (paper presented at the Dublin Seminar for New England Folklife, Deerfield, Mass., June 18, 2005) and grew into *Visiting the Shakers, 1778–1849* (Clinton, N.Y.: Richard W. Couper Press, 2007).

1. Asenath Clark, Ministerial Journal, August 21, 1836, HSV 1480, copy of SM original.
2. Ministry Sisters' Journal, July 2, 1837, WRHS 32, V:B-60; Records Kept by Order of the Church, 137, July 2, 1837, NYPL 2:7.
3. Betsy Bates, Journal of Events (1833–35), August 18, 1833, WRHS 35, V:B-128.
4. [Semantha Fairbanks] journal (1835–36) following John DeWitt Memorandum, May 31, 1835, WRHS 33, V:B-92.
5. Benjamin Waterhouse, 1794, Julian Niemcewicz, 1798, Charles Giles B. Daubeny, 1837, and "Shakers," 1838, in Wergland, *Visiting the Shakers, 1778–1849,* 143, 158, 266, 271.
6. "C.M.S." [Charles Montgomery Skinner], "Among the Shakers," *Shaker Manifesto* 16.4 (1886): 91, HCDC.
7. [Rufus Bishop,] Ministry Day Book (1815–29), August 1829, WRHS 33, V:B-85; Giles Avery, Journal of Times, Rhymes, Work & Weather (1836–38), August 1836, WRHS 34, V:B-106.
8. Seth Youngs Wells, comp., *Testimonies Concerning the Character and Ministry of Mother Ann Lee* (Albany, N.Y.: Packard and Van Benthuysen, 1827), 74.
9. Lawrence Pitkethly, 1842, in Wergland, *Visiting the Shakers, 1778–1849,* 303.
10. Benjamin Silliman, 1819, in ibid., 175.
11. [Rufus Bishop and Seth Youngs Wells, comps.], *Testimonies of the Life, Character, Revelation and Doctrines of Our Ever Blessed Mother Ann Lee* (Hancock, Mass.: J. Tallcott and J. Deming, Junrs., 1816), 265.
12. Julian U. Niemcewicz, 1798, in Wergland, *Visiting the Shakers, 1778–1849,* 159.
13. For decades the Shakers did not charge visitors for meals or lodging. Ibid.,109, 187, 206.
14. Anne Newport Royall, 1826, in ibid., 203–9. "Miss Betsey" may have been Betsey Darrow (1777–1860), an Eldress from 1834 to 1844 who, at five feet, seven inches, was probably the tall Betsey that Royall described. Isaac N. Youngs, Domestic Journal (1834–46), January 1, 1840, NYSL 10.
15. Eliza Bridgham, 1818, in Wergland, *Visiting the Shakers, 1778–1849,* 173–74.
16. Ibid.,174–75.
17. Julia Mayo Cabell, 1842, in ibid., 307.
18. "C.," 1796, in ibid., 150.

19. Dona Brown, *Inventing New England: Regional Tourism in the Nineteenth Century* (Washington, D.C.: Smithsonian Institution Press, 1995), 36.
20. Margaret Hall, 1827, in Wergland, *Visiting the Shakers, 1780–1849,* 214.
21. Barbara Welter, "The Cult of True Womanhood: 1820–1860," *American Quarterly* 18 (1966): 151–74.
22. William Plumer, "Original Shaker Communities in New England," ed. F. B. Sanborn, *New England Magazine,* May 1900, 305, Cornell University Making of America collection of nineteenth-century publications, http://cdl.library.cornell.edu/moa.
23. Elkanah Watson, 1790, in Wergland, *Visiting the Shakers, 1780–1849,* 136.
24. Liancourt, 1796, in ibid., 152–54.
25. Niemcewicz, in ibid., 158. Choir: Isaac N. Youngs, Family and Meeting Journal (1815–23), September 17, 1816, March 1, April 8, 1819, LC 3: 42.
26. Believers' dancing dwindled in the late 1790s, but Wright revived it in 1808 and encouraged other types of physical worship, as well. Dances, marches, and songs were introduced "to enliven the sense, and make worship feel new and interesting." Jean Humez, *Mother's First-Born Daughters: Early Shaker Writings on Women and Religion* (Bloomington: Indiana University Press, 1993), 69; Isaac N. Youngs, Concise View of the Church of God and of Christ on Earth, WM 861, 83, 90.
27. James Silk Buckingham, 1838, in Wergland, *Visiting the Shakers, 1780–1849,* 72–73. In 1881, a visitor noted that Antoinette Doolittle gave a public address. "Mount Lebanon Shakers: A Sunday's Attendance upon their Religious Services," *Pittsfield Sun,* July 13, 1881, 4.
28. Frances Anne Kemble, 1835, in Wergland, *Visiting the Shakers, 1780–1849,* 235.
29. Charles Giles B. Daubeny, 1837, Dr. Benjamin Waterhouse, 1794, and Carl David Arfwedson, 1832, in ibid., 143, 228–29, 261.
30. Ibid., 266.
31. See Catherine A. Brekus, *Strangers and Pilgrims: Female Preaching in America, 1740–1845* (Chapel Hill: University of North Carolina Press, 1998), 343–46, for women preachers before 1800. In the 1700s, the Methodist evangelist Sarah Crosby preached for two decades, logging 960 miles in one year. Michael J. McClymond, ed., *Embodying the Spirit: New Perspectives on North American Revivalism* (Baltimore: Johns Hopkins University Press, 2004), 25. Fanny Wright was persecuted for public speaking in New England as late as 1830. William R. Waterman, *Frances Wright,* Studies in History, Economics, and Public Law, vol. 115, no. 256 (New York: Columbia University Press, 1924).
32. Daubeny, in Wergland, *Visiting the Shakers, 1778–1849,* 263–65.
33. Ibid., 266.
34. "Letters from a Traveller, No. III," *Salem Gazette,* August 5, 1831, 2.
35. Glendyne Wergland, "Validation in the Shaker Era of Manifestations: A Process Analysis," *Communal Societies* 26.2 (Fall 2006): 121–40.
36. Fanny Longfellow, 1839, in Wergland, *Visiting the Shakers, 1780–1849,* 275.
37. Ibid.
38. Buckingham, in ibid., 75.
39. Greeley, 1838, and Daubeny, 1837, in ibid., 65, 264.
40. Edward D. Andrews, *The People Called Shakers* (New York: Dover, 1963), 162.
41. Anonymous, "A Sabbath Visit to the Shakers," 1846, in Wergland, *Visiting the Shakers, 1780–1849,* 313. Jerry Grant kindly provided this account.
42. John S. Dwight, 1847, in ibid., 321; Bremer, *Homes of the New World* (London: A. Hall, Virtue, 1853), 1:561; "Godfrey Greylock," [J. E. A. Smith], *Taghkonic; or Letters and*

Legends about our summer home (Boston: Redding, 1852), 126, University of Michigan Making of America collection of nineteenth-century publications, http://moa.umdl.umich.edu.

43. "Life Among the Shakers," *New York Times*, August 8, 1865, 8; William Dean Howells, *Three Villages* (Boston: J. R. Osgood and Company, 1884), 79, 80, 87; Charles Nordhoff, *Communistic Societies of the United States* (New York: Harper & Brothers, 1875; reprint, New York: Dover, 1966), 143. Perhaps inspiration did not end. See Suzanne Skees, *God among the Shakers* (New York: Hyperion, 1998), for speculation about Shaker gifts in the 1990s.

CHAPTER 7. WORK, RECIPROCITY, EQUALITY, AND UNION

This chapter began as "Sisters' Work, Brethren, and Shaker Union," in *Handled with Care: The Function of Form in Shaker Craft*, by Christian Goodwillie and M. Stephen Miller (Pittsfield, Mass.: Hancock Shaker Village, 2006), and evolved through talks at the Enfield, New Hampshire, Shaker Museum Spring Forum and the Communal Studies Association conference in 2007. I am also grateful to Kathy Peiss for helping me work through these issues.

1. Theodore E. Johnson, ed., "The Millennial Laws of 1821," *Shaker Quarterly* 7.2 (1967): 49.
2. "Female Scribbler," 1792, in Glendyne R. Wergland, *Visiting the Shakers, 1778–1849* (Clinton, N.Y.: Richard W. Couper Press, 2007), 140.
3. D'Ann Campbell, "Women's Life in Utopia: The Shaker Experiment in Sexual Equality Reappraised—1810 to 1860," *New England Quarterly* 51.1 (1978): 32.
4. "The Shakers," 1829, in Wergland, *Visiting the Shakers, 1780–1849*, 48.
5. William Owen, 1824, in ibid., 41.
6. Teaching tailoresses: Isaac N. Youngs, Domestic Journal (1834–46), January 22, February 13, 19, 1839, NYSL 10. Interactions with Lucy Wright: Glendyne Wergland, *One Shaker Life: Isaac Newton Youngs, 1793–1865* (Amherst: University of Massachusetts Press, 2006), 51–57.
7. Isaac N. Youngs, Concise View of the Church of God (1856–60), WM 861, 182–90; Alonzo Hollister, Reminiscences by a Soldier of the Cross, written July 7, 1907, 162–63, WRHS 116, X:B-31.
8. Youngs, Domestic Journal, July 23, 1837, NYSL 10; Henry DeWitt Journal (1827–67), August 8, 1837, WRHS 33, V:B-97.
9. Youngs, Concise View, 59–63. Unless otherwise noted, individuals quoted lived at the Shaker village in New Lebanon, New York.
10. Joseph Meacham to Lucy Wright [before August 16, 1796], WRHS 19, IV:A-30.
11. *Mother Lucy's Sayings* (Poland Spring, Maine: United Society of Shakers, 1989), 105.
12. Joan N. Radner and Susan S. Lanser, "The Feminist Voice: Strategies of Coding in Folklore and Literature," *Journal of American Folklore* 100.398 (1987): 412, 420–21; Cecilia De Vere, "Our Water Works," in *Mount Lebanon Cedar Boughs: Original Poems by the North Family of Shakers,* [ed. Anna White] (Buffalo, N.Y.: Peter Paul Company, 1895), 226–27.
13. Ibid., 227–28.
14. [Rufus Bishop and Seth Youngs Wells, comps.], *Testimonies of the Life, Character, Revelations and Doctrines of Our Ever Blessed Mother Ann Lee* (Hancock, Mass.: J. Talcott and J. Deming, Junrs., 1816), 265.

15. More than seventy visitor comments on cleanliness and shining floors are indexed in Wergland, *Visiting the Shakers, 1780–1849.*

16. A visitor to Hancock recalled: "The women's work is all done by turns, so that the same women are only employed at one kind of work for a limited period annually. Thus, four to cook, four in the dairy, eight to wash, etc. for one month, when they are relieved by others." Different villages had different numbers of women working each job. Anonymous, 1846, and W. S. Warder, 1846, in Wergland, *Visiting the Shakers, 1780–1849,* 84, 101. See also Daniel Pidgeon, *Old-World Questions and New-World Answers* (London: Kegan Paul, Trench & Co., 1884), 125. My thanks to Christian Goodwillie for this source.

17. Youngs, Concise View, 295–96.

18. Lawrence Pitkethly, 1843, in Wergland, *Visiting the Shakers, 1780–1849,* 298–99.

19. Polly Lee, Groveland journal (1843–63), January 19, 1863, WRHS 30, V:B-28.

20. In 1849 they bought six gallons of maple syrup and had to clarify it to bring it up to Shaker standards. Betsy Crosman, Small Record Book (1848–72), April 27–28, 1849, WRHS 36, V:B-143. Cheese: "H.," 1837, and Luther Tucker, 1846, in Wergland, *Visiting the Shakers, 1778–1849,* 258, 316.

21. Hancock Shaker Village keepsake, 1961, WM 661.

22. Calvin Green, Sayings of Mother Lucy Wright, [37], WRHS 56, VII:B-60.1.

23. "Four Months Among the Shakers," 1842–43, in Wergland, *Visiting the Shakers, 1780–1849,* 85.

24. Youngs, Domestic Journal, yearend 1837, NYSL 10; Betsy Bates, Journal of Events (1833–35), September 8, 1835, WRHS 35, V:B-128.

25. Isaac N. Youngs, Personal Journal (1839–54), October 7, 1839, WRHS 35, V:B-134; Benjamin Gates Journal (1839–40, 1846–54), September 28, 1839, SM 10450.

26. Crosman, Small Record Book, September–December 1852, WRHS 36, V:B-143.

27. Ibid., October 17, 1853, January 18, 1854, WRHS 36, V:B-143.

28. Journal of Domestic Events . . . Kept by the Deaconesses, Chh 2nd Order, March–April 1857, HSV 1086a.

29. Youngs, Concise View, 212–13, WM 861.

30. Crosman, Small Record Book, March 10, 1854, WRHS 36, V:B-143.

31. Linda J. Borish, "'Another Domestic Beast of Burden': Nineteenth-Century New England Farm Women's Work and Well-Being," *Journal of American Culture* 18.3 (1995): 83.

32. Youngs, Domestic Journal, occupational lists to 1850 at end, NYSL 10.

33. Johnson, "Millennial Laws of 1821," 57.

34. Eliza Bridgham, 1818, and Luther Tucker, 1846, in Wergland, *Visiting the Shakers, 1780–1849,* 174, 317.

35. Andrew Bell, 1835, in ibid., 237.

36. Hester A. Pool, "Among the Shakers," *Shaker Manifesto* 18.10 (1888): 252.

37. A journal kept by Lucy Ann Hammond while on a journey to New Lebanon Hancock & Enfield (1830), November 16, 1830, WRHS 30, V:B-39.

38. "Philos Harmoniae" [Richard McNemar], *A Selection of Hymns and Poems for the Use of Believers* (Watervliet, Ohio: [for the Shakers,] 1833), extract in Charles Nordhoff, *Communistic Societies of the United States* (London: John Murray, 1875), 217–18. Millennial Laws prohibited "thronging" the kitchen or going into it unnecessarily when cooks were at work. Johnson, "Millennial Laws of 1821," 55.

39. Lawrence Pitkethly, 1842, in Wergland, *Visiting the Shakers, 1780–1849,* 301. A Shaker wash mill is at HSV. See also E. D. Andrews, *Community Industries of the Shakers,* New

York State Museum handbook (Charlestown, Mass.: Emporium, 1971), 43–44, 270. Enfield, New Hampshire, Shakers had a "centrifugal dryer." Nordhoff, *Communistic Societies,* 188.

40. Youngs, Domestic Journal, January 1, 1840, NYSL 10; Rules concerning Washing, end of [Semantha Fairbanks] journal (1835–36) following John DeWitt Memorandum, WRHS 33, V:B-92.

41. DeWitt Journal, August 10, 1832, WRHS 33 V:B-97.

42. Susan I. Hautaniemi and Deborah L. Rotman, "To the Hogs or to the House? Municipal Water and Gender Relations at the Moors Site in Deerfield, Massachusetts," in *Shared Spaces and Divided Places: Material Dimensions of Gender Relations and the American Historical Landscape,* ed. Deborah Rotman and Ellen-Rose Savulis (Knoxville: University of Tennessee Press, 2003): 135–59.

43. Sally McMurray, *Families and Farmhouses in Nineteenth-Century America* (New York: Oxford University Press, 1988), chap. 4.

44. "Farming in New England," *Atlantic Monthly,* August 1858, 341, quoted in Thomas Dublin, *Women at Work: The Transformation of Work and Community in Lowell, Massachusetts, 1826–1860* (New York: Columbia University Press, 1979), 55.

45. This was the case when Hancock Shakers built their new brick dwelling in 1830. See Hancock Bishopric correspondence, William Deming to Beloved friends, January 8, 1832, HSV Red 9768.H2 D369 4541-2.

46. [Marcia Bullard?], Canaan Lower Family Sister's Memoir (1813–69), 1838, [13, 23, 25, 33], WRHS 33, V:B-84.

47. Crosman, Small Record Book, November 28, 1854, WRHS 36, V:B-143.

48. Ibid., September 26, 1849, December 4, 1850.

49. Youngs, Domestic Journal, May 20–26, 1853, WRHS 32, V:B-70 (apprentices); Youngs, Domestic Journal, January 22, February 13–19, 1839, December 7, 1840, NYSL 10 (helping tailoresses); Youngs, Personal Journal, June–July 23, 1853, WRHS 35, V:B-134 (sewing machines).

50. Isaac N. Youngs, Taylor's Journal, October 6, 10, 1853, WRHS 36, V:B-139; Crosman, Small Record Book, November 12, 14, December 13, 17, 1853, WRHS 36, V:B-143.

51. Bates, Journal, March 20, 1835, WRHS 35, V:B-128.

52. A "new wood house, bonnet shop, soap house &c inclusive" was built in August 1836. Giles Avery, Historical Sketches (1834–43), 41, LC 4:53.

53. Youngs, Concise View, 266, WM 861; Bates, Journal, April 11, 1835, WRHS 35, V:B-128.

54. Crosman, Small Record Book, December 16–19, 1848, February 4, 18, March 26, 31, 1852, WRHS 36, V:B-143; Youngs, Domestic Journal, yearend, 1852, WRHS 32, V:B-70.

55. Youngs, Domestic Journal, December 31, 1845, NYSL 10; Gates, Journal, October 30–31, 1839 (cutting palm leaf) and February 21, 1852 (ironing leaf), SM 10,450. Crosman, Small Record Book, February 11, 1869 (popple), WRHS 36, V:B-143.

56. Thurman rebuts Karen Nickless and Pamela Nickless's argument that brethren's work was the real work of the Shaker family. Suzanne Thurman, *"O Sisters Ain't You Happy?" Gender, Family, and Community among the Harvard and Shirley Shakers, 1781–1918* (Syracuse, N.Y.: Syracuse University Press, 2002), 67, 74–75.

57. [Second Family Sisters' Employments] January 15, 1860, WRHS 14, III:A-8; Don Gifford, ed., *An Early View of the Shakers* (Hanover, N.H.: University Press of New England and Hancock Shaker Village, 1989), 23, 49, 51.

58. Bates, Journal, September 7, 1833, WRHS 35, V:B-128; Fairbanks, Journal, October 30, 1835, WRHS 33, V:B-92; Youngs, Domestic Journal, yearend report, 1839, NYSL 10.

59. Youngs, Domestic Journal, January 1, 1840, NYSL 10.

60. "Dolly Stetson," *Pittsfield Sun,* June 28, 1876; "New Lebanon: A Venerable Shaker," *Pittsfield Sun,* May 12, 1880.

61. Youngs, Domestic Journal, December 16, 1853, WRHS 32, V:B-70.

62. Harvard Sisters' Journal (1845–52), January 1, 1845, FM 1.11.

63. Seth Youngs Wells, comp., *Testimonies Concerning the Character and Ministry of Mother Ann Lee* (Albany, N.Y.: Packard and Van Benthuysen, 1827), 57 (Zipporah Cory); Laurel Thatcher Ulrich, *Age of Homespun* (New York: Alfred A. Knopf, 2001), 201–4.

64. Youngs, Personal Journal, December 31, 1850, WRHS 35, V:B-134. Lucy Smith's glove mender is at HSV.

65. Crosman, Small Record Book, December 14, 1853, WRHS 36, V:B-143.

66. Youngs, Personal Journal, December 31, 1850 WRHS 35, V:B-134 (bone bodkins and stocking needles with ivory handles); Fairbanks, Journal, March 24, 1835, WRHS 33, V:B-92 (weaver's reed).

67. [Abigail Crosman et al.], A Journal of Domestic Events & transactions . . . Kept by the Deaconesses, Chh 2nd Order (1843–64), June 19–21, 1850, HSV 9758 MtL. Xc.

68. Youngs, Concise View, 238–39, WM 861; Ministry Sisters' Book, May 1834, WRHS 32, V:B-60. One sister was employed spinning on the jenny. Youngs, Domestic Journal, January 1, 1840, NYSL 10. Youngs had to fix Watervliet's "jenne." Freegift Wells, Memorandum of Events (1816–19), June 22–28, 1816, WRHS 45, V:B-286.

69. Nordhoff, *Communistic Societies,* 188. My thanks to Arthur Gagnon, who showed me how Enfield Shaker Museum's sock-knitting machine worked.

70. Mary Rose Boswell, "Enfield and Canterbury Shaker Textile Industries" (talk at Enfield Shaker Museum Spring Forum, May 19, 2007).

71. Nancy F. Cott, *Bonds of Womanhood: "Woman's Sphere" in New England, 1780–1835* (New Haven: Yale University Press, 1977), chap. 1. In Barbara Welter, "The Cult of True Womanhood: 1820–1860," *American Quarterly* 18.2 (1966): 151–74, women seemed to do little work other than sewing and caring for the sick.

72. Elizabeth Lovegrove journal, June 28, 1827, WRHS 33, V:B-94.

73. This list was compiled from entries for May through November in Crosman, Small Record Book; Fairbanks, Journal; and Bates, Journal, as well as Annie Williams journal (1832–55), WRHS 35, V:B-127.

74. Crosman, Small Record Book, June 26–27, 1849, July 28, 1852, WRHS 36, V:B-143; Bates, Journal, November 2–6, 1833, WRHS 35, V:B-128; Williams journal, September 8, 1841, WRHS 35, V:B-127.

75. Hammond journal, October 1830, WRHS 30, V:B-39; Bates, Journal, September 6, November 1, 1833, WRHS 35, V:B-128; Youngs, Domestic Journal, December 31, 1838, NYSL 10.

76. Dr. Benjamin Waterhouse, 1794, in Wergland, *Visiting the Shakers, 1778–1849,* 142.

77. Freegift Wells, Records of the Church at Watervliet, August 28, 1814, WRHS 44, V:B-279; Anna White and Leila Taylor, *Shakerism: Its Meaning and Message* (Columbus, Ohio: for the Shakers, 1905), 134–35.

78. Thurman, *"O Sisters Ain't You Happy?"* chaps. 4 and 5.

79. [Marcia Bullard?], Canaan Lower Family Sister's Memoir, 1810s, WRHS 33, V:B-84.

80. Susan Starr Sered, "Ideology, Autonomy, and Sisterhood: An Analysis of the Secular Consequences of Women's Religions," *Gender and Society* 8.4 (1994): 495, 500–1.

Chapter 8. Gendered Conflict among the Shakers

1. Philemon Stewart, Daily Journal No. 3 (1834–36), April 12, 1834, WRHS 35, V:B-130.
2. 1845 Millennial Laws, in Edward D. Andrews, *People Called Shakers: A Search for the Perfect Society* (New York: Dover, 1963), 268.
3. Polly Reed journal, February 24, 1872, WRHS 35, V:B-165.
4. Jean Humez, *Mother's First-Born Daughters: Early Shaker Writings on Women and Religion* (Bloomington: Indiana University Press, 1993), xxii, 15.
5. Ibid., 112, 141–42.
6. Isaac N. Youngs, Meeting Journal (1823–28), extract in Alonzo Hollister, Book of Remembrance, 209, WRHS 58, VII:B-109.
7. The same poem says that when sisters "provoke and aggravate, it ill becomes their gender"; neither sex was perfect. Robert Fowle, Ephraim Dennett, Marcia Hastings, and Mira Bean, "Plain Dealing with Square Work," 9, WRHS 116, X:B-1.
8. Humez, *Mother's First-Born Daughters,* 67–68.
9. Isaac N. Youngs, Family and Meeting Journal (1815–23), August 17, 1816, LC 3:42.
10. Lauren A. Stiles, "'Rather Than Ever Milk Again': Shaker Sisters' Refusal to Milk at Mount Lebanon and Watervliet—1873–1877," *American Communal Societies Quarterly* 3.1 (2009): 13–25.
11. [Marcia Bullard?], Canaan Lower Family Sister's Memoir (1813–69), [1–4, 23, 28–29, 35], WRHS 33, V:B-84. I believe Bullard was the author of this memoir, because she arrived at the Lower Family the same month as its anonymous female author; see [68]. She lived at Canaan until 1870, at least. Having come from the North Family, she knew that Canaan sisters' lot was unnecessarily hard. [Levi Shaw, Daniel Fraser, and Daniel Sizer], Canaan journal (1813–75), January 1844, LC 3:41.
12. [Bullard?], Canaan Lower Family Sister's Memoir, [30], WRHS 33, V:B-84, cited in Priscilla Brewer, "'Tho' of the Weaker Sex': A Reassessment of Gender Equality among the Shakers," *Signs: A Journal of Women in Culture and Society* 17 (Spring 1992): 621.
13. Ibid.
14. The Shaker names index shows two William Evans, neither the right age to have been the one expelled. WRHS 123. Frederick Evans claimed only one natural brother, George H. Evans, a friend of Horace Greeley's (editor of the *New York Tribune*). Frederick Evans, "Autobiography of a Shaker," *Atlantic Monthly,* April 1869, 417.
15. [Bullard?], Canaan Lower Family Sister's Memoir, [30–31], WRHS 33, V:B-84. Hannah Bryant (1785–1877) was about fifty-one when she expelled Evans. Bryant, a tailoress, may have been Canaan's Eldress. When she moved to the North Family in 1838, Harriet Sellick (1804–1840) took her place. Shaker names index, WRHS 123; Tom Donnelly card file, HSV.
16. [Bullard?], Canaan Lower Family Sister's Memoir, [31], WRHS 33, V:B-84.
17. Ibid., [1–2, 10].
18. Evans was not the only such example of a Believer who was cast out by sisters. After Harvard Elder John "got completely through with him," the Eldresses expelled Jonas Warren in 1894. Why they, rather than the Elders, did so is unclear. Maria Foster, Harvard Shaker Journal (1893–1911), July 1–2, 1894, April 26, 1896, FM 3.2.
19. [Bullard?], Canaan Lower Family Sister's Memoir, [31], WRHS 33, V:B-84.
20. Karen Nickless and Pamela Nickless, "Trustees, Deacons, and Deaconesses: The Temporal Role of Shaker Sisters 1820–1890," *Communal Studies Journal* 7 (1987): 16–24.
21. [Bullard?], Canaan Lower Family Sister's Memoir, [35], WRHS 33, V:B-84.

22. Susan Carol Rogers, "Female Forms of Power and the Myth of Male Dominance: A Model of Female/Male Interaction in Peasant Society," *American Ethnologist* 2.4 (1975): 727–56.
23. Nicholas Briggs, "Forty Years a Shaker," *Granite Monthly*, February 1921, 62.
24. Hervey Elkins, *Fifteen Years in the Senior Order of Shakers* (Hanover, N.H.: Dartmouth Press, 1853), 26.
25. Theodore E. Johnson, ed., "The Millennial Laws of 1821," *Shaker Quarterly* 7.2 (1967): 46–47.
26. David R. Lamson, *Two Years' Experience Among the Shakers* (West Boylston [Mass.]: for the author, 1848), 166.
27. Cynthia Barton, "Robert Leavitt and his Enfield Shaker Friends," *Friends Quarterly* (Enfield Shaker Museum) 17.4 (Spring 2008): 1.
28. Anne Newport Royall, 1826, in Wergland, *Visiting the Shakers, 1778–1849* (Clinton, N.Y.: Richard W. Couper Press, 2007), 204.
29. "Notes About Home: Mount Lebanon, N. Y.," *Shaker Manifesto* 22.3 (1892): 62, HCDC.
30. Diane Sasson, "'Dear Friend and Sister': Laura Holloway-Langford and the Shakers," *American Communal Societies Quarterly* 1.4 (2007): 180.
31. Isaac N. Youngs, A Concise View of the Church of God and of Christ on Earth, 282–91, WM 861.
32. "Four Months Among the Shakers," Wergland, *Visiting the Shakers, 1778–1849*, 85.
33. Betsy Bates, Journal of Events (1833–35), October 31, 1833, WRHS 35, V:B-128.
34. Giles Avery Journal (1834–36), December 3, 1834, WRHS 33, V:B-105; Derobigne Bennett and Isaac N. Youngs, Family and Meeting Journal (1840–41), October 22, 1840, WRHS 77, VIII:B-138.
35. Calvin Green, Sayings of Mother Lucy Wright, 14, 36–37, WRHS 56, VII:B-70.
36. Bates, Journal, September 2, 1835, WRHS 35, V:B-128.
37. Isaac N. Youngs, Domestic Journal (1834–46), September 16, 1835, NYSL 10.
38. Ibid., August 17, 1836.
39. Aaron D. Bill, Journal or Day Book (1834–40), August 5, 1837, WRHS 35, V:B-132.
40. Youngs, Concise View, 291, WM 861.
41. Youngs, Domestic Journal (1847–55), January 1, 1850, WRHS 32, V:B-70.
42. Youngs, Concise View, 300–302, WM 861.
43. Betsy Crosman, Small Record Book (1848–72), year-end report, 1849, and September 4, 1852, WRHS 36, V:B-143.
44. J. N. the Tanner, "Hoggish Nature," in [Richard McNemar], *A Selection of Hymns and Poems for the Use of Believers* (Watervliet, Ohio: [Shakers,] 1833), 168–69.
45. 1845 Millennial Laws, 279, 287.
46. J. N. the Tanner, "Hoggish Nature," 169.
47. When the Ministry advocated reduced pork consumption, they tried not to offend cooks who preferred to season food with animal fat. Margaret Pushkar-Pasewicz, "Kitchen Sisters and Disagreeable Boys: Debates over Meatless Diets in Nineteenth-Century Shaker Communities," in *Eating in Eden: Food and American Utopias,* ed. Etta M. Madden and Martha L. Finch (Lincoln: University of Nebraska Press, 2006), 114–16.
48. Youngs, Family and Meeting Journal (1815–23), May 28–30, June 30, 1819, LC 3:42; Beverly Chiñas, *The Isthmus Zapotecs: Women's Roles in Cultural Context* (New York: Holt, Rinehart and Winston, 1973), 108–9. The sisters may have wanted to avoid anti-Shaker attacks by parents wanting to break their children's indentures. See Elizabeth

De Wolfe, *Shaking the Faith: Women, Family, and Mary Marshall Dyer's Anti-Shaker Campaign, 1815–1867* (New York: Palgrave, 2002).

49. Edward D. Andrews, *The Gift to Be Simple: Songs, Dances, and Rituals of the American Shakers* (New York: Dover, 1962), 54.

50. Hannah Brownson, "Poison of the Tongue," [untitled hymnal], 28–31, WRHS 98, IX:B-165. These poems suggest that gossip was gendered female, but another blamed both sexes. "The Tale Bearer," [untitled book of verse] (1820–30), 24–25, WRHS 91, IX:B-41.

51. Lucy S. Bowers, "The Bird Legislator," in *Mount Lebanon Cedar Boughs,* [ed. Anna White] (Buffalo, N.Y.: Peter Paul Company, 1895), 177–79.

52. [Bullard?], Canaan Lower Family Sister's Memoir, [1–3, 10, 35].

53. "The Slug," "Philos Harmoniae" [Richard McNemar], *A Selection of Hymns and Poems for the Use of Believers* (Watervliet, Ohio: [for the Shakers,] 1833) 162, extract in Charles Nordhoff, *Communistic Societies of the United States* (London: John Murray, 1875), 216.

54. Abigail May Alcott (Mrs. Bronson), in *Journals of Bronson Alcott,* ed. Odell Shepard (1938; reprint, Port Washington, N.Y.: Kennikat Press, 1966), 1:154–55.

55. Royall, in Wergland, *Visiting the Shakers, 1778–1849, 205.*

56. Isaac N. Youngs et al., Taylor's Journal, January–June, 1851, WRHS 36, V:B-139.

57. Elkins, *Fifteen Years,* 26. At New Lebanon, Joseph Bennet, Isaac N. Youngs, Benjamin Gates, and an unknown man (Elisha Blakeman?) encrypted journal entries; at Hancock, Thomas Damon did. Complaints: Jean Humez, "The Problem of Female Leadership in Early Shakerism," in *Shaker Design,* ed. Jean Burks (New Haven: Yale, 2008): 93–119.

CHAPTER 9. ABUSE BY SPIRIT MESSAGES DURING THE ERA OF MANIFESTATIONS

Acknowledgments: My thanks to Jane Crosthwaite's Mount Holyoke College Shaker research seminar students, March 25, 2008, and to the Communal Studies Association conference attendees at Estero, Florida, October 4, 2008, for their comments on the presentations that evolved into this chapter.

1. Rufus Bishop and Seth Youngs Wells, comps., *Testimonies of the Life, Character, Revelations and Doctrines of Our Ever Blessed Mother Ann Lee* (Hancock, Mass.: J. Talcott and J. Deming, Junrs., 1816), 226.

2. Abijah Worster, Sayings of Mother Ann, Thomas Hammond, comp., 1–2, WRHS 54, VII:B-22.

3. Theodore E. Johnson, ed., "The Millennial Laws of 1821," *Shaker Quarterly* 7.2 (1967): 46–47.

4. Stephen J. Stein, "Shaker Gift and Shaker Order: A Study of Religious Tension in Nineteenth-Century America," *Communal Societies* 10 (1990): 102–13.

5. The Deans lived in Dudley, Mass., in 1797, Windham, Conn., in 1799, and Savoy, Mass., in the 1810s. Sally had lived also in Washington County, N.Y. The numerous moves indicate economic marginality. Names of the Brethren and the Sisters in the First and Second Order April 1835, LC 5:92; Tom Donnelly card file, HSV; Shaker names index, WRHS 123; "Sally Dean and Her Letter to 'Respected Friend Phineas,'" *American Communal Societies Quarterly* 1.3 (2007): 99–116.

6. Isaac N. Youngs, Concise View of the Church of God, 93–94, WM 861.

7. Isaac N. Youngs, Meeting Journal (1823–28) extract in Alonzo Hollister, Book of Re-

membrance 3:210, WRHS 58, VII:B-109; Priscilla Brewer, *Shaker Communities, Shaker Lives* (Hanover, N.H.: University Press of New England, 1986), 115.

8. Ministry Sisters' Journal (1780–1841), September 1832, WHRS 32, V:B-60; Isaac N. Youngs, Domestic Journal (1834–46), March 10, 1834, March 26, 1836, and caretaker list at end, NYSL 10; [Semantha Fairbanks] journal (1835–36) following John DeWitt Memorandum, October 14, 1836, WRHS 33, V:B-92; Records Book No. 2 (1825–1929), 36, NYPL 2:6.

9. Shaker names index, WRHS 123; Betsy Bates, Journal of Events (1833–35), September 13, 1835, WRHS 35, V:B-128; Youngs, Domestic Journal, March 26, 1836, September 1837, January 1, 1840, NYSL 10.

10. Rufus Bishop, Daily Journal of Passing Events (1830–39), October 1, 8, 1837, NYPL 1:1.

11. Glendyne R. Wergland, "Validation in the Shaker Era of Manifestations: A Process Analysis," *Communal Societies* 26.2 (2006): 121–40.

12. Isaac N. Youngs, Sketches of Visions (1838), January 1838, 7–8, and n.d., 32, WRHS 75, VIII:B-113.

13. Diane Sasson, "Individual Experience, Community Control, and Gender: The Harvard Shaker Community during the Era of Manifestations," *Communal Societies* 13 (1993): 47–48.

14. Youngs, Sketches, May 1838, 43, WRHS 75, VIII:B-113.

15. Ibid., May 14, 1838, 49, 50, 53.

16. Bishop, Daily Journal, May 9, 1838, NYPL 1:1.

17. Youngs, Sketches, May 11, 1838, 47, WRHS 75, VIII:B-113.

18. Contending visionists were not unique to New Lebanon. At Harvard, Mary Hill delivered a spirit message that tried to control her natural sister, the visionist Minerva Hill. Sasson, "Individual Experience," 57–58.

19. Records Kept by Order of the Church (1780–1850), 191, NYPL 2:7.

20. Youngs, Concise View, 105.

21. David R. Lamson, *Two Years' Experience among the Shakers* (West Boylston [Mass.]: author, 1848), 41. By July 1839, Harvard Elders tried to control manifestations by appointing visionists and requiring them to submit gifts for approval before revealing them to others. Sasson, "Individual Experience," 53.

22. Some suspected that girls' gifts were only "childish fancies." Youngs, Sketches, June 14, 1838, 67, WRHS 75, VIII:B-113.

23. List of children's caretakers (1787–1850), Youngs, Domestic Journal, at end, NYSL 10; Jean Humez, *Mother's First-Born Daughters: Early Shaker Writings on Women and Religion* (Bloomington: Indiana University Press, 1993), 213, 238.

24. Johnson, "Millennial Laws of 1821," 45–47.

25. Lawrence Foster, "Shaker Spiritualism and Salem Witchcraft: Social Perspectives on Trance and Possession Phenomena," *Communal Societies* 5 (1985): 185; Stein, "Shaker Gift and Shaker Order," 102–13; Stephen J. Stein, *The Shaker Experience in America: A History of the United Society of Believers* (New Haven: Yale University Press, 1992), 187–88. According to Jean Humez, the instrument Margaret O'Brien ousted McNemar. Humez, *Mother's First-Born Daughters*, 215. See also Lawrence Foster, *Women, Family, and Utopia: Communal Experiments of the Shakers, the Oneida Community, and the Mormons* (Syracuse, N.Y.: Syracuse University Press: 1991), chap. 3.

26. Bishop, Daily Journal, May 30, 1839, NYPL 1:1.

27. Sasson, "Individual Experience," 54.
28. Sally Promey, *Spiritual Spectacles: Vision and Image in Mid-Nineteenth-Century Shakerism* (Bloomington: Indiana University Press, 1993), 52, citing Copies of Letters begun 1833, 309, February 23, 1839, WRHS 27, IV:B-8.
29. Anna Dodgson, Prophetic Warning Concerning Reprobates, June 1, 1840, 45–46, SM 12,341.
30. Derobigne Bennett and Isaac N. Youngs, Journal of Inspirational Meetings (1840–41), October 4, 1840, WRHS 77, VIII:B-138, corroborated by Joseph W. Babe, Journal of Inspirational Meetings (1840–41), October 4, 1840, WRHS 77, VIII:B-139.
31. Rufus Bishop, Daily Journal of Passing Events (1839–50), October 7, 1840, NYPL 1.2. Such divisiveness during the Ministry's absences indicates that the 1840 Ministry influenced visionists as the Church Family's Elders did not.
32. Bennett and Youngs, Journal, October 7, 1840, WRHS 77, VIII:B-138. In a separatist group, doubts invite criticism. Ruth Garret, as an Old Order Amish teenager, did not show skepticism because she feared excommunication. "Thinking aloud too much, analyzing too much, would raise suspicions. And that would make life hard, if not unbearable. The Amish are always watching to see if a person appears vulnerable to doubt." Garrett, *Crossing Over: One Woman's Escape from Amish Life* (San Francisco: HarperCollins, 2003), 43.
33. Bennett and Youngs, Journal, October 7, 1840, WRHS 77, VIII:B-138.
34. Youngs, Domestic Journal, September 14, 1837, January 1, 1840, NYSL 10.
35. Bennett and Youngs, Journal, October 8, 1840, WRHS 77, VIII:B-138.
36. Archibald Montgomery Maxwell, in Glendyne R. Wergland, *Visiting the Shakers, 1778–1849* (Clinton, N.Y.: Richard W. Couper Press, 2007), 277.
37. Bennett and Youngs, Journal, October 9, 1840, WRHS 77, VIII:B-138. If the Ministry had considered the matter urgent, they could have made the return trip in about nine hours. Bishop, Daily Journal, November 5, 1840, NYPL 1:2.
38. Babe, Journal, October 25, 1840, WRHS 77, VIII:B-139.
39. Ibid., November 1, 7, 1840. "Sufficient unto the day": Matthew 6:34. Leah Taylor was the only "l.t." over age six. Youngs, Domestic Journal, January 1, 1840, NYSL 10.
40. Calvin Green, Prophetic Warning, November 9, 1840, 8–9, WRHS 66, VIII:A-34.
41. Babe, Journal, January–February 1841, WRHS 77, VIII:B-139.
42. Lamson, *Two Years' Experience among the Shakers,* 66–67.
43. Hervey Elkins, *Fifteen Years in the Senior Order of Shakers* (Hanover, N.H.: Dartmouth Press, 1853), 42.
44. Records Kept by Order of the Church, November 1842, NYPL 2:7.
45. Sian E. Lewis and Jim Orford, "Women's Experiences of Workplace Bullying: Changes in Social Relationships," *Journal of Community & Applied Social Psychology* 15 (2005): 41–42.
46. The term *clique* goes beyond its synonyms (group, faction). A clique can exist for mutual support. A toxic clique, however, forms around a "Queen Bee" with a desire for power, little tolerance for dissent, and malicious intent toward selected individuals. These Shaker visionists were between the ages of twenty-one and thirty-five, but there is no age limit for toxic cliques. See Leslie Parrott, "How Do I Handle Cliques at My Church?" *Today's Christian Woman* 29.3 (May–June 2007): 16; Patricia Zavella, "Abnormal Intimacy: The Varying Work Networks of Chicana Cannery Workers," *Feminist Studies* 11.3 (1985): 541–57; Jane Eisner, "Finally Coming into Focus: Violence against Women by Women," *Philadelphia Inquirer,* March 22, 2002; Sonia Salari, Barbara B.

Brown, and Jacqueline Eaton, "Conflicts, Friendship Cliques and Territorial Displays in Senior Center Environments," *Journal of Aging Studies* 20.3 (September 2006): 237–53. The best research on adolescent cliques' bullying is Rachel Simmons, *Odd Girl Out: The Hidden Culture of Aggression in Girls* (New York: Harcourt, 2002): "Girls use backbiting, exclusion, rumors, name-calling, and manipulation to inflict psychological pain on their targeted victims." (3). Another author says, "Girls form cliques, held together by dirty tricks, gossip, ostracism, and ridicule." Kay S. Hymowitz, "The Weaker Sex? Putting to Rest the Feminist Shibboleth That Our Culture Silences Girls," *City Journal,* February 27, 2002, online edition, www.city-journal.org.

47. Bullying often begins with a job change or new boss. Charlotte Rayner, "The Incidence of Workplace Bullying," *Journal of Community and Applied Social Psychology* 7 (1997): 199–208. Turnover in Shaker sisters' employment was not unusual. Dean served three years, Potter two. Records Book No. 2, December 17, 1840, 36–37, NYPL 2.6; Ministry Sisters' Journal, December 19, 1840, WRHS 32, V:B-60.

48. Deborah E. Burns, *Shaker Cities of Peace, Love, and Union: A History of the Hancock Bishopric* (Hanover, N.H.: University Press of New England, 1993), 41, 180.

49. Ebenezer and Rufus Bishop were the male half of the Ministry from 1821 to 1849. Their nephew Daniel Crosman was a deacon in 1839 and Elder 1844–85. Betsy Crosman became lead family deaconess in 1839 after serving eighteen months as a junior deaconess. Records Book No. 2, 17–18, 22–23, 44–47, 388, NYPL 2.6.

50. Bennett and Youngs, Journal, April 11, 1841, WRHS 77, V:B-138; Babe, Journal, April 11, 1841, WRHS 77, VIII:B-139. A Record of Holy Mother's first Visitation on the Holy Mount . . . June 1st, 1842, WRHS 79, VIII:B-159, contains twenty-two messages in more than 130 pages attributed to Miranda Barber, March–August 1841.

51. Bennett and Youngs, Journal, May 22–23, 1841, WRHS 77, V:B-138.

52. Ibid., May 26, 1841.

53. Rayner, "Incidence of Workplace Bullying."

54. Bennett and Youngs, Journal, May 26, 1841, WRHS 77, V:B-138.

55. Youngs, Domestic Journal (1834–46), May 27, 1841, NYSL 10. Thomas Munson and Alex McArthur were "very much married together." Calvin Green was accused of doing "that which led to the flesh." Isaac N. Youngs, Private Journal (1837–59), March 21, July 23, 1837, SM 10,509.

56. Giles Avery, Journal of Times, Rhymes, Work and Weather (1836–47), June 4, 1841, WRHS 34, V:B-107.

57. Julia Kasdorf, *The Body and the Book: Writing from a Mennonite Life* (Baltimore, Md.: Johns Hopkins University Press, 2001), 78. In *Crossing Over,* Ruth Garret tells how wrenching it is to leave family, friends, and church.

58. Youngs, Domestic Journal (1834–46), June 3, 1941, NYSL 10.

59. Bennett and Youngs, Journal, October 23, November 4, 1841, WRHS 77, V:B-138.

60. Records Kept by Order of the Church, November 6, 1841, NYPL 2:7; Ministry Sisters' Journal, November 6, 1841, WRHS 32, V:B-60.

61. A True Record of Sacred Communications, 7:163–67, November 6, 1841, WRHS 76, VIII:B-122. At age fourteen, Barber had written to Isaac N. Youngs of her progress in controlling temper. Promey, *Spiritual Spectacles,* 48, citing Barber to Youngs, August 14, 1833, WRHS 20, IV:A-36.

62. Anna Dodgson, From Father William to the Elder Sisters, November 11, 12, 1841, 28–29, 30–36, Book of Rolls, Letters, Messages, and Communications to the Ministry and Elders (1840–43), vol. 15, SM 12,332.

63. Bennett and Youngs, Journal, November 13, 1841, WRHS 77, V:B-138.
64. Anna Dodgson, Mother Lucy's Word to Betsy Bates, November 15, 1841, 43–45, Book of Rolls, SM 12,332.
65. Anna Dodgson, Words of the Holy Angel, November 17, 1841, 45–46, ibid.
66. Bennett and Youngs, Journal, November 17, 1841, WRHS 77, V:B-138.
67. Anna Dodgson, Mother Lucy's Word to S.D., November 18, 1841, 46–54, Book of Rolls, SM 12,332.
68. Miranda Barber, Words of solemn and weighty truth, November 23, 1841, A True Record of Sacred Communications, 8:96–103, WRHS 76, VIII:B-123.
69. Bennett and Youngs, Journal, November 23, 1841, WRHS 77, V:B-138.
70. Holy Mother Wisdom: Bishop, Daily Journal, September 2, 1841, NYPL 1:2. Recommendations: Bennett and Youngs, Journal, November 28, 1841, WRHS 77, V:B-138.
71. Bennett and Youngs, Journal, November 28, 1841, WRHS 77, V:B-138.
72. Semantha Fairbanks, A short communication from Mother Ann to the Ministry and Trustees, November 28, 1841, True Record, 8:132–35, WRHS 76, VIII:B-123.
73. Bennett and Youngs, Journal, November 29, 1841, WRHS 77, V:B-138.
74. True Record, 8:140, November 29, 1841, WRHS 76, VIII:B-123.
75. Church Order Journal (1841–46), November 29, 1841, WRHS 35, V:B-135.
76. Bennett and Youngs, Journal, November 30, 1841, WRHS 77, V:B-138.
77. Ibid., 1841 yearend review.
78. Records Kept by Order of the Church, April 13, 15, June 23, 1842, September 22, 28, 1843, NYPL 2:7.
79. Polly Reed, Journal of Miscellaneous Items Kept by the Elder Sisters (1855–64), November 11, 1857, SM 10,452.
80. New Lebanon Church Family deaconesses in 1857: Betsy Crosman (served 1837–72), Matilda Reed (served 1854–75), Jane Blanchard (served 1839–48 and 1854–58). Records Book No. 2, 43–47, 388, NYPL 2.7.
81. Isaac N. Youngs and John M. Brown, Domestic Journal (1856–77), November 16, 1857, WRHS 32, V:B-71.
82. Ann Buckingham diary (1864–78), April 3–4, 1868, NYSL 2.
83. Fairbanks died in March 1852. A stroke paralyzed Barber at age fifty-two; she died about a month later, in December 1871. Youngs and Brown, Domestic Journal, November 26, 1871, WRHS 32, V:B-71; Shaker names index, WRHS 123.
84. Anna Dodgson, Domestic Journal (1873–79), May 28, June 26, 1874, August 31, 1875, November 1, 1878, SM 10,462.
85. Thomas Brown, *Account of the People Called Shakers: Their Faith, Doctrines, and Practice* (Troy, N.Y., 1812; reprint, New York: AMS 1972), 58; Youngs, Meeting Journal, March 1824, in Hollister, Book of Remembrance, WRHS 58, VII:B-109.
86. I want to thank Mario De Pillis, Diane Sasson, and Cori Munro for answering my questions about church regulation of spiritual gifts at the 2008 Shaker Seminar.
87. Records Book No. 2, 17–18, NYPL 2.6.
88. Elder Giles B. Avery, "Autobiography," in *Translated* (East Canterbury, N.H.: Shakers, 1891), 13.
89. Frederick W. Evans, *Tests of Divine Inspiration; or, the Rudimental Principles by which True and False Revelation, in all eras of the world, can be unerringly discriminated* (New Lebanon: Shakers, 1853), 93–94. My thanks to Larry Foster for pointing out this source.

90. Henry C. Blinn, *Manifestation of Spiritualism among the Shakers, 1837–1847* (1899), 61.

91. Morton Klass, *Mind Over Mind: The Anthropology and Psychology of Spirit Possession* (Lanham, Md.: Rowan and Littlefield, 2003), 11, 44–45, 76.

92. [Untitled book of verse] (1820–30), 24–25, WRHS 91, IX:B-41.

93. Henry Youngs' book of writings (1835–57), 4–7, WRHS 56, VII:B-72.

94. William Hepworth Dixon, *New America* (Philadelphia: J. B. Lippincott, 1867), 311, University of Michigan Making of America collection, http://moa.umdl.umich.edu.

95. Rodney Stark, "A Theory of Revelations," *Journal for the Scientific Study of Religion* 38.2 (1999): 287–308, provides a twelve-point model of revelations. Clarke Garrett, *Spirit Possession and Popular Religion: From the Camisards to the Shakers* (Baltimore: Johns Hopkins University Press, 1987) covers the history of Shaker spirit gifts. Skeptics might be interested in Edith Turner, an anthropologist whose education had not prepared her for seeing an actual spirit. "The Reality of Spirits," *Shamanism Magazine* (Foundation for Shamanic Studies) 10.1 (Spring–Summer 1997), http://www.shamanism.org/articles/article02.html.

96. Judith T. Irvine, "Creation of Identity in Spirit Mediumship and Possession," in *Semantic Anthropology*, ed. David Parkin (New York: Academic Press, 1982), 241–60.

97. Foster, "Shaker Spiritualism," 191.

98. Mother Ann's Message, April 22, 1838, WRHS 75, VIII:B-112.

99. [Marcia Bullard?], Canaan Lower Family Sister's Memoir (1813–69), [35], WRHS 33, V:B-84.

100. Erika Bourguignon, "Introduction: A Framework for the Comparative Study of Altered States of Consciousness," in *Religion, Altered States of Consciousness, and Social Change,* ed. Erika Bourguignon (Columbus: Ohio State University Press, 1973), 3–35, points out that psychologists view altered states of consciousness as pathology, even though religions worldwide use them in culturally patterned ways. Ashwin Budden, "Pathologizing Possession: An Essay on Mind, Self, and Experience in Dissociation," *Anthropology of Consciousness* 14.2 (2003): 27–59, describes efforts to understand how psychology, behavior, and culture shape possession behavior. Theorists believe that questions about spirit possession could be "weighed on an absolute scale of pathology and normalcy."

101. Klass, *Mind Over Mind,* 72–73, 115, 117.

102. For this insight, I thank John Schachter. Personal communication, September 20, 2008.

103. Edward A. Alpers, "'Ordinary Household Chores': Ritual and Power in a Nineteenth-Century Swahili Women's Spirit Possession Cult," *International Journal of African Historical Studies* 17.4 (1984): 677–702.

104. I. M. Lewis, *Ecstatic Religion: A Study of Shamanism and Spirit Possession* (New York: Routledge, 1989), says spirit possession is a bid for power by "marginal" individuals, a conclusion that does not necessarily apply to the Shakers. Anthropologists distinguish between those who communicate with spirits and those who are possessed by spirits.

105. Records Book No. 2, 17, 36–37, 44, NYPL 2.6; Promey, *Spiritual Spectacles,* 228n9.

106. "Cliques Give White Staff Advantage in Getting Top Jobs," *Nursing Standard* 22.7 (October 24, 2007): 8–9. Kin ties can help, but ambitious individuals without family support may have formed alliances toward the same ends.

107. Sasson, "Individual Experience," 66–67.

108. Youngs, Concise View, 162–81, WM 861; Records Kept by Order of the Church, June 2, 1844, NYPL 2:7. HSV, NYPL, NYSL, and WRHS own some of Reed's valentines.

109. Daniel W. Patterson, "The Place of Gift Drawings in Shaker Life," in *The Human and Eternal: Shaker Art in Its Many Forms,* ed. Michael S. Graham (New Gloucester, Maine: Sabbathday Lake Shaker Museum, 2008), 8; Daniel W. Patterson, *Gift Drawing and Gift Song* (Sabbathday Lake, Maine: United Society of Shakers, 1983), 61–65, 76–85.

110. Youngs, Concise View, 168–69, cited in Promey, *Spiritual Spectacles,* 162.

111. Suzanne Thurman, "'Dearly Loved Mother Eunice': Gender, Motherhood, and Shaker Spirituality," *Church History* 66.4 (1997): 755.

CHAPTER 10. THE NEW LEBANON DEACONESSES' BONNET BUSINESS, 1835–1850

1. Karen Nickless and Pamela Nickless, "Trustees, Deacons, and Deaconesses: The Temporal Role of Shaker Sisters 1820–1890," *Communal Studies Journal* 7 (1987): 16.

2. Records Book No. 2, 32–33, NYPL 2.6.

3. Leila S. Taylor, *A Memorial to Eldress Anna and Elder Daniel Offord* (Mt. Lebanon, N.Y.: Shakers, 1912), 48.

4. Suzanne Thurman, *"O Sisters Ain't You Happy?" Gender, Family and Community Among the Harvard and Shirley Shakers, 1781–1918* (Syracuse, N.Y.: Syracuse University Press, 2002), 70.

5. Mary Farrell Bednarowski, "Outside the Mainstream: Women's Religion and Women Religious Leaders in Nineteenth-Century America," *Journal of the American Academy of Religion* 48 (1980): 212.

6. Carl D. Arfwedson, in Glendyne R. Wergland, *Visiting the Shakers, 1778–1849* (Clinton, N.Y.: Richard W. Couper Press, 2007), 229.

7. Deaconesses' writings: New Lebanon: [Semantha Fairbanks] journal (1835–36) following John DeWitt Memorandum, WRHS 33, V:B-92; Journal kept by the Deaconesses at the Office (1830–71), January 4, 1832, WM 844b; Mount Lebanon Church Family Trustees' Account Book, November 1835–September 1839, HSV 9784.N5, #364; Betsy Crosman, Small Record Book (1848–72), WRHS 36, V:B-143; [Abigail Crosman et al.], Journal of Domestic Events . . . Kept by the Deaconesses, Church 2nd Order (1843–64), HSV 1086a; Anna Dodgson, Domestic Journal Kept by Order of Deaconesses (1873–79), SM 10,462; Watervliet: [Polly Vedder?], An Account of the Sisters' Work . . . First Order Watervliet (1830–41), esp. 1835–36, WRHS 47, V:B-315; Account of bonnets, baskets, &c, [Watervliet] Account Book (1836–57), WRHS 12, II:B-109; Book Containing an Account of the Income & Expenses of the Sisters at the South Family Watervliet (1840–60), WRHS 12, II:B-113. Harvard: Journal of the Domestic Work Performed by the Sisters; In the Church at Harvard Mass. Kept by the Deaconesses. Book No. 4 (1853–67), FM 31.2. For names of New Lebanon deacons and deaconesses, see Isaac N. Youngs, Domestic Journal (1834–46), NYSL 10, list at end; Records Book No. 2 (1825–1929), 34–40, NYPL 2.6.

8. According to a Watervliet "winter Shaker," three deacons oversaw farm, outside business, and mechanical operations; three deaconesses did so for women's work. Narrative of Four Months' Residence among the Shakers at Watervliet, WM 1711, in Wergland, *Visiting the Shakers, 1778–1849,* 83.

9. A Trip to the Berkshires: The 1860 Summer Diary of Lucius Manlius Sargent, Jr., HSV photocopy, 72.

10. Nathaniel S. Shaler, "Summer's Journey of a Naturalist, I," *Atlantic Monthly,* June 1873, 716.

11. James Silk Buckingham, in Wergland, *Visiting the Shakers, 1778–1849,* 76.

12. Aaron D. Bill, meeting journal at end of Journal or Day Book (1834–40), February 12, 1837, WRHS 35, V:B-132.

13. Visitors also described two Elders as good-looking. Joseph Wicker: David R. Lamson, *Two Years' Experience among the Shakers* (West Boylston, [Mass.]: for the author, 1848), 61. Ebenezer Bishop described by Carl David Arfwedson, 1832, in Wergland, *Visiting the Shakers, 1778–1849,* 226. Using attractive salespeople is a marketing ploy. See George C. Engel, "Importance of Salespeople in Ready-to-Wear Stores," *Journal of Marketing* 11.3 (1947): 282–85; Stephanie Saul, "Gimme an Rx! Cheerleaders Pep Up Drug Sales," *New York Times,* November 28, 2005.

14. Isaac N. Youngs, Concise View of the Church of God (1856–60), 266, WM 861.

15. "S.," in Wergland, *Visiting the Shakers, 1778–1849,* 186.

16. E. D. Andrews and Faith Andrews, *Work and Worship* (Greenwich, Conn.: New York Graphic Arts Society, 1974), 131.

17. "Items of News," *Newport Mercury,* March 2, 1839, 3.

18. Isaac N. Youngs, Domestic Journal (1856–69), December 1, 1864, WRHS 32, V:B-71.

19. Daniel Pidgeon, *Old-World Questions and New-World Answers* (London: Kegan Paul, Trench & Co., 1884), 125. My thanks to Christian Goodwillie for this account.

20. Lorenzo de Zavala, 1830, Andrew Bell and Harriet Martineau, 1835, in Wergland, *Visiting the Shakers, 1778–1849,* 221, 237, 248.

21. Youngs, Domestic Journal, December 31, 1835, NYSL 10; Journal kept by the Deaconesses at the Office, January 4, 1832.

22. Anonymous, 1842, "The Community of Shakers," in Wergland, *Visiting the Shakers, 1778–1849,* 295.

23. Caroline Sloat, "'A great help to many families': Straw Braiding in Massachusetts before 1825," in *House and Home,* Dublin Seminar for New England Folklife Annual Proceedings, ed. Peter Benes, ed. (Boston: Boston University, 1988), 98.

24. [Louis McLane], *Documents Relative to the Manufactures in the United States,* vol. 1 (1833; reprint, New York: Augustus M. Kelley, 1969), 69, 70, 75.

25. Lois Banner, *American Beauty* (Chicago: University of Chicago Press, 1983), 40–41, 53.

26. [Rufus Bishop and Seth Youngs Wells, comps.], *Testimonies of the Life, Character, Revelations and Doctrines of Our Ever Blessed Mother Ann Lee* (Hancock, Mass.: J. Talcott and J. Deming, Junrs., 1816), 278; Seth Youngs Wells, comp., *Testimonies Concerning the Character and Ministry of Mother Ann Lee* (Albany, N.Y.: Packard and Van Benthuysen, 1827), 93. Bareheaded women were conspicuous. After a theft in Pittsfield, a witness recalled two women who were notable for being hatless. Criminal Cases #1 (1870–71), case 419, Berkshire County District Court Records, Superior Court vault, Pittsfield, Mass.

27. Lucy Stone took her bonnet off in church and had to explain why to the Ladies' Board. Abigail Scott Duniway, *Path Breaking* ([New York]: Source Book Press, [1970]), 290.

28. "Inklings," *Berkshire Courier,* October 2, 1872, 2.

29. Wells, *Testimonies (1827),* 63. Bats and moles: [Bishop and Wells], *Testimonies (1816),* 265. List of forbidden articles, LC 22: 305.

30. "Connecticut Leghorn Bonnets," *Albany Gazette,* November 8, 1819; "Wethersfield Bonnet," *Pittsfield Sun,* November 15, 1820. A spear grass bonnet was auctioned for thirty dollars. "Farmer's Department," *Hampden Federalist and Public Journal,* November 8, 1820.
31. Sloat, "Straw Braiding," 98; Thomas Dublin, "Women's Work and the Family Economy: Textiles and Palm Leaf Hat Making in New England, 1830–1850," *Tocqueville Review* 5.2 (1983): 299–300.
32. Christopher Clark, *The Roots of Rural Capitalism: Western Massachusetts, 1780–1860* (Ithaca, N.Y.: Cornell University Press, 1990), 186–88.
33. [Shirley journal] (1816–29), February 4, 1828, WRHS 38, V:B-197.
34. [Rhoda Blake], Sketch of the Life & Experiences of Rhoda Blake, written 1864–92, Alonzo Hollister transcription, 36, 42, WRHS 51, VI:B-33; Freegift Wells, Records of the Church at Watervliet (1788–1851), 113, December 12, 1829, WRHS 44, V:B-279.
35. [Fairbanks], Journal, March 1835, WRHS 33, V:B-92.
36. Betsy Bates, Journal of Events (1833–35), November 14, 1833, WRHS 35, V:B-128.
37. Henry Blinn, "Historical Notes about the Change of Dress among Believers," *World of Shaker,* Winter 1974, 2.
38. Bell, 1835, in Wergland, *Visiting the Shakers, 1778–1849,* 240.
39. Charles Giles B. Daubeny, 1837, and Fanny Appleton Longfellow, 1839, in ibid., 261, 274.
40. Henry Blinn, "Notes from our Diary," *Manifesto* 28.10 (October 1898): 149, HCDC.
41. Harriet Hanson Robinson, *Loom and Spindle,* 65–66, quoted in Thomas Dublin, *Women at Work* (New York: Columbia University Press, 1979), 81.
42. [Vedder?], Account of the Sisters' Work, 4–7, June 1835, March, July 18, 1836, WRHS 47, V:B-315; [Watervliet] Account Book (1836–57), WRHS 12, II:B-109.
43. [Fairbanks], Journal, March 31, May 18, June 3, 20, July 4, 25, 28, August 7, September 15, October 22, December 23, 1835, WRHS 33, V:B-92; Youngs, Domestic Journal, December 31, 1835, NYSL 10.
44. [Fairbanks], Journal, December 18, 1835, WRHS 33, V:B-92; Annie Williams journal (1832–55), December 15, 1835, WRHS 35, V:B-127.
45. Williams journal, December 31, 1835, WRHS 35, V:B-127.
46. Blake was promoted from weaver to deaconess in 1835, perhaps because of her initiative in the bonnet business. [Blake], Sketch of Life, 36, 38, WRHS 51, VI:B-33.
47. [Fairbanks], Journal, March 1, 1836, WRHS 33, V:B-92.
48. Calvin Green, Sayings of Mother Lucy Wright, WRHS 56, VII:B-60.1, 53–54.
49. [Fairbanks], Journal, March 2, 1836, WRHS 33, V:B-92.
50. Ibid., March–May 1836.
51. Asenath Clark, Ministerial Journal, New Lebanon and Watervliet, NY (1834–36), June 2, 1836, HSV ms. 1480, photocopy of SM original; [Fairbanks], Journal, December 1836, WRHS 33, V:B-92; Journal kept by the Deaconesses at the Office, 16–17, WM 844b.
52. Journal kept by the Deaconesses at the Office, 14, WM 844b.
53. Mount Lebanon Church Family Trustees' Account Book, November 1835–September 1839, HSV 9784.N5, #364.
54. Edna Bryner, *Dressmaking and Millinery* (Cleveland: Survey Committee of the Cleveland Foundation, 1916), 46–47, 104, 106, 108–9; *The Ladies' Hand-book of Millinery and Dressmaking* (New York, 1844), 11.
55. Some Shaker-style bonnets in museum collections show construction too shoddy to meet

Believers' high standards. They were presumably either practice pieces or made by the world's people.

56. [Blake], Sketch of Life, 38, WRHS 51, VI:B-33; [Fairbanks], Journal, May 15, 1836, WRHS 33, V:B-92.
57. [Fairbanks], Journal, May 1836, WRHS 33, V:B-92.
58. Williams journal, May 6, 14, 1836, WRHS 35, V:B-127.
59. Ibid., June 15, July 5, 25, December 31, 1836.
60. Youngs, Domestic Journal, March 1836, NYSL 10.
61. Ibid., January 1, 1840.
62. Youngs, Domestic Journal, January 1, 1860, WRHS 32, V:B-71.
63. Rowley: Youngs, Domestic Journal, December 31, 1845, NYSL 10. Men's palm leaf work: Benjamin Gates, Journal (1839–40, 1846–54), October 30–31, 1839 (cutting leaf), February 21, 1852 (ironing leaf), SM 10,450; Henry DeWitt journal (1827–67), April 16, 1844 (cutting leaf), WRHS 33, V:B-97; Philemon Stewart, Daily Journal, No. 3 (1834–36), March 28, 1834, WRHS 35, V:B-130 (splitting leaf).
64. Williams journal, January 21, 1836, WRHS 35, V:B-127.
65. [Fairbanks], Journal, May 1836, WRHS 33, V:B-92.
66. For this insight I thank Jessica Kuhnen, who trekked across Hancock Shaker Village's grounds on a bitter December day and searched through bonnets, molds, patterns, and cutters. Cutters at HSV have teeth the same distance apart that palm leaf strips are wide. Fruitlands' splitter, ostensibly used on straw, resembles HSV's poplar splitters. Sloat, "Straw Braiding," 93.
67. One HSV bonnet uses two widths of palm leaf strips: 1/16-inch warp and 1/8-inch weft. Beverly Gordon, *Shaker Textile Arts* (Hanover, N.H.: University Press of New England, 1980), 180, gives an overview of the process. New Lebanon's directions, however, did not mention wetting the chip. Andrews and Andrews, *Work and Worship*, 125.
68. The phrases "Emily Wilkinson" and "size 12" appear on a cardboard bonnet pattern from 1863, now at HSV.
69. Andrews and Andrews, *Work and Worship*, 124–25, offers the best description of assembly.
70. I have found only two Shaker-style palm leaf bonnets that have documented Shaker provenance, both at HSV. The Grace Dahm (1874–1958) bonnet is covered with maroon silk, which hides many construction details. Another bonnet, circa 1840, has green silk lining over a wool bat, tacked at one-inch intervals. The brim is ten inches, and the crown has six 3/8-inch pleats. The braid used palm leaf for warp and weft.
71. Andrews and Andrews, *Work and Worship*, 123.
72. [Watervliet] Day Book [bonnet sales] (1836–55), WRHS 12, II:B-108; Clarissa Jacobs, New Lebanon bonnet prices, WM 1131.
73. Edgar W. Martin, *The Standard of Living in 1860* (Chicago: University of Chicago Press, 1942), 193, 195.
74. Youngs, Domestic Journal, June 30, 1837, August 31, December 31, 1838, NYSL 10; [Watervliet] Day Book, WRHS 12, II:B-108.
75. Andrews and Andrews, *Work and Worship*, 123; Martha Osbourne Barrett diary, December 4, 1858, Essex Institute Library, Peabody-Essex Museum.
76. Youngs, Domestic Journal, December 31, 1839, NYSL 10; Journal kept by the Deaconesses at the Office, December 31, 1839, WM 844b; New Lebanon Annual Inventory (1839–64), 1839, WRHS 9, II:B-38.
77. [Watervliet] Account Book, 1836–1839, WRHS 12, II:B-109.

78. By 1840, the Second Order had only six bonnet makers, including Rhoda Blake. Youngs, Domestic Journal, January 1, 1840 and list of deacons at end, NYSL 10.

79. Mabel S. Maitland, "Aunt Thank's First Journey," *Peterson's Magazine,* January 1856, 55–56.

80. "Among the Shakers: A Visit to Whitewater Village," *Cincinnati Commercial,* July 21, 1871, 2. My thanks to Christian Goodwillie for this source.

81. Journal kept by the Deaconesses at the Office, December 31, 1840, WM 844b; Youngs, Domestic Journal, yearend reports 1840–46, NYSL 10. The palm leaf trade was most profitable from 1830 to 1837. Caroline Sloat, "The Center of Local Commerce: The Asa Knight Store of Dummerston, Vermont, 1827–51," *Vermont History* 53.4 (1985): 205–20.

82. Molly Smith, 65, wove bonnets and fans. Mary Hazard, 34, and Anna Dodgson, 27, made bonnets and baskets. Youngs, Domestic Journal, January 1, 1845, NYSL 10.

83. Youngs, Domestic Journal, January 1, 1850, WRHS 32, V:B-70.

84. Crosman, Small Record Book, January 1855, WRHS 36, V:B-143.

85. [Benjamin Gates], "Extracts from the Journal of a Shaker Journey," ed. Robert G. Newman, *New England Galaxy* 4.1 (Summer 1962), 26.

86. Reports of sisters' work: Youngs, Domestic Journal, December 31, yearly, NYSL 10. Fancy goods: Beverly Gordon, "Victorian Fancy Goods: Another Reappraisal of Shaker Material Culture," *Winterthur Portfolio* 23.2/3 (1990): 111–29.

87. Journal kept by the Deaconesses at the Office, December 31, 1854, WM 844b; Youngs, Domestic Journal, December 31, 1854, WRHS 32, V:B-70; Gordon, *Shaker Textile Arts,* 210, fig. 111.

88. Thurman, *"O Sisters Ain't You Happy?"* 5.

Conclusions on Shaker Equality of the Sexes

1. The late Jeanne Boydston concluded that historians had bogged down in gender theory, hindering the study of women's lives. Boydston, "Gender as a Question of Historical Analysis," *Gender and History* 20.3 (2008): 558–83.

2. "Shakers," *Shaker and Shakeress,* January 1875, 4, reprinted from *New Haven Daily Press.*

3. D'Ann Campbell, "Women's Life in Utopia: The Shaker Experiment in Sexual Equality Reappraised – 1810 to 1860," *New England Quarterly* 51.1 (1978): 27.

4. Catherine A. Brekus, *Strangers and Pilgrims: Female Preaching in America, 1740–1845* (Chapel Hill: University of North Carolina Press, 1998), 343–46.

5. Aurelia Mace, *The Aletheia: Spirit of Truth,* 2nd ed. (Farmington, Maine: Knowlton and McLeary, 1907), 28. Shakers have acknowledged Mother Ann as a protofeminist foremother since the nineteenth century. Tisa J. Wenger, "Female Christ and Feminist Foremother: The Many Lives of Ann Lee," *Journal of Feminist Studies in Religion* 18.2 (Fall 2002): 5–32.

6. Benjamin West, *Scriptural Cautions Against Embracing a Religious Scheme. . . .* (Hartford, Conn.: Bavil Webster, 1783), 7.

7. Wenger, "Female Christ." Wenger traces the evolution of Shaker portrayals of Mother Ann Lee (see esp. 31–32), but without acknowledging that those portrayals rest on the Shaker belief that Mother Ann was head of the church. Wenger suggests "there is room for doubt even that she was the sole leader of the society" (8). That view ignores Shakers' own beliefs, which credit Ann Lee above her contemporaries.

8. The term "deputy husband" was popularized by Laurel Thatcher Ulrich, *Good Wives: Image and Reality in the Lives of Women in Northern New England, 1650–1750* (New York: Oxford University Press, 1983), chap. 2.

9. Jean Humez, *Mother's First-Born Daughters: Early Shaker Writings on Women and Religion* (Bloomington: Indiana University Press, 1993), 5, 11n18, 15.

10. Karen R. Blaisure and Katherine R. Allen, "Feminists and the Ideology and Practice of Marital Equality," *Journal of Marriage and the Family* 57.1 (1995): 6.

11. Isaac N. Youngs, A Concise View of the Church of God and of Christ on Earth, Edward Deming Andrews Memorial Shaker Collection, WM 861, 33.

12. Records Book No. 2, 16, 32, 42, NYPL 2.6.

13. Humez, *Mother's First-Born Daughters*, 141.

14. Alison M. Newby, "Shakers as Feminists? Shakerism as a Vanguard in the Antebellum American Search for Female Autonomy and Independence," in *Locating the Shakers: Cultural Origins and Legacies of an American Religious Movement*, Mick Gridley and Kate Bowles, eds. (Exeter, England: University of Exeter Press, 1990): 96-103.

15. Christian Goodwillie and Jane Crosthwaite, eds., *Millennial Praises: A Shaker Hymnal* (Amherst: University of Massachusetts Press, 2009), 49, 115–16. My thanks to Christian for pointing out these lyrics.

16. David Darrow, John Meacham, and Benjamin Seth Youngs, *Testimony of Christ's Second Appearing*, 2nd ed. (Albany, N.Y.: Hosford, 1810), 526, 551–52, 601.

17. Seth Youngs Wells and Calvin Green, *A Summary View of the Millennial Church or United Society of Believers* (Albany, N.Y.: Packard and Van Benthuysen, 1823), 213–34.

18. Youngs, Family and Meeting Journal, April 1, 1821, LC 3:42.

19. Anne Newport Royall, 1826, in Glendyne R. Wergland, *Visiting the Shakers, 1778–1849* (Clinton, N.Y.: Richard W. Couper Press, 2007), 205.

20. Betsy Bates, Journal of Events (1833–35), March 20, 1835, WRHS 35, V:B-128; Giles Avery, Historical Sketches (1834–43), 41, LC 4:53.

21. D. A. Buckingham, "Epitomic History of the Watervliet Shakers, No. 4," *Shaker Manifesto* 7 (August 1877): 59.

22. Hester A. Pool, "Among the Shakers," Shaker *Manifesto* 18 (1888): 252. See also Eliza Bridgham, 1818, and Luther Tucker, 1846, in Wergland, *Visiting the Shakers, 1778–1849*, 174, 317; and a Joseph Becker image of a Shaker kitchen in *Frank Leslie's Illustrated Newspaper*, September 13, 1873.

23. Carmen Knudson-Martin and Anne Rankin Mahoney, "Language and Processes in the Construction of Equality in New Marriages," *Family Relations* 47.1 (1998): 81–91; Blaisure and Allen, "Feminists," 5, 12–14.

24. Gender customs could be changed by altering the ways in which women and men practice "femininities" and "masculinities." By recognizing their harmful effects, it might be possible to challenge and eliminate them. Yancey Martin, "'Said and Done' versus 'Saying and Doing': Gendering Practices, Practicing Gender at Work," *Gender and Society* 17.3 (2003): 342–66.

25. Hervey Elkins, *Fifteen Years in the Senior Order of Shakers* (Hanover, N.H.: 1853), 26.

26. Lauren A. Stiles, "'Rather Than Ever Milk Again': Shaker Sisters' Refusal to Milk at Mount Lebanon and Watervliet—1873-1877," *American Communal Societies Quarterly* 3.1 (2009):13–25.

27. William Leonard, *A Discourse on the Order and Propriety of Divine Inspiration and Revelation* (Harvard, Mass.: United Society, 1853), 51, 54–55, quoted in Wenger, "Female Christ," 22.

28. Frederick W. Evans, *Shakers. Compendium of the Origin, History, Principles, Rules And Regulations, Government, and Doctrines of the United Society of Believers in Christ's Second Appearing* (New York: D. Appleton, 1859), 43, University of Michigan Making of America collection, http://moa.umdl.umich.edu.
29. Chauncey Sears, "Duality of the Deity," *The Shaker*, January 1871, 6-7; Asenath C. Stickney, "The Shaker Woman's Rights," and Rosie Morse, "Woman's Sphere," *Shaker and Shakeress* 4:7 (July 1874): 54, 55, HCDC.
30. Wendy R. Benningfield, Appeal of the Sisterhood: The Shakers and the Woman's Rights Movement (University of Kentucky Lexington doctoral dissertation, 2004), 73. Benningfield documents Shaker efforts to promote women's rights among the world's people.
31. "Shakers," *Shaker and Shakeress* 5:1 (January 1875), 4.
32. William A. Hinds, *American Communities* (Oneida, N.Y.: American Socialist, 1878), 104. Hinds (1833–1919) joined the John Humphrey Noyes community in Vermont in 1846, moved to Oneida, New York, with them, and was associated with Oneida for the rest of his life. Robert P. Sutton, *Modern American Communes: A Dictionary* (Westport, Conn.: Greenwood Press: 2005), 74.
33. Isaac Pierce, 1887, in Glendyne R. Wergland, *Visiting the Shakers, 1850-1899* (Clinton, N.Y., Couper Press/Hamilton College, 2010), 374.
34. Elie Reclus, 1878, in Wergland, *Visiting the Shakers, 1850-1899*, 295.
35. "Among the Shakers," *Boston Daily Globe*, August 7, 1881, 6, reprinted from the *New York Tribune*. Brethren's complaints about the sisters' power persisted through the nineteenth century. See Jean Humez, "The Problem of Female Leadership in Early Shakerism," in *Shaker Design*, ed. Jean M. Burks (New Haven: Yale University Press, 2008): 93–119.
36. Anonymous, 1899, in Wergland, *Visiting the Shakers, 1850-1899*, 3.
37. Lida A. Kimball, 1897, in Wergland, *Visiting the Shakers, 1850-1899*, 394.
38. "Innominato," in 1899, writing of thirty years earlier, in Wergland, *Visiting the Shakers, 1850-1899*, 103.
39. Isaac N. Youngs, Family and Meeting Journal, August 17, 1816, LC3:42.
40. Despite the anonymous visitor's comments about Canterbury in 1899, other evidence suggests inequality there earlier in the century. In a talk at Enfield's Spring Forum in 2008, Mary Boswell mentioned that the Canterbury sisters were not "allowed" to get a sewing machine until they had earned enough money to buy it. In 1815 a Maine visionist prophesied that the Canterbury lead would never be a woman, even though eldresses led at New Lebanon and Harvard, and he expected that at Alfred, too. A Dream or Night Vision as related by Benjamin Bailey to the Author, in Otis Sawyer's History of Alfred (1876-80), Sabbathday Lake Shaker Library. My thanks to Steve Paterwic for the vision.
41. My thanks to Kathy Peiss for this insight, which widens the discussion of Shaker influence beyond Shakerism into the national political culture of the United States.
42. Youngs, Concise View, 33, WM 861.
43. *New York Tribune* quoted in Isaac N. Youngs and John M. Brown, Domestic Journal (1856–77), June 11, 1869, WRHS 32, V:B-71.
44. "Among the Shakers," pt. 3, *American Socialist* 4.49 (December 4, 1879): 389. For the influential visitors who published accounts of trips to Shaker villages, see Wergland, *Visiting the Shakers, 1778–1849*, and Wergland, *Visiting the Shakers, 1850–1899*; Hyland, *Sexism Is a Sin: The Biblical Basis of Female Equality* (Sarasota, Fla.: Viatoris Publications, 1995), 115.

INDEX

family as economic safety net, 27
family influence in conversion. *See* bandwagon effect
family ties within Shakerism, 59, 135. *See also* bandwagon effect
fancy goods, *illus.,* 89, 90, 109, 150, 160, 166
farm economy, 88
farmwives, 105, 107
Farnham, James, 118–19
Farrington, John, 25–26
Farrington, Mehitabel, 44
fashion, worldly, 74, 88, 154, 159
Fay, Clarissa, 77
femininities, 168, 215n24
feminists, twentieth century, 4
fictive kin, 2; Cory's, 50. *See also* love; pull factors
Finch, Marianne, 53
flood, 111
food, 14, 49, 55, 89, 104–6, 111, 121–23, 149, 196n13, 203n47; bread and water, 141. *See also* Grahamism; kitchen; work, sisters'
Forester, Emeline and Lydia, *illus.*
foundlings, 58. *See also* Phillips, Aurelia
French and Indian Wars. *See* Native Americans

Gallup, Mazella, *illus.*
Garvey, Elizabeth, 79
Gates, Benjamin, 105, 157, 204n57
Gates, Lucy, 159
Gates, Olive, 130, 132–34, 156, 159
gathering in, 2, 40, 51, 183n40, 184n54
gathering order. *See* Canaan
gender norms: on frontier, 31; sisters beyond, 16, 17–18, 21–22, 24, 40–41, 43–44, 53, 94, 95–96, 98, 112, 118–19, 120, 163–64, 166, 169–70, 171. *See also* petticoat government
gender, 5–10, 16, 21–22, 24, 31, 76, 88, 112–13, 168; in children's behavior, 57, 60, 72, 192n99; dress issues, 75; flexible, 112, 160; in persistence, 72; in religion, 17–18, 20, 43, 112; socially constructed, 81; theory, 214n1. *See also* authority;

caps; equality of the sexes: androgynous ideal; governance
gendered conflicts, 115, 116–17, 118, 121, 124–25, 202n7, 204n50. *See also* petticoat government
genetics of religiosity, 47
gift, xiii. *See also* healing gifts; spiritual gifts
Gillette, Mariah, 65
Gilman, Nicholas, 33
Girls' Order, 60, 77. *See also* work, girls'
glossolalia. *See* speaking in tongues
gluttony, 106, 124
God, biune. *See* biune God
Goodrich, Charles, 33
Goodrich, Daniel, 16, 17, 19, 25, 33, 35, 119
Goodrich, Elizur, death, 41, 184n60; debt, 182n25; gift of mortification, 39; life with Lucy Wright, 32–34; merchant, 34, 40; militia service, 31–32; not selected for Ministry, 40–41; opposed collecting testimonies, 41; scarlet coat, 39
Goodrich, Elizur, Jr. ("young" in 1798), 182n22
Goodrich, Hannah (Fuller) (wife of Nathan), 35
Goodrich, Lucy (Wright). *See* Wright, Lucy
Goodrich, Molly, 115
Goodrich, Nathan, 35
Goodrich, Thankful, 46, 78
Goodrich family, 17, 35, 47
Goodwin, Ann Eliza, 131
Goodwin, Harriet, 60, 68, 131
gossip, 8–9, 116, 120, 125, 177n34, 204n50, 207n46
Gothra, Robena, 62
governance gender-balanced, 2–3, 6–7, 44
Grahamism, 122–24, 203n47
Green, Calvin, 2, 31, 32, 38, 41, 50, 59, 131, 134, 143, 145, 207n55
Groveland, N.Y., 81
gynécratie or gynocracy, 10, 171; sisters' hegemony, 127, 168

Hacker, Jeremiah, 66
hair, girls', 194n29; sisters', 77
Hall, Emily, 78
Hall, Margaret, 94

Niemcewicz, Julian, 89, 95
Niskeyuna, N.Y. *See* Watervliet
Noble, Capt. James, 32

occupations: Shaker women's (*see* work, sisters'); worldly women's, 2, 150–51, 183n45
Offord, Daniel, *illus.*
Offord, Emily, *illus.*
Old Order River Brethren, 74, 83, 194n26
Oneida, 216n32
opening the mind. *See* confession
organizational Darwinism, 170
overwork. *See* farmwives

pacifism, 20, 32, 84
palm leaf. *See* bonnets; fancy goods
Panic of 1837, 57, 158
Parker, Mrs. Phineas, 31
particular affection, 3
Partington, Mary, 35
party spirit, xiii, 3, 108, 118, 122–24, 146, 172
patriarchy, 6, 54, 75–76, 103, 163, 168, 173. *See also* marriage; married women's legal disabilities
peer pressure, 22–23, 57. *See also* band-wagon effect
perfectibility, 45
Perkins, Tryphena, 22
personal property donated, 26–27
petticoat government, 6, 9, 41, 116, 120, 127, 163–64, 171
Phillips, Aurelia, and daughter Jane, 57
Pierce, Eleanor, 23
Pillow, William, Sr. and Jr., 58
Pittsfield, Mass., 17, 30–31, 64
Plumer, William, 43, 94
poetry: "The Bird Legislator," 125; "Come, Sister, Come," 125; "Hoggish Nature," 124; "Lines on a Shaker Dress," 74; "Old Slug," 106; "Look if you please / On yonder cheese," 105; "On the Improved Muslin Caps," 81; "Our Water Works," 104; "Plain Dealing with Square Work," 81; "The Poison of the Tongue," 125; "The Scholar's Soliloquy," 65;

"Slanderous Tongue," 143; "The Tale Bearer," 143; "We thank the Sisters," 104
politics, national, Shaker influence in, 172–73
Polly (New Lebanon girls' caretaker), 65
Pontoosuck plantation, 30–31
Poole, Hester, 106
pork, 203
Potter, Ada Zillah, 60, 69, 124–26, 129, 130, 131, 133, 135
Potter, Eleanor, 124–26, 132, 134, 160
Poughkeepsie, N.Y., jail, 37
poverty: early Shakers', 13; non-Shakers', 27, 57; proselytes', 49
power of God, 17–19, 43, 51–52, 53; Pentecostal, 185n4
Presbyterians, 44, 47, 52. *See also* Barker, Sarah; Johnson, Elizabeth; Johnson, Samuel
Prescot, Martha, 23
prosperity, Shakers'. *See* temporal success
puberty, 70, 76–77
public speaking, worldly women's, 97, 197n31
pull factors: in conversion, 21; economic support, 48–49; equality, 54; food, 14; love for Shaker individuals, 50, 58; sinlessness, 15–16, 44–45; spiritual gifts, 45–47. *See also* bandwagon effect; celibacy; commitment mechanisms; healing gifts; Lee, Ann; push factors; sin, conviction of; temporal success
push factors: abuse or persecution, 50–52; disappointed in former church, 44–45

Quakers, 51, 165, 192n2, 194n26

Rathbun, Valentine, 16, 19–20, 21, 22, 27, 33, 52
Rayson, Eliza, *illus.*, 47
Rea, Sarah Jane, *illus.*, 159
reciprocity, xi, 7, 54, 103, 106, 107–9, 112, 126, 169. *See also* equality of the sexes; union
Reed, Amy, 60, 159
Reed, Hannah, 154, 156
Reed, Matilda, *illus.*, 129, 208n80

39–40; milking, 117, 168; membership jump, 49; proselytes' visits, 16–17, 34–36, 88, 178n17; rebuking visitors in worship, 95–96; Sally Dean at, 142; school, 67; separation of sexes, 102–3; spinning jenny, 201n68; weaving palm leaf, 152. *See also* Fairs, Eleanor Brooks; Hulings, Martha; Sherburne, Trudy Reno; Slater, Catherine

waterworks, 103–4

Watson, Elkanah, 27, 95

Webster, Mariah, 56

Wells, Jennie, *illus.*

Wells, Nancy, 65

Wells, Seth Youngs, xi, 55, 60, 64, 72, 146

Wells family, 47, 48

West, Benjamin, 162

Wheeler, Olive, 64, 159

whirling in worship. *See* turning

White, Anna, *illus.,* 2

Whitefield, George, 33

Whittaker, James, 26

Wicker, Joseph, 211n13

Wicks, Mary, 155, 156, 157

widow's dower, 1

Wight, Lucy, 17, 26, 46

Wilkinson, Emily, 213n68

Williams, Annie, 78, 153, 156, 157

Williams, Elizabeth, 18, 51–52

Wilson, James, 187n50

Wilson, Nancy, 79

Wilson, Rhoda, 60, 156

Winship, Ella, *illus.,* 64

winter Shakers, 117–18

witchcraft, 21, 50, 52

woman-ocracy. See gynécratie

women's property, 1. *See also* married women's legal disabilities

women's rights: and school play, 67; promoted by Shakers, 169, 216n30; and Shaker influence on national politics, 172–73

Wood, Daniel, 106

Wood, Elizabeth, 21

work ethic, 27–28, 62–63. *See also* Elders: sense of entitlement; laziness

work, girls', 60–64, 70, 157, 190n52

work, sisters', *illus.,* 89–91, 92, 129–30, 189n39; bonnet making, 148–60; in brethren's businesses, 109; cap bee, 78; cleaning road and dooryard, 114; clearing brush, 111; demolishing building, 112; drying food for storage, 105; flood cleanup, 111; gathering wild foods and herbs, 111, 142; ironing, 79, 80–81; laundry, 79, 107; painting, 129; picking produce, 111, 129; raising vegetables, 111; rotation, 61, 104, 149–50, 199n16; spring cleaning, 129; stacking firewood, 111; tailoring, 108. *See also* baskets; butter; cheese; extracts; fancy goods; food; hospitality; knitting; kitchen; meals; reciprocity; tailoresses; textile manufacture

work, women's, invisible to men, 189n38

world's people, xiii. *See also* visitors

worship, 19–20; admonished to attend, 87–88; dull, 129; Elder's address, 93; family, 70–71. *See also* dancing; shaking; singing; sisters: as leaders in worship; sweeping; turning; visitors: at public worship

Worster, Abijah, 23

Wright, Eleanor Hayes, 53–54

Wright, Grove, 183n44

Wright, John and Mary (Robbins), 30

Wright, Josiah, 31

Wright, Lucy, 49, 50, 78, 80, 103, 105, 111, 112; childhood, 30–31; collection of 1816 testimonies, 41; considerations in ending marriage, 37–38; death of, 41; demolishing building, 112; described, 31; established equality, 165; marital relationship, 32–34; as Ministry lead, 40–41, 116–17; partnership with Joseph Meacham, 2–5, 40, 44; preaching, 103, 154; sent missionaries West, 41; on sexual self-control, 76; shaped worship, 95, 197n26; wedding of, 29

Wright, Susanna (poet), 54

Wright, Woodbridge, 183n44

Wright family, 181n4, 183n44; characterized, 36

Year Without a Summer (1816), 49
Youngs, Benjamin Seth, 115
Youngs, Isaac Newton, xi, 4, 49, 60–61, 69, 71, 79, 103–5, 108, 110, 111, 116, 122–23, 130–31, 134, 135, 136–37,

141, 146, 156, 158, 163, 171, 172, 204n57
Youngs, Seth Jr. and Martha (Farley), 48–49
Youngs family, 47, 48